Knausgård and the Autofictional Novel

Knausgård and the Autofictional Novel

CLAUS ELHOLM ANDERSEN

SUNY
PRESS

Published by State University of New York Press, Albany

© 2023 State University of New York

All rights reserved

Printed in the United States of America

No part of this book may be used or reproduced in any manner whatsoever without written permission. No part of this book may be stored in a retrieval system or transmitted in any form or by any means including electronic, electrostatic, magnetic tape, mechanical, photocopying, recording, or otherwise without the prior permission in writing of the publisher.

For information, contact State University of New York Press, Albany, NY
www.sunypress.edu

Library of Congress Cataloging-in-Publication Data

Name: Andersen, Claus Elholm, 1972– author.
Title: Knausgård and the autofictional novel / Claus Elholm Andersen.
Description: Albany : State University of New York Press, [2023] | Includes
    bibliographical references and index.
Identifiers: LCCN 2023009073 | ISBN 9781438495668 (hardcover : alk. paper) |
    ISBN 9781438495675 (ebook) | ISBN 9781438495651 (pbk. : alk. paper)
Subjects: LCSH: Knausgård, Karl Ove, 1968– Min kamp. | LCGFT: Literary
    criticism.
Classification: LCC PT8951.21.N38 M56326 2023 | DDC
    839.823/74—dc23/eng/20230517
LC record available at https://lccn.loc.gov/2023009073

10 9 8 7 6 5 4 3 2 1

Contents

Acknowledgments   vii

Introduction   1

Chapter 1   A Commitment to Reality   31

Chapter 2   Reforming the Form   57

Chapter 3   A Son of Shame   81

Chapter 4   Fiction and Trust   107

Chapter 5   The Very Edge of Fiction   135

Afterword   After Autofiction   165

Notes   171

Bibliography   217

Index   237

Acknowledgments

This book would not have been possible had it not been for the support of brilliant friends and colleagues on both sides of the Atlantic who took time away from their own work to engage with mine: Dean Krouk, Gísli Magnússon, Alison Gibbons, Stefan Kjerkegaard, Yi-Ping Ong, Peter Sjølyst-Jackson, Andrew Nestingen, Pernille Ipsen, Olivia Noble Gunn, Mario Ortiz-Robles, Stig Olsen, Cara L. Lewis, Hadle Oftedal Andersen, Julia Dominguez, Jay Shelat, Julie Orlemanski, Elizabeth Peterson, Viren Murthy, and Sarah Ensor. I am especially grateful to Arnaud Schmitt, Russ Castronovo, B. Venkat Mani, Richard Goodkin, and Toril Moi who at a pivotal stage read the manuscript in its entirety and provided invaluable feedback. Special thanks to Toril whose continued support and encouragement from start to finish made all the difference.

Megan Pugh's phenomenal editing skills helped strengthen the arguments and the overall structure of the book. And my talented research assistant, Marek Makowski took on the role of a senior editor and made my broken English readable. Once again, Marlene Hastenplug provided ready feedback and always asked the right questions. In the last phase of writing, my discussions with Marta Figlerowicz—the best conversation partner anyone could ask for—made a world of difference.

The University of Wisconsin-Madison gave me stable and supportive working conditions for writing this book. The encouragement of my colleagues in the Department of German, Nordic, and Slavic+ has been second to none, and my mentor, Kirsten Wolf, believed in me when I didn't. A faculty fellowship at the Institute for the Humanities gave me an intellectual home for a semester and the Center for the Humanities First Book Program showed me what constructive feedback looks like at its best. I would like to thank the directors, Steven Nadler and Russ Cas-

vii

viii | Acknowledgments

tronovo. The research for this book was made possible by funding from the Office of the Vice Chancellor for Research and Graduate Education at the University of Wisconsin-Madison.

Rebecca Colesworthy is the smartest, sharpest, sweetest, and most supportive editor anyone could dream of. Working with her and the team at SUNY Press has been a true joy. Also, thanks to Andrew Hnatow for his creative and stellar indexing.

I am also indebted to the graduate students in the two seminars on *My Struggle* that I have had the fortune to teach. I have benefitted from the comments and questions from fellow scholars when presenting early versions of some of the chapters at conferences and seminars. Karin Sanders hosted me for a talk at UC Berkley in what became a turning in my work on the book. My friends on Twitter have contributed in numerous ways: through their knowledge, support, and camaraderie. And I have learned from every single one of the hundreds of conversations I have had about *My Struggle* over the years.

Finally—and most importantly—thanks to my family: my children, August and Andrea; and wife, Morgan; to whom I dedicate this book. Without her, I would never have written a single word.

Introduction

This is a book about the novel in the twenty-first century. It is about novels that leap over or push through fiction—novels that are often referred to as autofiction. More than anything else, though, it is about Karl Ove Knausgård's *My Struggle*, a monumental novel in six volumes and more than 3,600 pages that has become the preeminent example of autofiction and has changed how we conceive of novels.[1] Widely hailed for its heroic exploration of selfhood, compulsive readability, and restless experimentation with form and genre, *My Struggle* provides a sense of authenticity and intimacy that the contemporary novel has long been missing.[2]

Knausgård, I suggest, diagnoses a crisis in contemporary literature, and in his own life. Fiction has become stale, and his life as a harried father leaves him scant room to work. The remedy he prescribes is to write honestly about himself, not in the form of a memoir or autobiography, but in a novel.[3] He consciously engages with, and undermines, a long critical history of equating novels with fiction. I argue that Knausgård decouples the novel from fiction, muddling the boundary between the two. Doing so, he renews and revitalizes the genre.

Autofiction, as I use the term throughout the book, is a subgenre of the novel. It involves a blurring of fiction and reality that would be seen as duplicitous in traditional autobiographies, with the paradoxical effect of suggesting a sincerity widely held to have been absent in contemporary literature. It evokes what Philippe Lejeune calls the autobiographical and the fictional pacts, which he envisions as invisible contracts between the reader and the author determined by genre designations on the cover and by the corresponding attitude of the readers; I join other critics in seeing this blurring as the product of what David Shields calls "reality hunger." That hunger was already present in reaction to postmodernism, with its

2 | Knausgård and the Autofictional Novel

insistence on sincerity and authenticity, and it peaked in the wake of the Financial Crisis of 2008, which revealed a system of exchange based on fictitious evaluations of worth. Autofiction shows that there is a reality and that it matters—albeit in a complex and contradictory manner that simultaneously contrasts and arises from the heightened understanding of postmodern fictionality.[4]

My Struggle is one of many new autofictional novels that make it impossible to maintain the kind of clear and fundamental distinctions between fiction and nonfiction advanced by critics like Dorrit Cohn.[5] Today, autofiction "is everywhere," as it was pronounced in the *Guardian* in 2018, while the *New York Times* in 2021 wrote about "the autofiction boom of the last decade."[6] Three writers who repeatedly have been named English-language practitioners of Knausgård-style autofiction, Ben Lerner, Sheila Heti, and Rachel Cusk, all of whom I discuss in the book, share Knausgård's mistrust of fiction in various forms, and like him they experiment with form and genre. But they choose radically different ways to handle what can come off, variously, as skepticism, disappointment, or fatigue with fiction. Heti follows Knausgård, as she tries to slough off the unreal to find what lies underneath, while exposing the difficulties of writing as a woman, and Cusk practices a close attention that becomes a kind of a gendered truth-finding mission. Lerner, on the other hand, embraces the blurring of fiction and reality to play out several possible futures and, ultimately, to further a case for sincerity. *My Struggle* shares many of these concerns and techniques, but it stands apart in its monumental aspect, its omnivorousness, its faithfulness to facts, and what I call its "autofictionalization."

The term arises from my reading of narrative stance and point of view and reflects how Knausgård fictionalizes his former self by placing the narrative consciousness in the past. While autofiction purports to define a literary genre, autofictionalization, as I define it, refers to this specific narrative technique. It is one of many ways that Knausgård—contrary to what critics who misread *My Struggle* as a "novel without form" suggest— uses and reimagines central tropes from the novelistic genre to manage his literary balancing act, which depends upon modes of reading and writing both fiction and autobiography.[7] As such, my book is also about reading, where I make the case for a certain way of reading autofiction.

My readings of Knausgård and others move from affect to aesthetics, from feeling to form. The book opens with a backward glance at Knausgård's career before beginning *My Struggle* and provides a historical and

Introduction | 3

theoretical account of the rise of autofiction. The first part lays out the groundwork of my argument, exploring Knausgård's commitment to reality and the ways he invokes it, with particular focus on Books 1 and 2. Building on the insights from the early part of the book, I then explore how shame is integrated into the novelistic form throughout all six volumes, before examining the relationship between fiction, form, and trust in the light of *My Struggle*'s closing. Toward the end, I extend these insights to a discussion of autofictional novels by Sheila Heti, Rachel Cusk, and Ben Lerner, showing why autofiction has begun to dominate the literary landscape in the early twenty-first century and why *My Struggle* remains the pinnacle of this autofictional trend.

Karl Ove Knausgård ascended into international literary stardom with *My Struggle*. The six-volume novel chronicles Knausgård's life from his childhood, youth, and first marriage into the time of writing and led him to be hailed, among other things, as a "Norwegian Proust." In *My Struggle*, Knausgård, as James Wood wrote in a five-page review in the *New Yorker* when Book 1 came out in English in 2012, rescues things, objects, and sensations that otherwise are "pacing towards meaninglessness" by bringing "meaning, color, and life back to the soccer boots and to the grass, and to cranes and trees and airports, and even to Gibson guitars and Roland amplifiers and Ajax."[8] Today, phrases like "literary phenomenon" and "Norwegian sensation" are still invoked when the name Knausgård appears in media. And *My Struggle* is referred to as the autofictional novel par excellence that both designated the advent and peak of this new subgenre in contemporary literature.

My Struggle brought Knausgård to a wide international audience, but by the time it was published, he was already a well-established writer in his native Scandinavia, where his earlier novels lay the groundwork for the experiments in *My Struggle*: the themes, the affects, the narrative tricks, and so on. His first novel, *Ute av verden* (*Out of the World*), was published in 1998. The novel is narrated by Henrik Vankel, a man in his late twenties who, in the opening pages, arrives in a small, desolate town in northern Norway to work as a schoolteacher for one year. He becomes obsessed with, and has a relationship with, his thirteen-year-old student Miriam.[9] In many ways, the book resembles Knut Hamsun's 1894 *Pan*. Both *Pan* and *Ute av verden* focus on their protagonists' memories of northern Norway; both are structured as frame stories; and both feature disturbing obsessions with a girl or young woman (Lieutenant Glahn, the protagonist of *Pan*, lusts after Edvarda, the daughter of a local merchant).

4 | Knausgård and the Autofictional Novel

Where Hamsun's interest in the past is embodied in Glahn's unreliable narration, Knausgård's interest extends to a continual and explicit engagement with the questions of time, memory, and truth. In a one hundred–page excurse, Vankel tells the story of his parents and how they met, trying to understand how he ended up as he did: a highly educated intellectual without any actual self-insight. But mostly, the novel—as he sits and looks back at his time in northern Norway, just a few months prior, still longing for Miriam—is dominated by his shame, as he continually hides and suppresses his inner feelings. Toril Moi, in an excellent short essay, called the novel "one long investigation of the phenomenology of shame," noting that "no one has written better about shame than Knausgård."[10] A decade after the novel's publication, Knausgård wrote in *My Struggle* about how Hamsun's novel followed him in his earliest youth to a point where he even identified with Lieutenant Glahn.[11] Such an identification suggests that the storyline of Knausgård's first novel was autobiographically informed.

Ute av verden became a bestseller, selling thirty thousand copies in Norway alone—an incredible number considering the density of the novel and the fact that it was Knausgård's debut.[12] In one of the national newspapers, a critic referred to the novel as "the sensation of the fall," arguing that Knausgård was trying to merge the realism of Flaubert and Stendhal with Proust, Dickens with Joyce and Woolf, while another national newspaper declared the novel "a monument on modern man."[13] *Ute av verden* was awarded the prestigious Kritikerprisen, the Critic's Prize, an honor that for the past fifty years had never been bestowed for a writer's first novel, and publishers in neighboring countries soon brought the book out in Danish, English, and Lithuanian translations.[14]

In 2004, Knausgård published his second novel, *En tid for alt* (*A Time for Everything*). By then, he had moved from his native Norway to Stockholm, Sweden, where he lived with his second wife, the author Linda Boström Knausgård, and their first daughter. The novel opens with the story of the fictitious renaissance scholar Antonio Belloris, whose understanding of angels leads the novel's narrator to rewrite the Old Testament stories of Cain and Abel, Noah, and Ezekiel. The narrator's retellings seem to suggest both that historical perspectives shape our ability to see and that history could easily have unfolded in very different ways.

Some fifty pages before the novel's nearly six hundred pages come to a close, we discover that Belloris has been a fiction, and that all along we have been hearing from Henrik Vankel, the protagonist of Knausgård's first novel. Vankel's father—who was generally distant and authoritarian, and

Introduction | 5

has recently died—once commented upon the similarities between seagulls and fallen angels. The book is Vankel's attempt to recreate a moment of intimacy with him. As readers of *My Struggle* later discovered, Vankel's story, and especially his vexed relationship to his father, mirrors to a large degree that of Knausgård's. The novel also reflects Knausgård's evolving dissatisfaction with fiction, with Knausgård later, in *My Struggle*, leaving the fictional persona behind.

En tid for alt never made it to the bestseller lists, but it was nominated for the Nordic Council Literature Prize (Scandinavia's equivalent of the Man Booker Prize), and critics loved it. A Norwegian critic wrote that the novel made it evident that Knausgård had a "unique talent," while a Danish critic assured readers that "Nordic novelistic history" had been written with Knausgård's new book.[15] It was soon translated into even more languages than his first novel—Swedish, Danish, German, English, Dutch, Polish, and Rumanian—and helped expand Knausgård's reputation as a writer.

It took another five years before Knausgård published his third novel, which his publisher announced would come out in six volumes over the span of a single year. *My Struggle*, Book 1, was published in September 2009 in Norway. Book 2 came out in November that same year and Book 3 was released in December. Book 4 followed in February 2010, while Book 5 came out in June. But Norwegian readers had to wait almost a year and a half until Book 6—more than 1,100 pages long—was published in November 2011.

In *My Struggle*, Knausgård writes about his own life as a father of three, living as a Norwegian expat with his second wife, Linda Boström Knausgård, in Malmö in southern Sweden. He describes in painstaking details his ambivalence toward being a parent and how, in the midst of diapers needing to be changed, piles of laundry needing to be washed, and kids needing to be dressed, fed, and taken to and from daycare, he struggles to find time to write. *My Struggle*—a novel where he writes about himself using not only his name but also the actual names of friends and family—investigates how he ended up in that situation.

The release of Book 1 led to a string of controversies in Norway. Half of Knausgård's family publicly distanced themselves from him and his novel, and his uncle threatened to sue both him and his publisher. Newspapers asked lawyers, philosophers, and other experts to weigh in on the legal and ethical issues related to writing about other real people in a novel: Who is allowed to tell whose stories? Where should the line

6 | Knausgård and the Autofictional Novel

be drawn when we speak of respecting other people's privacy? Does Knausgård cross that line by revealing intimate details not only about his own life but also about his family, his friends, and his acquaintances? Pages upon pages were dedicated to comparisons between the novel and Knausgård's actual life. The media revealed details that Knausgård had never even touched upon in the novel and waited outside his apartment to take pictures of him as he walked his children to day care, turning some of the ethical questions upside down: now it was the media that controlled the narrative of Knausgård's story, just as he in the novel had controlled the narrative of other real people.

But the novel was not just met with controversy: the feverish coverage of and conversations around *My Struggle* included heaps of critical praise. In *Aftenposten*, Norway's largest daily, the critic Hans Skei wrote: "It should be impossible. But Karl Ove Knausgård gives literary form to something that not only seems personal but almost private. It could have turned out to be self-absorbing and subject to the limitation of self-representation. Instead, it turns out to be artistic writing of the highest quality and a well-composed novel."[16] Other critics agreed. In the tabloid *VG*, Norway's second largest newspaper, Morten Abrahamsen rejoiced that in Knausgård, Norway finally had a writer "at the level of the international top-class," noting that there was "no doubt that *My Struggle* is great literature [*stor literatur*]."[17]

Book 1 far outsold any other of Knausgård's novels. While the first printing was ten thousand copies—a number Knausgård in Book 6 reveals he thought was too high for the kind of book he had written—Book 1 ended up selling more than 140,000 copies in Norway alone.[18] The following volumes each sold a little less, with Book 6 "only" selling around fifty thousand copies. In total, all six volumes have sold close to half a million copies in Norway, a country with a population of just 5.4 million.[19]

As the six books rolled out, Knausgård seemed ever present in the Norwegian media. *Dagbladet*, a major national newspaper, printed a special section, "Knausgård for dummies," with a guide to the novel so its readers could, the cover said, take part "in the discussion without having to read 3,000 pages."[20] The Language Council in Norway recorded the newly minted verb *to knause*, meaning to tell seemingly insignificant details from your life after reading *My Struggle*.[21] And in December 2010, more than a year after the publication of Book 1, Norwegian *Elle* named Knausgård the "sexiest man in Norway"—though he had lived in Sweden for the past eight years.[22]

Introduction | 7

After the publication of the first three volumes, the public coverage expanded from enthusiasm about the books, and debate over their ethics, to questions about the literary merits of Knausgård's novel, and whether, indeed, it was a novel in the first place. The occasion was an op-ed by the author Jan Kjærstad, published in January 2010. Kjærstad—a giant in Norwegian literature who was known in the 1980s as the postmodern author par excellence, and whose style the nineteen-year-old Knausgård tries to copy in Book 4 of *My Struggle*—criticized not Knausgård himself but the adoring critics who had compared "Knausgård to authors such as—I pinch myself in the arm, but I am awake—Ibsen and Hamsun and Proust."[23] What the critics missed, he argued, was Knausgård's immediate context: a trend in contemporary Scandinavian literature in which a number of writers had created a hybrid genre consisting of a mixture of fiction, essay, and autobiography.[24] This new trend, Kjærstad continued, was particularly prevalent among writers in Sweden, where Knausgård happened to have lived for the past eight years.

Kjærstad's op-ed is a good reminder that Knausgård did not write *My Struggle* in a vacuum, but at a time when numerous Scandinavian authors had been working in different forms of autobiography. Knausgård himself often singles out the Swedish poet Stig Larsson and his 1997 *Natta de mina* as a book that changed his outlook on literature. Indeed, Larsson integrates his own life in a radical exploration of what literature is, whereby challenging conventional literary forms establishes a literary freedom. In the 1990s, the Swedish writers Carina Rydberg and Maja Lundgren also sparked controversy by using, in their mixtures of fiction and autobiography, the actual names of members of the Swedish cultural elite. In neighboring Denmark, Claus Beck-Nielsen staged his own disappearance and used the media stories that ensued as raw material for the biography *Claus Beck-Nielsen (1963–2001)*, which ends with the death of the author of that name. (He has since published novels using numerous different names.) And in Knausgård's native Norway, in 2002, after three decades writing fictional novels, Dag Solstad published the novel *16.07.47* (the day, month, and year of his birth), in which we follow the character Dag Solstad traveling from Berlin to a school reunion that takes place in his childhood home, and back to Berlin, where he starts writing this novel about his life.

The literary turn toward autobiographical writing also meant that a number of scholars were becoming more interested in the genre, and in what it meant to write from life. One of them was Arne Melberg, a

8 | Knausgård and the Autofictional Novel

Swedish professor of comparative literature at the University of Oslo who had published a book on autobiography in 2009, and who responded to Kjærstad's op-ed just a few days later, turning the discussion of *My Struggle* into a question of genre, as Melberg defined *My Struggle* as a "literary centaur: the body of a novel with a biographical head."[25] The discussion of genre also spilled into some of the first scholarly accounts of *My Struggle*, where numerous new terms—such as "fictionless fiction" and "performative biographism," to name just two—were introduced to characterize what was at stake in Knausgård's novel.[26] Among this early scholarship, Poul Behrendt's pioneering article "Autonarration som skandinavisk novum" ("Autonarration as Scandinavian Novum"), written and published before the release of Book 6, and to which I return several times in this book, stands out for its precise analysis of central narrative features of *My Struggle*.

As the scholarly debates began, sales kept increasing. Just nine months after Book 1 had hit the Norwegian bookstores, it appeared in a Danish translation—and a few months after that, a Swedish translation was published.[27] The Italian translation appeared that same year, in 2010, followed by French and German translations in 2011. And in 2012, the first translation of *My Struggle* appeared in English. For Western readers, Knausgård seemed to be everywhere.[28]

Autofiction: Fiction and Finance

The term "autofiction" has made it into the public imagination fairly recently, serving a perceived need: how to refer to what has seemed a spate of literary projects blurring autobiography and fiction. Several of the authors most often associated with Anglophone autofiction, like Sheila Heti and Chris Kraus, have distanced themselves from the term; Knausgård, for his part, has claimed to know nothing about it.[29] Autofiction, however, and as I use it, is a subgenre of the novel that involves a blurring of fiction and reality that has created a new sense of sincerity that suggests a departure from the poetics of postmodernism.

The term first appeared in print in English in 1972 in a review in the *New York Times* by novelist and critic Paul West. Four years later, in 1976, West introduced the term in a scholarly context in a *New Literary History* article where he used it to describe how fiction can often be read "as a mode of tethered autobiography, or *autofiction*."[30] The following year, the French author Serge Doubrovsky described his novel *Fils*, on its back cover, as "fiction, of strictly real events and fact; *autofiction*, if you like."[31] Since Doubrovsky spent the coming decades championing the term with more volume and frequency than West ever did, his usage of it has been much better remembered, and he is almost always mentioned in discussions of its origins.[32] In the span of his career, he defined autofiction "at least three different ways," as Hywel Dix argues: stylistically, sociologically, and historically.[33] What's more, it was in his native France that, in the ensuing decades, the notion of autofiction caught on among a group of authors that included, most notably, Annie Ernaux and Christine Angot.[34]

In French and Francophone studies, Karen Ferreira-Meyers writes, autofiction has been "described, discussed and debated at length" with Doubrovsky remaining "one of the main contributors to the fine-tuning of the genre."[35] Two contradictory definitions of autofiction emerged from these discussions. In one, advanced by Philippe Gasparini, autofiction is a genre wherein the events are true and the fictive is limited to "the very form of the narrative," or how the author shapes the facts into a story.[36] In the other, advanced by Gérard Genette, autofiction is seen as "authentically fictional," a genre in which "I, the author, am going to tell you a story of which I am the hero but which never happened to me."[37]

In Scandinavia, autofiction became popular in the wake of *My Struggle* and other celebrated autofictional novels. But the popularity mostly extended to the public imagination, as only a few Scandinavian scholars embraced and started studying the term systematically. Scholars in the Anglophone world were also late to pick up the term, but by the 2010s, critics and readers were deploying it with some frequency. In the anthology *Autofiction in English* from 2018, a number of scholars show "that various recent developments in research about life writing have brought the field of autofiction to a moment of effective emergence in English in both theory and practice," as the editor of the anthology, Hywel Dix, writes in his introduction (7). The anthology gives evidence of the sprawling and emerging scholarship on autofiction, though the individual contributors don't seem to agree on what autofiction is or whether it is a contemporary phenomenon.

According to Marjorie Worthington, in her 2018 book *The Story of "Me,"* contemporary American autofiction is the result of a trend that started in the 1960s. Autofiction is the result of how the poststructuralist notion that "all writing by its very nature merely [is] a representation of reality and, therefore, a fiction"[38] has been accepted by mainstream

10 | Knausgård and the Autofictional Novel

audiences. As such, contemporary autofiction is essentially a postmodern genre, Worthington argues. Central to Worthington's argument is that American autofiction is mostly "written by write men" (19). As feminist literary theory began challenging the notion that an author necessarily is male, the white male writers of literary fiction turned to self-conscious writing to promote their masculinity.[39]

In contrast to Worthington's argument about autofiction mainly being written by men, Hywel Dix points out that many practitioners of autofiction are women and suggests that autofiction as we see it today would not have been possible without the heighted status of women's writing. Many female writers, he asserts, have in autofiction found a "freer and freeing experimentation" where the new form has helped to represent women's experience in the twenty-first century.[40] Accordingly, autofiction has deliberately steered these writers away from postmodernism and poststructuralism.

Worthington's and Dix's conflicting arguments can be attributed to their different definitions of autofiction and its history. Where Worthington reads autofiction as a postmodern genre that spans the past fifty years, Dix is interested in autofiction as a recent twenty-first-century phenomenon that tries to move beyond the aesthetics of postmodernism. Yet, on the final pages of his anthology, Dix lists a "Select Bibliography of Primary Texts" of autofiction in English. Of the seventy-one works of autofiction listed on this eclectic list only a little more than a third is by female writers.[41] It is also hard to ignore the fact that the author of a novel hailed as the pinnacle of contemporary autofiction is a white, Norwegian man whose nominal distinction between fathering and literature on the one hand and politics on the other is steeped in male privilege, as evidenced when he, for instance, in Book 2 of *My Struggle*, continually mocks the gender ideal of equality in Sweden and in the Swedish welfare state.[42]

Worthington's second charge—that autofiction in essence is a "white" genre—is not easily qualified.[43] Indeed, in an essay in the *New Republic* from 2020, the novelist Tope Folarin asks, as the headline of the essay reads, "Can a Black Novelist Write Autofiction?" Folarin opens his essay by asking what names come to mind when we hear the term autofiction. "Let me guess," he continues, "you are probably thinking about Rachel Cusk, Karl Ove Knausgaard, Ben Lerner, and Sheila Heti, among a few others"—all of whom have in common "that they are white."[44] Listing a number of novels by people of color that by all accounts would qualify as autofiction, including Michael Thomas's *Man Gone Down*, Zinzi Clemmons's *What We Lose*, and Akwaeke Emezi's *Freshwater*, Folarin points out that when critics have addressed the autobiographical aspect of these novels "it is simply described as being, well, autobiographical." To be sure, Folarin's own 2019 novel, *A Particular Kind of Black Man*, written, as he says, "under the influence of autofiction," was never described as such by critics but instead seen as an immigrant novel and a bildungsroman.

The reason for this, Folarin argues, is a literary landscape "dominated by white editors, white critics, and white readers" in which writers of color rarely are seen as "innovators who might establish trends that permanently shift literary culture writ large." While white writers share the privilege that their lives "are worthy of being transformed into literature regardless of how prosaic and boring they might be," writers of colors whose work could qualify as autofiction are placed in "literary categories—e.g., immigrant literature—that read as "exotic," even if their subject matter is utterly normal to those writers and the people for whom they are writing."[45] The result, Folarin insists, is that writers of colors aren't understood to be capable of the same artistic and creative freedom as white writers and that the genre of fiction misses a "fresh infusion of perspectives and ideas and talent."

My study of contemporary autofiction is undeniably very white, but I agree with Folarin that his novel, as well as those he mentions in his piece, are also autofictional; I would also add to his list Ocean Vuong's *On Earth We're Briefly Gorgeous*, Ayad Akhtar's *Homeland Elegies*, and Brandon Taylor's *Real Life*—books that have at least been referred to as autofiction, though critics, as Folarin claims, seem to have focused more on their content than on their place within a contemporary autofictional landscape.[46] All of these novels were published a few years after the novels I discuss in this study, and they form what I would argue is a second wave of contemporary autofiction well worth attending to. I focus here on the first wave of autofiction by Knausgård, Heti, Cusk, and Lerner in order to explore, among other things, how their formal features have led them to be grouped together, and how they have shaped our understandings of what autofiction is today.

Autofiction has also been criticized as a commercial genre, tailored to satisfy "the marked need for 'relatable' protagonists while at the same time appearing to offer a new mode through which to deliver content," as Sarah Wasserman opines.[47] This view is shared by Lee Konstantinou, who sees autofiction as "an aesthetic gesture or practice or mode (or whatever you want to call it) that takes place at the intersection of genre and marketing."[48] The critic Christian Lorentzen turns to Doubrovsky's blurb on the back of the novel *Fils* to express a similar sentiment, arguing that autofiction "came to us as part of the language of commercial promotion, a way of marketing as new something almost as old as writing itself: the blending of the real and the invented."[49] Autofiction, Lorentzen warns, allows writers to stand "at a distance from the world—the ethics and the politics—on display in their novels, as far or farther than authors of fictions that aren't autobiographical at all."

In this criticism we find a tacit perception that autofiction is a gimmick and, above all else, about selling books. While Doubrovsky's early definition of the term was in the form of a blurb on a novel, it was, as I discuss in chapter 2, also a direct response to the theoretical writings on autobiography by his friend Philippe Lejeune. To be sure, autofiction has been theorized and discussed in academia for decades by a host of mainly French scholars, though these discussions only sporadically have made it to the English-speaking world.[50] In Book 6 of *My Struggle*, Knausgård refers to the publication of his novel in numerous volumes as "a gimmick" and as such a shortcut to literary value premised upon emptying out the literary (6.67). But he also writes that neither he nor his publisher thought the book would have "any major impact," though the first print of Book 1 was, after Scandinavian standards, an impressive ten thousand copies, presumably mostly due to Knausgård's name recognition among Norwegian readers. In addition, none of the novels examined in this book were promoted as autofictional when first published. In fact, the term autofiction was applied to these novels by critics, not by the publisher or the writers themselves, often long after their initial publication.[51]

In recent years, objections about the mere notion of autofiction have become a default gesture among a number of US-based scholars. Some seem to dislike the term itself; others, the idea that autofiction offers anything new.[52] Certainly, the term autofiction is not perfect. But Fredric Jameson's description of the term "postmodernism" as "internally conflicted and contradictory," but nevertheless a term so popular that "we cannot *not* use" it, seems applicable to autofiction too.[53] Autofiction designates an important development of the twenty-first-century novel, and however contested it might be, the term—as Jameson reasoned with the term postmodernism—provides "something to call it that other people seem to acknowledge by themselves using the word" (xxii).

To understand my embrace of the term autofiction, I turn to autobiography myself, and more specifically, the 2012 University of Frankfurt

Introduction | 13

symposium where I met Knausgård. I had been invited to give a talk on the history of pan-Scandinavian literature, and I included a final section on Knausgård, whose six-volume novel I had started reading a few weeks earlier but still had not completed.[54] Arguing that *My Struggle* had shown the emergence of a new pan-Nordic literary public, I prefaced my remarks by declaring how I read the book: "And perhaps I should start by saying that I read *My Struggle* as a novel, with an emphasis on the word 'novel,' with a protagonist and narrator named Karl Ove who might share the same name and identity with the author, but also that this is not what makes it interesting."[55] And then I turned my attention to the novel's criticism of the Nordic welfare state.

At the lunch following my talk, I was confronted with a different reality—literally. I was at a table with the hosts and other speakers at the symposium, and was talking with the Finnish author Monika Fagerholm, when Knausgård, who had been invited to the symposium too, arrived. He had missed the morning sessions because his flight had been delayed but made it in time to read from Book 2, which had just been published in German, later in the afternoon. Now, he politely shook hands with everyone in our little group, sat down next to me, and joined our conversation. It turned out that Knausgård and Fagerholm already knew each other, and soon the two of them were engaged in conversation.[56]As I sat there listening to the conversation, adding a comment here and there, I started thinking about the relationship between the man sitting next to me and the protagonist by the same name in *My Struggle*. I recognized traits in him that I knew from what I had read of the novel, such as when he spoke of how nervous he had been when his flight was delayed. This recognition was unnerving, as though I knew more than I should, but it was accompanied by the opposite feeling: that I, in fact, did not know anything about the man sitting next to me. The feeling came about as he talked his way through the events of the day that seemed vastly different from those described in his novel and I realized the person next to me did not fit the mold of the novelistic character by the name Karl Ove Knausgård. As a result, I could not get myself to bring up *My Struggle* in my conversation with him, although in the past I had often talked with writers about their work. Somewhat shaken, I realized that I had been wrong in my reading of *My Struggle* that morning: that it certainly, but in a complex and ambiguous interplay between the two, matters that the author of the novel is the same as the character—and that this is, in fact, part of what is most interesting about it.

14 | Knausgård and the Autofictional Novel

Karl Ove Knausgård exists.[57] Claiming that he does not—or that he is purely a literary character indistinctive from any fictional character, as several other scholars have suggested and as I myself once wanted to believe—is ridiculous. That the character shares his name with the author inevitably informs our reading of the novel. It forces us to ask what the relationship is between these entities. I ask this question not historically or biographically, which would involve collating sources to examine similarities and differences, but formally, in terms of how this relationship obtains and signifies in his novel. How does *My Struggle*, through autofictionalization, make the past seem present? How does it blur the difference between fiction and reality? How does it simultaneously evoke both the autobiographical and the fictional pacts? Knausgård's insistence on the shared identity of character and author seems imperative for any reading of *My Struggle* to consider.

For other autofictional novels, too, we cannot—or at least, we should not—ignore the reality that they embrace. But it does not follow that we cannot simultaneously read them as novels. To this duality *My Struggle* serves both as a testament and a validation. In addition to employing the autobiographical pact, *My Struggle* invokes the novelistic pact and uses formal features typically associated with fiction. Using these features does not turn all of *My Struggle* into a fictional novel. Instead, it reinforces how we are dealing with a trope that involves two otherwise contradictory ways of reading. And that is precisely what I experienced in Frankfurt and what came to inform my approach to reading *My Struggle*: the uncanny feeling that Karl Ove Knausgård—the author I sat next to during lunch—was simultaneously identical to and different from the Karl Ove Knausgård I had met in *My Struggle*.

In this book, I use the term autofiction to distinguish those novels whose authors, as Annabel L. Kim puts it, use "the strategy of playing their biographical, or real, identities against their thinly disguised autobiographical protagonist in ways that enchant and frustrate readers" from traditional, memoiristic life narratives.[58] Autofiction, as Kim observes, is not autobiography; it is a subgenre of the novel. It involves a blurring of fiction and reality that would be a detriment in a traditional autobiography of, say, a former president or well-known athlete. It is, as Alison Gibbons writes, an "explicitly hybrid form of life writing that merges autobiographical fact with fiction."[59] Autofiction often employs tropes that are rarely found in autobiography, including metafictional passages, digressions, and what Myra Bloom lists as "metatextuality, fragmentation,

Introduction | 15

formal experimentation, and narrative hybridity."[60] I add to this list the technique I call "autofictionalization," where Knausgård narrates his former self as if it were a fictional character.[61]

Bloom asserts that autofiction's methods "are cribbed from the post-modern playbook." But, she continues, the "earnest existential and ethical investment" of autofiction signals "a renewed faith in the possibilities of personhood."[62] Indeed, autofiction is a far cry from a postmodernism that, according to Jameson, is characterized by a lack of depth, a waning of affect, and a departure from an inside/outside dichotomy.[63] Instead, a belief in depth, affect, and the dualism of the inside/outside dichotomy is precisely what describes many of the novels often labeled as autofiction, including *My Struggle*.[64] Following Jonathan Sturgeon, we might say that autofiction reveals that "the postmodern novel is dead."[65] In its place, autofiction in its current iteration has injected a sincerity and sense of authenticity that otherwise seem to have been missing in contemporary literature, part of what Alison Gibbons refers to as an "affective turn" in contemporary autofiction.[66] Where autofiction was often associated with postmodernism in France in the 1980s, contemporary authors blur fiction and nonfiction to evoke a reality that helps their novels engage readers. And by narrating their own genesis in what Johannes Voelz, in relation to autofiction, has coined the "*making-of* novel"—albeit with explicit considerations of truthfulness, unreliability, and faulty memories—these novels paradoxically develop a sense of authenticity.[67]

The desire for such authenticity—or as David Shields called it in a 2010 manifesto of the same name, "reality hunger"—is itself a product of postmodernity. Knausgård identifies this desire when, in Book 2 of *My Struggle*, he diagnoses a crisis of contemporary literature in which we are "totally inundated with fiction and stories." Literary fiction, he suggests, has lost its value because of its fictionality: "Wherever you turned you saw fiction" (2.561). Sheila Heti expresses a similar fatigue, telling one interviewer that she has become "less interested in writing about fictional people, because it seems so tiresome to make up a fake person and put them through the paces of a fake story."[68] David Shields, for his part, writes that he finds it "very nearly impossible to read a contemporary novel," before denouncing the entire genre: "The novel is dead. Long live the antinovel, built from scraps."[69]

To Shields, the novel has become too outdated and boring to seriously reflect the ever-changing and chaotic world we live in today. We have turned, he says, from novels to reality TV, documentaries and

16 | Knausgård and the Autofictional Novel

mockumentaries, sampling and celebrity DJs—work that in some way or other invokes reality as its raw material. Where literature is concerned, he hails the memoir, the lyric essay, and collage ("an evolution beyond narrative") as the genres best suited for a new artistic movement. This new movement, he says, consists of "a burgeoning group of interrelated but unconnected artists" who are "breaking larger and larger chunks of 'reality' into their work." Shields frames his own book, plundering and fragmentary, as the movement's ars poetica (3–5).[70]

It is not surprising that Shields's book has often been invoked in discussions about autofiction as well as readings of *My Struggle*.[71] Shields, Günter Leypoldt writes, "provided resonant concepts," and Knausgård gave "these concepts a new life by providing a compelling readable example."[72] *My Struggle* certainly affirms Shields's diagnosis of how we "yearn for the 'real' " and "want to pose something nonfictional against all the fabrication" (81). When Knausgård was asked about *Reality Hunger* in an interview, he answered that he "didn't read David Shields until I was done with these books [the *My Struggle* series]" but that he "related to his views in many ways."[73] He did not offer further details, but it seems safe to say that Knausgård does not want to join the movement Shields describes: Shields advocates for even more, and shorter, fictions, which Knausgård wants—in a series of sprawling tomes—to move beyond.

Shields advances his cause via a discussion of the controversy surrounding James Frey's *A Million Little Pieces*. In 2005, Frey appeared on *The Oprah Winfrey Show* to discuss his memoir, which he presented as the true story of his way back to sobriety after a decade of drug and alcohol addiction.[74] Soon after, the website *The Smoking Gun* revealed that large chunks of the book were fabrications. At first, Oprah Winfrey defended Frey, but a few weeks later she invited him back on her show for what Shields refers to as a "whipping." Frey profusely apologized for misleading both Oprah and his readers. But he should not have apologized, Shields writes: "I'm disappointed not that Frey is a liar but that he isn't a better one. He should have said, *Everyone who writes about himself is a liar. I created a person meaner, funnier, more filled with life than I ever could be*" (43, original italics). Suggesting that Frey should have insisted that every autobiographical account necessarily is fictitious, Shields implies that our reality hunger can never be satisfied: every new attempt to write about ourselves and engage reality cannot help but be a fiction. Rejecting any notion of authenticity, Shields offers "advice" to Frey that is not even his own, but a quote he plundered, without in-text attribution, from an

Introduction | 17

unpublished manuscript by the memoirist Alice Marshall.[75] Shields's quotations suggest a view of language as a prison house that we can never escape:[76] because a signifier only refers to other signifiers and never to the signified, language itself is a kind of fiction, pointing only to itself, never to some other, deeper, "real."[77] "If this is right," says Toril Moi about Shields's reading of Frey, "everything in *My Struggle* would be fiction."[78] In Shields's account, all autobiographical attempts are fictional and all pursuits of authenticity illusory.

I too find Shields's prescription—that is, for more fiction—wanting, but his description of a condition of "reality hunger," in which we "yearn for the 'real'" and want to "pose something nonfictional against all the fabrication," is convincing. It helps us understand and name the attempts to engage reality in our culture generally, and in autofiction specifically, even though he pays scant attention to causes—which is to say, history.[79]

To understand what caused a reality hunger so deep that numerous authors simultaneously started writing about their own lives in the form of a novel around 2010, we must turn to recent history. Here, the notion of post-truth that has dominated politics in the Western world for the past decade offers one model of explanation, as we, in the words of Ralph Keyes, "live in a post-truth era." Post-truthfulness, he asserts, exists in an "ethical twilight zone" because it allows us to justify dishonesty if the truth conflicts with our values.[80] Though the term was coined as early as 1992, it became a dominant theme in discussions of politics in the wake of the US invasion of Iraq in 2003, when, in a speech to UN Security Council, then–secretary of state Colin Powell infamously presented the "facts" of the case against Saddam Hussein—facts that turned out not to be facts at all. In 2016, the election of Donald Trump, as well as new paradoxical terms as such "fake news," "truthiness," and "alternative facts," marked a culmination of this tendency.

It would be tempting to see contemporary literature's insistence on a reality of sorts as a response to this development where political discourse has been divorced from reality. But that the divorce of political discourse from reality is only a symptom of a larger historical development of the 1990s and the early 2000s, in the course of which it became increasingly clear that capitalist society rests on what Marx called "fictitious capital," was made explicit by and peaked with the advent of the Financial Crisis of 2008.

Knausgård started writing what eventually became *My Struggle* in February 2008, just a few weeks after the word "subprime," referring to the subprime mortgage crisis, had been voted "Word of the Year" by the

American Dialect Society. In Scandinavia, most major news outlets had been covering the credit crisis since the summer of 2007, with newspaper articles explaining subprime loans.[81] Over the course of the year, the debt that continually had accumulated in the previous decades defaulted; two of the world's largest investment banks went bankrupt; the housing market crumbled; and unemployment soared.[82]

Suddenly, the world faced a major financial crisis. Initially, this seemed like a wake-up call for finance capitalism, with Alan Greenspan, the former chair of the Federal Reserve and a lifelong champion for deregulation and neoliberalism, admitting that he had made a "mistake" in assuming that banks were "best capable of protecting their own shareholders and their equity in the firms."[83] But, as history has shown, that wake-up call was greeted with another snooze.

The halt in predatory lending practices was temporary: finance capitalism continues at full speed, with subprime loans continuing under a new name, "non-prime loans"; they make up an increasing share of mortgages taken out.[84] But the crisis exposed what critics had long claimed: that our whole financial system, based on "fictitious capital," has, in Fredric Jameson's phrase, taken a "dialectical leap from quality to quantity, and a transformation so central to the system—and so momentous in its consequences—as to be considered a historically new phenomenon in its own right."[85] Consequently, Jameson's assessment of our current financial system suggests that we have moved beyond the economic conditions that were reflected in the aesthetic of postmodernism as he had defined it.

That we are witnessing a "historically new phenomenon" might be the reason numerous attempts to understand autofiction in the context of postmodernism, including Jameson's own attempt, seem inadequate. Jameson, in a review of Book 6 of *My Struggle*, focuses solely on Knausgård's itemization, arguing that in postmodernism all there is left is "to list the items that come by."[86] But Jameson, whose reading of Knausgård I discuss in chapter 2, is far from alone in his attempt to insist on understanding autofiction in a postmodernist context. Sarah Wasserman asks why it is that "autofiction has so many scholarly admirers" and answers that it is because it "satisfies the desire for something new, and the need for a humane ethical position that can be articulated through writing itself." The problem, however, is that when we try to "diagnose the newness of contemporary fiction by engaging with rhetorical and genre innovations and variations," we do so "while insisting that the global economic order" that helped solidify and diagnose postmodernism "remains operative"

(578, 580). As such, Wasserman asserts, the real question to ask when it comes to autofiction is: "How new, how contemporary is it, really?" (580).

To Lee Konstantinou, autofiction is a gesture or mode that "takes place at the intersection of genre and marketing" and reveals the "internalization of marketing into literary form."[87] Autofiction, he continues, confronts the reality "that under neoliberalism, the individual is increasingly charged with the job of managing his own portfolio of human capital."[88] This is the very reason writers of autofiction supposedly are obsessed with "the process of publishing and the mechanics of the writer's life" because they "must, like any independent firm, hire and fire agents, editors, and publishers and must navigate personal and professional relationships."

Anna Kornbluh historicizes autofiction by turning to what she calls the "macroeconomic structures" and the restructuring of work with deindustrialization, privatization, and deskilling of labor from the 1970s to the present.[89] The intensification of work with an "omni temporality and the 24/7 workday" is "exerting a lot of pressure on circulation" with demands of "rapid exchange, fluent and direct messaging, and instantaneous logistical management," to name just a few of these infrastructures of "instant contact and rapid relay." This provides the context for explaining an aesthetic mode of "self-emanation, disclosure, and no filter, the kinds of modes of manifestation that are often very stylized but with the pretense that they have no style: the author is the character, the self is without boundaries."

What these accounts have in common is a desire to situate autofiction in the context of neoliberalism and postmodernism. But while their cultural and economic analysis is both fascinating and seductive, it also makes it difficult to distinguish between a bestselling memoir or autobiography from the 1980s and an autofiction novel from the 2011, as both are considered symptoms of the same historical conditions. With this comes a rejection of the reality claim that is central to many autofictional novels as nothing but a style or a fiction, thus invoking the proposition that it is impossible to move beyond the fictional. Such a proposition not only seems archaic here in the twenty-first century; it also ignores how writers of autofiction deliberately position a thinly veiled protagonist against their actual identities.

Some of these attempts to understand autofiction in the context of postmodernism seem more interested in rejecting or belittling a certain literary genre than in trying to understand it. In a discussion of autofiction, Mitch R. Murray, for instance, goes to great lengths to inform us that he thinks "often and with bitter resentment" about Elif Batuman's 2017

20 | Knausgård and the Autofictional Novel

novel *The Idiot* because his "experiences as an undergraduate and graduate student look nothing like Batuman's." This leads him to conclude that the reason autofiction "is a very vocal and well-promoted niche, at least within literary critical circles" is that it offers "a comfortable narrative about what universities are supposed to [do]: produce educated, successful, upwardly mobile, white-collar neoliberal subjects."[90] He supports this claim not with analysis of other novels, but with a ranking of the universities attended by eight autofiction writers, including Knausgård, Heti, Cusk, and Lerner. (Murray conveniently ignores that the scholars who work closely on autofiction rarely are products of or work at elite American institutions, while the deriders of autofiction—many of whom are mentioned earlier—are and do. Indeed, the four scholars whose work on autofiction my definition of the term derives from—Alison Gibbons, Myra Bloom, Arnaud Schmitt, and Stefan Kjerkegaard—are all employed and trained outside the US.[91] In contrast, Lee Konstantinou received his PhD from Stanford University, Sarah Wasserman from Princeton University, and Anna Kornbluh from University of California–Irvine, while Murray received his PhD from the University of Florida and currently is a postdoctoral fellow at Emory University.) In a similar tone, Sarah Wasserman dismisses autofiction as a "critical darling" that presents "its exploration of the self with enough novelty to seem experimental, even when it is formally conventional."[92]

The rejection of autofiction by these scholars should not come as a surprise. In an essay on *My Struggle*, Toril Moi writes that applying "conventional criteria" to understand *My Struggle* will predictably lead to the conclusion that it "is a complete failure."[93] But a literary critic could choose another path: "she could try to figure out how to read this novel in new ways, drawing on completely different criteria for good writing. Instead of looking for symbols, she could consider the text's authenticity, passion and integrity, the quality of its descriptions, its capacity to convey reality, or its world-building abilities, just to mention some options." In this book, I attempt to follow Moi's path.

In recent years, a number of scholars have offered a host of new terms to describe what comes after postmodernism. Several of these accounts point to the centrality of the financial crisis and a few even suggest a correlation between the crisis and autofiction. Arne De Boever and Paul Crosthwaite both paint a picture of the complex ways contemporary literature confronts its inevitable participation in a financialized economy by mobilizing the tension between reality and fiction. The former explores in *Finance Fictions* (2018) how contemporary novels, including Ben Lerner's

10:04, exist at the "crossroads between the disavowal of reality and the affirmation of it," as he writes.[94] In *The Market Logics of Contemporary Fiction* (2019), Paul Crosthwaite suggests the term "market metafiction" to describe a body of authors who are "less concerned with the fictionality of the text as such, and more with the ways in which that fictionality solicits or spurns the approval of the literary marketplace."[95] This includes writers of autofiction such as Sheila Heti and Ben Lerner who "work out their positioning in the cultural field in and through dialogues with aspects of contemporary financial capitalism" (190). Crosthwaite insists that the financial crisis made it possible to "theorize a new intimacy between cultural production and economic value under contemporary conditions of financialization" (14).

Timotheus Vermeulen and Robin van den Akker have also, in their writings on what they call metamodernism, suggested a connection between current crises and a renewed commitment to reality. Though the term "metamodernism" appeared as early as 1975 (that is, if we are to trust *Wikipedia*), it was not until Vermeulen's and van den Akker's manifesto-like essay "Notes on Metamodernism" from 2010 that it became a viable term to describe what comes after postmodernism. In the essay they argue that "financial crises, geopolitical instabilities, and climatological uncertainties" have revealed that "the postmodern years of plenty, pastiche, and parataxis are over."[96] Metamodernism, on the other hand, is characterized by "the oscillation between a typically modern commitment and a markedly postmodern detachment" or between "a modern enthusiasm and postmodern irony" that can be "conceived as a kind of informed naivety, a pragmatic idealism" (2, 5). In the anthology *Metamodernism: Historicity, Affect, and Depth after Postmodernism*, Vermeulen and van den Akker further argue that metamodernism has become "the dominant cultural logical of Western capitalist societies."[97] It "emerges from, and reacts to, the postmodern as much as it is a cultural logic that corresponds to today's stage of global capitalism" that has been "bracketed by the collapse of the 'double bubble' consisting of the dot-com crash (1999–2000) and the global financial crisis (2007–2009)" (5, 14).

Writing with Alison Gibbons, Vermeulen and van den Akker turn to autofiction, asserting that metamodern texts "produce a 'reality effect'—a performance of, or insistence on, reality—and ironically, they create this effect by using the same postmodernist devises [Marie-Laue] Ryan identifies as panfictionalising techniques."[98] Invoking the comedian Stephen Colbert and his term "truthiness"—"the truth felt in one's gut as opposed to estab-

22 | Knausgård and the Autofictional Novel

lished through reason or empirical research"—the three authors coin the term "depthiness" as a response to Fredric Jameson's "depthlessness," used to characterize postmodernism. Depthiness, they write, "designates a renewed need or wish to experience the world as possessing depth, *as real*, even amidst a lingering postmodernism skepticism of such as an attempt" (54). Autofiction, and other metamodern genres, does not designate a return to earlier models of realism or the real. Rather, it displays "intimations of depth—performances of depthiness—dressed up as truth-claims that are, by necessity, fictional or fictionalised" (65).

Vermeulen and van den Akker, borrowing Raymond Williams's term, see metamodernist sentiment as "a structure of feeling" whose causes we might not be able to track precisely, but "whose results are visible in artistic commonality."[99] And this is precisely what we see with autofiction. Though metamodernism might not be the most eloquent or suitable term, it helps name the condition after postmodernism and in the wake of the financial crisis. It staves off the insufficient readings of autofiction in the light of postmodernism that inevitably ends with a rejection of the works in question and with little interest in understanding how these novels actually work. Instead, it opens up for a reading of the current iteration of autofictional novels as a phenomenon in its own right and as uniquely tied to the material conditions of the twenty-first century.

The reality hunger inherent in metamodernism with its "performance of, or instance on, reality" is apparent everywhere we look in the literary world. We find it in a diverse group of genres spanning from autobiographies, documentary novels, and true crime novels to autofiction and exofiction. We find it in the general perception of Elena Ferrante's Neapolitan novels as autobiographical despite the fact that the writer behind the pseudonym remains anonymous.[100] We find it institutionalized when the Nobel committee awards its literature prize to Svetlana Alexievich in 2015 and to Annie Ernaux in 2022. And we find it invoked when talking about a host of important contemporary Anglo-American writers, including those most often discussed in relation to Knausgård—Sheila Heti, Rachel Cusk, and Ben Lerner—as well as Jenny Offill, Teju Cole, Tope Folarin, Maggie Nelson, Brandon Taylor, Olivia Laing, Ocean Vuong, Edward St Aubyn, Ayad Akhtar, Chris Kraus, Tao Lin, and many others.

My Struggle is the pinnacle of this insistence on and engagement with reality. It is a departure from postmodernism both as an aesthetics and a condition. The novel expresses a longing and a striving for reality that might be utopian, but which nevertheless seems to resonate with

Introduction | 23

readers across the world. Writing a novel about what he in Book 6 calls "exclusively everyday events," Knausgård engages in world-building, where he recreates his own world literarily: not a fictional world but the world he lives in and which he inhabits.[101] If the financial crisis revealed a system based on fiction, Knausgård and other autofictional writers, in a complex and contradictory manner that simultaneously contrasts and arises from it, show that there is a reality, that it matters, and that it cannot be understood in a simple dichotomy against fiction.[102]

The Form of Autofiction

For years, formalism has had a bad reputation in literary studies. Formalism, especially as practiced by the New Criticism, treated literature as coherent and self-contained wholes, likened, in Cleanth Brooks's formulation, to a ballet or musical composition with "a pattern of resolutions and balances and harmonizations, developed through a temporal scheme."[103] Formalists focused on literary techniques such as plotting, structure, narration, imagery, and language at the expense of social, historical, or biographical understandings of any given text. Such an approach made it appear that texts existed in a vacuum, where all that mattered was close reading. More recently, a different kind of formalism, under the name new formalism, has become popular, in which, as Timothy Aubry and Florence Dore write, an "attention to form can serve ethical or political ends."[104] New formalism contends that literary forms reflect or respond to political and economic conditions. But it is less a theory or method, as Marjorie Levinson argues in a critical essay on new formalism, than it is "a movement," or perhaps more precisely, a diverse group of scholars who in various and often different ways are interested in the relationship between the political and literary form.[105]

I hesitate to align myself with new formalism, but formalism plays a key role in this study. It joins the cast as an understudy who eventually takes the lead. My readings of Knausgård and others move from affect to aesthetics, from feeling to form. I zoom in on specific passages to investigate the narration and narrative voice. These readings are typically contextualized in the larger theoretical discussions that they invoke—such as the genre of autobiography, the novel, narrative theory, and theories of fiction and fictionality—and I use formalism to argue that these autofictional novels challenge a number of theoretical assumptions about autobiography, narrative fiction, and the novel. My readings are not explicitly political but, I would argue, inevitably fight on the ground of what Joseph North calls "the terrain of sensibility."[106]

My view of what form is and can do is informed by scholars often seen as on the periphery of new formalism—scholars who not only link formalism and political readings but who also attempt to rethink what form is.[107] Caroline Levine, for instance, reminds us that form is more than specific literary techniques but something that "always indicates *an arrangement of elements—an ordering, patterning, or shaping*."[108] Levine borrows the term "affordance" from design theory, where it describes "the potential uses or actions latent in materials or designs." In the study of literary form, and as I use it here, affordance helps us see how different forms lay claim to different affordances. As Levine writes, "The sonnet, brief and condensed, best affords a single idea or experiences, 'a moment's monuments,' while the triple-decker novel affords elaborate processes of character development in multiplot social context" (6). Addressing a form's affordance is not an attempt to restrict what certain forms can do. Rather, it helps us see when certain forms are "put to use in unexpected ways" and examine what happens when different forms collide (6). In my reading of *My Struggle*, I use the concept of affordance to show how Knausgård, within the novelistic form, uses the form of the diary, which affords him a sense of intimacy, authenticity, and secrecy, such that we, readers of his six-volume novel, feel we are being let in where no one else has ever been. I also use affordance to explain the radicality of autofictionalization, where the monumentality of *My Struggle*'s six volumes affords an expanded and expansive use as Knausgård recounts episodes from his life.

Form is, however, more than affordance; as Sarah Chihaya writes, it is also "a verb, not just a noun."[109] As a verb, to form means to make, construct, or shape. And what literary form does—according to Anna Kornbluh—is to construct worlds where "we build works of worldly art, such as the novel, in order to push the bounds of possibility; we build social relations 'without origin.'"[110] Asking what realism builds, Kornbluh shows how theories of the novel, spanning Henry James, Georg Lukács, and Fredric Jameson, think of the novel in terms of architecture. She characterizes this as "the deliberate building of social space" and sees it "as the trope of realist form" (47). By approaching literary form through the concepts of affordance and architecture, it is possible to show what the form of autofiction both allows and builds. Formalism, then, need no longer be solely about identifying certain techniques or narrative modes but can also be a way to recognize what different forms can instigate. It can help us see the complexity of form: how different forms interact, overlap, and collide while building new structures, new genres, new literary worlds.[111]

My study reveals the literary forms that autofiction evokes as it seeks to satisfy a contemporary reality hunger by turning to reality. Central to this endeavor is the specific kind of narration, one that dominates *My Struggle*, that I call "autofictionalization." Other critics have noted that something unique is at stake in Knausgård's narration; I am in debt to the pioneering work of Danish scholar Poul Behrendt, whose early readings of *My Struggle* identified aspects of this narration. Joshua Rothman writes that Knausgård chronicles "the minute details of his own existence, but not from the perspective of himself," while Martin Hägglund characterizes Knausgård's narration as "not simply an act of remembering but of reliving."[112] I use the term "autofictionalization" to emphasize the distinctiveness of this narrative mode and to indicate its connection to autofiction as a genre.

Autofictionalization places the voice or the narrative consciousness not with the narrator, as we have come to accept it in autobiography, but with the author's former self. It can resemble free indirect discourse in third-person narrations; but with autofictionalization, there is no "third position" between narrator and character, as there is in free indirect discourse. The narrative voice is specifically and explicitly that of the former self. This mode of narration means that the narrator's knowledge of events is oftentimes not extended to the former self. It becomes a way to make the past present, as if certain events in the past were happening here and now. It also adds drama and intensity to the narration: in an episode I analyze in chapter 2, Knausgård's eight-year-old self wonders how his father knew he had been running when he was not supposed to: "How on earth did he know I had been running?" his former self ponders, while we experience how Knausgård as the narrator writes from the perspective of his eight-year-old self, almost as if he is reliving it. Knausgård as the narrator knows the answer to the question posed by his former self but only reveals it later in the narration when the eight-year-old self realizes how.[113] Knausgård's radical use of autofictionalization at varying degrees throughout *My Struggle* makes it a governing narrative trope in the novel.

I use the terms "fiction" and "fictionality" in numerous iterations throughout my study. But I specifically employ a notion of fictionality that

26 | Knausgård and the Autofictional Novel

I derive from newer rhetorical definitions in my definition of autofictionalization to help me understand it as a formal feature of Knausgård's novel. Instrumental in this endeavor are Henrik Skov Nielsen, James Phelan, and Richard Walsh. In "Ten Theses about Fictionality," their much-discussed article from 2015, they propose an understanding of fictionality based on relevance theory, through which they circumvent the discussion of fiction versus reality. To them, fictionality is not a textual marker but a contextual assumption. Fictionality is "a basic human ability to imagine," always a means to an end.[114] It is "a means for negotiating an engagement with that world" whether in fictive or nonfictive discourses (63).

Approaching fiction and fictionality rhetorically is a departure from attempts to distinguish fiction and reality formalistically. These attempts have been spearheaded by Dorrit Cohn in *The Distinction of Fiction* from 1999, and in recent decades, have been taken up by scholars such as Timothy Bewes and Catherine Gallagher.[115] These thinkers are united by a belief in what Cohn calls "signposts of fictionality." If these signposts can be identified in any text, then the text is to be considered fiction. Indeed, this is precisely what Bewes concludes in his reading of Knausgård, which I relay in chapter 1, and where he sees *My Struggle* as no different than any other fictional novel.

Such attempts to determine the fictional status of a literary text based on isolated formal characteristics are yet another reason formalism has had a bad reputation in literary studies in the past few decades. They sidestep commonsense perceptions of reading novels. While any fictional novel is characterized by what J. Hillis Miller calls "displacements," where the author, narrator, and main character decidedly not are identical, we take notice when they are. It informs our reading when they are one and the same. In other words, it matters that Karl Ove Knausgård is not only the author of the novel but also its narrator and protagonist. This homology affects our reading and creates an autobiographical pact between Knausgård and the reader, where we are invited to read *My Struggle* autobiographically. Simultaneously, Knausgård seems to go out of his way to convince us that he has a faulty memory, even claiming that large parts are made up, thus invoking a fictional pact. I argue that these two opposite trends in *My Struggle* do not undermine or even out each other. This duality—that *My Struggle* simultaneously invokes the autobiographical and fictional pacts—is a fundamental tenet of my reading of Knausgård. And examining form—what it is, what it can do, and how Knausgård uses it—is how I get there.

Introduction | 27

Knausgård and the Autofictional Novel

Knausgård and the Autofictional Novel consists of five chapters, four of which are dedicated to *My Struggle*. Chapter 1 is about Knausgård's desire to engage with reality in the form of a novel. It opens with a reading of his reflections on death, which correspond to the novel's considerations of fiction versus reality. The chapter argues that Knausgård's desire to move beyond what he refers to as a "purely linguistically structured world" to engage reality directly is a common thread throughout his writing. I show that the several scholars who have rejected this vital aspect of the novel, and who have dismissed *My Struggle* as fiction, are influenced by Paul de Man's essay "Autobiography as De-facement." After a critical reading of de Man's essay, I argue that Knausgård uses the literary form of the diary to bring about the reality in the novel he longs for. The chapter concludes where it opens, with a reading of death, but in a new iteration that reflects Knausgård's novelistic ambition.

Chapter 2 discusses how Knausgård turns to traditional features of the novel, as he seeks to write about his own life. With *My Struggle*, he embraces dualism—a dualism that I situate in the grand theories of the novel as a literary form—while also employing what Philippe Lejeune called, some decades ago, an "autobiographical pact," as well as a novelistic or fictional pact. The specificity, range, and quantity of details he includes in his novel create a sense of truthfulness, particularly when he's imagining—and fictionalizing—his former self. I call this mode of writing "autofictionalization," to distinguish the technique itself from the generic term autofiction.[116]

Chapter 3 is about shame in *My Struggle*, and about how shame is integrated into the novelistic form. Knausgård treats shame as a gateway to the past and a way to insist on the existence of a subject that otherwise has been deemed dead in postmodernity. Shame, in *My Struggle*, is not performative, like the shame described by Silvan Tomkins and Eve Sedgwick. Informed by Giorgio Agamben's understanding of shame as "the absolute concomitance of subjectification and desubjectification," Knausgård seems to use shame in part because it depends upon the existence of an actual subject.[117] Shame is also reflected in the novelistic form. And it results from the seeming incommensurability of ethics and aesthetics that leads Knausgård to renounce, in the very last sentence of *My Struggle*, his identity as a writer.[118] Finally, shame is also what reveals how much Knausgård and his father are alike and leads him to "fasten

28 | Knausgård and the Autofictional Novel

his gaze," which is a phrase he first hears at his father's funeral, but which in the novel takes on a metaphorical quality to express the existential quest of his novel, where he through his writing fastened his gaze on his own life and on his family in an attempt to solve the struggle between writing and family.[119]

Chapter 4 examines the relationship between fiction and the novel. Through a close reading of an episode from Book 6 of *My Struggle*, and drawing on Sianne Ngai's writing on tonality, I argue that the relation is reflected in the tone of Knausgård's novel. Turning to a larger discussion of the shared history of the novel and fiction, I engage a critical reading of Catherine Gallagher's influential article "The Rise of Fictionality" to conclude that Knausgård's attempt to do away with fiction is precisely what has led readers—both professional and others—to emphasize absorption and identification as integral to the experience of *My Struggle*. The chapter concludes with a reading of *My Struggle* in light of the narration versus description dichotomy that has been discussed in literary studies for decades, where I show how Knausgård's challenge to that dichotomy is a vital part of his novelistic project.

By turning to contemporary books most often named in connection with *My Struggle*—Heti's *How Should a Person Be?* (2010), Lerner's *10:04* (2014), and Rachel Cusk's *Outline* trilogy (2014–2018)—chapter 5 investigates autofiction more broadly and in the wake of Knausgård.[120] In *How Should a Person Be?* the titular question reflects both an existential concern about imitation and uncertainty about what it means to write novels in the twenty-first century—as a person and, the text itself makes clear, as a woman. In the *Outline* trilogy, Cusk creates presence through the apparent absence of her main protagonist, Faye, as the act of listening and observing becomes central to the novel's relentless pursuit of truth and reality. For Cusk, too, gender is integral to her autofictional project as the novel seeks a narrative form that adequately reflects the lived experience of women. And inspired by Knausgård, Lerner's autofictionalization in *10:04* complicates any distinction between fiction and reality further than the other writers under consideration in my study, as fiction simultaneously has become a problem and a possibility for the ambiguously named narrator of the novel.

The book concludes with a short afterword in which I discuss the implication of my study of autofiction in the twenty-first century, as well as how Knausgård, Heti, Cusk, and Lerner have approached writing in the wake of their autofictional novels.

That a novel is a "fictional prose narrative," as defined in the *OED*, is integral to our understanding of the genre from its earliest iteration in Cervantes's *Don Quixote* through its prime in the nineteenth century to the present. But Knausgård, and other authors following his lead, have challenged this assumption by writing about their own lives in novels. The results have made clear that the novel still is the most able and nimble genre we have for interpreting and understanding both our own lives and the world we inhabit.

Knausgård's *My Struggle* is one of the most important literary achievements of the twenty-first century. My book explains why, as I argue that Knausgård confronts, challenges, and rejects the symbiotic relationship between novels and fiction.

Chapter 1

A Commitment to Reality

My Struggle opens with a reversal of the typical narrative of life: it begins with death. In a hyperrealist description of what happens to the body when death sets in, Knausgård portrays death as a purely physical phenomenon.[1] Yet, after one long paragraph—a little more than one page—Knausgård leaves the description of the dead body behind and launches into an essayistic account of our unwillingness to face death in everyday life, even as it surrounds us in art and the media.[2] That essayistic passage anticipates what is to come in the six volumes of *My Struggle*: an ongoing commitment to represent reality, and an attempt to do away with fiction.

In his account on death, Knausgård describes society's immense "distaste" for it. He describes how we hide dead bodies in "discrete, inaccessible rooms" of hospital basements and how we cover them up, transport them in "vehicles with tinted glass," and keep them in "closed coffins until they are lowered into the earth or cremated in the oven" (1.4). There is no practical purpose for going to such lengths to conceal the dead, he says, but we engage in a "collective act of repression" anyway.[3] But at the same time that we hide death from our lives, we are constantly exposed to it in newspapers and on TV. Death, as we see it in the media, is everywhere:

> Yet, *that* kind of death does not seem threatening. Quite the contrary, it is something we are drawn to and will happily pay to see. Add the enormously high body count in fiction and it becomes even harder to understand the system that keeps death out of sight. If the phenomenon of death does not frighten us, why then this distaste for dead bodies? (1.5)

32 | Knausgård and the Autofictional Novel

The answer, Knausgård speculates, is that there are two kinds of death: "our conception of death and death as it actually turns out to be" (1.5). These two kinds of death are relayed to us differently in two separate and distinct systems: "One is associated with concealment and gravity, earth and darkness, the other with openness and airiness, ether and light" (1.6). While the first is concrete and based in reality, the other is abstract and seems removed from reality.

Knausgård's writing about two kinds of deaths resembles his conceptualization of fiction and reality, which he considers throughout *My Struggle*. His ambition, as I will show in this chapter, is to make the kind of death we conceal and hide away as visible and concrete as the kind of death we are exposed to everywhere. It is a longing for reality, which in his version translates into an ontology of being and an engagement with the physical world. But it is equally a longing to break the layer of fiction that penetrates everything and is exemplified in our view of death. As such, his thoughts on death are emblematic of his overall aspiration in *My Struggle*: doing away with fiction by writing honestly and sincerely about his own life in the form of a novel. No wonder that, as Knausgård tells it in Book 6, he insisted on having *My Struggle* open with these pages on death despite his editor's recommendation against it.[4] Death is how he fuels, and begins to realize, his ambitions.

A Linguistically Structured World

Knausgård first introduced his idea about the two kinds of death in an essay titled "On the Future" ("Om framtiden"), published in the Norwegian journal *Samtiden* a full year before Book 1 of *My Struggle* hit Norwegian bookstores. In the essay, Knausgård sees death as the only future we can be sure of while, in times less rational than ours, "it was the return of Jesus that was thought of as the future."[5] With *My Struggle*, Knausgård repurposes much of the essay, cutting and pasting some of the text directly: the sentence that became the opening of *My Struggle*, the physiological description of what happens when death sets in, and his own thoughts about how he previously, and unsuccessfully, had been trying "to combat fiction with fiction" as an author. He also reuses the essay's final words to close Book 1, where Karl Ove, as I refer to the character in the novel to distinguish him from the narrator and author, sees the corpse of his deceased father and realizes that death "is no more than a pipe that springs a leak, a branch that cracks in the wind, a jacket that slips off a clothes hanger and falls to the floor" (1.441). By placing these passages at both the opening and conclusion of Book 1, death is announced as a major theme in *My Struggle* and directs our reading of what is to come.

Knausgård is not the first to theorize about the existence of two kinds of death. In his 1936 essay "The Storyteller," Walter Benjamin observes that death has become less visible in daily life. "Dying was once a public process in the life of the individual and a most exemplary one," he writes, and there was "no house, hardly a room, in which someone had not died."[6] But today— which for Benjamin means the interwar period—we stow the dying away in sanatoria or hospitals and, as a result, live in houses and rooms "that have never been touched by death" (84). Instead of witnessing death ourselves, we experience representations and descriptions of it: "No event any longer comes to us without already being shot through with explanation" (81). As Knausgård later describes, this means that death reaches us in mediated forms.

Because we no longer derive knowledge of death from its presence in our lives, we turn to the novel. Novels serve as compensation, Benjamin argues, showing us deaths that are both concrete, when characters die, and more metaphorical, when the novel itself ends. As Peter Brooks puts it in his reading of Benjamin, all "narrative may in essence be obituary" in that the "retrospective knowledge it seeks, the knowledge that comes after, stands on the far side of the end, in human terms on the far side of death."[7] In other words, the ability to encounter death at safe distances gives the novel its power. Benjamin writes:

> The novel is significant, therefore, not because it presents someone else's fate to us, perhaps didactically, but because this stranger's fate by virtue of the flame which consumes it yields us the warmth which we never draw from our own fate. What draws the reader to the novel is the hope of warming his shivering life with a death he reads about." (88)

Knausgård, too, warms his shivering life by writing about death. He never mentions Benjamin's essay by name, but, as James Wood writes, *My Struggle* "is so powerfully alive to death that it sometimes seems a kind of huge, ramshackle annex to Benjamin's brief thesis."[8] Benjamin's ghostly presence suggests that, in writing about death, Knausgård also has in mind the status of the novel and writing itself. Both writers situate the two kinds of death within a frame of fiction versus reality, but while Benjamin sees the two kinds of death develop historically with one form of death replacing another, Knausgård sees them as simultaneous with both existing at once.

34 | Knausgård and the Autofictional Novel

Knausgård concludes his reflections on the two kinds of death with several examples of death as it appears in the media, the last of which sends the narration of Book 1 off in a different direction: the story of when Knausgård at the age of eight watched a TV news report about a shipwrecked fishing boat whose entire crew had drowned. After that, the essayistic considerations on death disappear from the narration for more than two hundred pages. When returning to the subject, halfway through Book 1, Knausgård makes the relationship between the two kinds of death and fiction and reality explicit. He writes how, at the age of nineteen, he was introduced to the "contention that the world is linguistically structured." At first, he rejected it: "it was obviously meaningless, the pen I held, was that supposed to be language?" (1.220). But years later, he began "to view this differently" when he happened upon Nietzsche's description of the world as "*a purely fabricated world*" (1.221, original italics).

The phrase helps young Knausgård understand the notion of the world as linguistically structured—a view attributed to what has been called the "linguistic turn."[9] To him, a purely fabricated world means the world "as a superstructure" and a world that "after three hundred years of natural science is left without mysteries." It is a world where everything can be explained and understood, for it lies "within humanity's horizon of comprehension" (1.221). It is also, I would add, a world that emerges from and with the transition from early to late capitalism; the "almost incestuous" feeling that Knausgård identifies is bound up with the way capitalism penetrates every aspect of life (1.221). He seems to have this in mind as well, using the Marxist term "superstructure" (or *overbygning* in the Norwegian original) to describe the linguistically structured world.

Knausgård contends that a purely fabricated and linguistically structured world depends upon a layer of fiction that prevents us from accessing reality. He writes that it makes the world feel "small, tightly enclosed around itself." That particular feeling is what he wants to escape: "The longing I always felt, which some days was so great it could hardly be controlled, had its source here . . . It was partly to relieve this feeling that I wrote" (1.221). Thus, he writes because he longs for a reality outside of the fictional superstructure the world has become.

To show that such reality exists—that there truly is something beyond the fictional superstructure—Knausgård points to the moments "where for a few seconds you catch sight of another world from the one you were in only a moment earlier" (1.222). These moments show that not everything in the world can be explained, and Knausgård is convinced that they expose the existence of something that falls outside of language.[10] He mentions how he once experienced such a moment while riding a commuter train in Stockholm. It was, he explains, a gray and foggy day with "red rays [of sunlight] fading into the mist" as the train passed through an industrial area with "empty railway cars, gas tanks, factories" (1.222). Suddenly, he says, he felt a pleasure so powerful "that it was indistinguishable from pain." By contrasting colors and natural phenomena, such as the fog and the sun with the man-made and deserted industrial landscape, Knausgård describes something akin to a modernist epiphany and configuration of the sublime, albeit, as Alexandra Kingston-Reese notes, in "a quieter, domestic version."[11] Unable to explain what exactly happened, he stresses that it came to him with an unparalleled intensity: "What I experienced seemed to me to be of enormous significance," he writes, repeating the last part of the sentence for emphasis: "Enormous significance" (1.222).[12]

At this point in his narration Knausgård reintroduces his ideas about the two kinds of death from the opening pages. The proximity of these ideas to his longing for reality beyond the linguistically structured world reveals what was there all along: an abiding concern with the concepts of fiction and reality, situated in a tangible, concrete frame that readers will find relevant. As we recognize how society seems to operate within a system in which death is both something we hide away and something we are exposed to every single day, we can see how the fictional and "the linguistically structured world" allow us to forget that reality exists.[13] And we can track the larger argument about fiction and language that Knausgård advances throughout *My Struggle*.

Indeed, Knausgård concludes the second round of his thoughts on death with a reflection upon the word itself: the many mediated representations of death, he writes, have made the word itself a fiction, as this kind of "death is the same as the word 'death,' the bodiless entity referred to when a person's name is used" (1.226). Knausgård differentiates, here, between the form and content of the word "death": the form is the word we use to designates death, while the content is death as it actually occurs. With this, Knausgård situates his novelistic project in the midst of a discussion of the linguistic sign as consisting of signifier and signified that has been pivotal in literary studies from the early twentieth century to the present. He does so in an attempt to answer urgent questions about both life and literature.

The Reality of Fantasy

The terms "signifier" and "signified" were coined by Ferdinand de Saussure, whose lecture notes from the University of Geneva in the first decade of the twentieth century were compiled by his students into the book *Course in General Linguistics*. Widely considered the father of modern linguistics, Saussure argued that the only way to scientifically study language is synchronically. As an extension of his distinction between *language, langue,* and *parole* (that is language as such, *a* language such as English, and language in use), Saussure analyzed the word as a verbal sign consisting of two sides, a sound pattern and a concept. "A linguistic sign is not a link between a thing and a name," he states, "but between a concept and a sound pattern."[14] Renaming the sound pattern and the concept "signifier" and "signified" (or *signifié* and *signifiant*), Saussure stresses that the "*linguistic sign is arbitrary,*" by which he simply means that there is "no internal connection between, for example, the idea 'sister' and the French sequence of sounds *s-ö-r* which acts as its signified" (12, translation altered, original italics).[15]

Saussure's distinction between signifier and signified became such an important contribution to literary studies, and the humanities more broadly, that as Toril Moi puts it, "in the humanities today, the *doxa* concerning language and meaning remains Saussurean or, rather, post-Saussurean."[16] His study of language became, as Terence Hawkes writes, an "entry not only into structuralism and semiotics, but into the wide range of cultural and critical theories underpinned by these approaches."[17] It also led to theories of poststructuralism and deconstruction, based, in Hawkes's formulation, on the belief that "the signifiers have free play" (92).[18]

It is precisely this that Knausgård refers to when writing about a linguistically structured and purely fabricated world. But as a novelist, and not a language philosopher, he still experiences a longing to represent the real, and this is what made him write in the first place: "I wanted to open the world by writing," he says (1.221).[19] That desire, he explains in Book 1 of *My Struggle*, animated his first two novels as well—the novels *Out of the World* (1998) and *A Time for Everything* (2004)—just in a different way: "What I was trying to do, and perhaps what all writers try to do—what on earth do I know?—was to combat fiction with fiction" (1.222).[20] He was, in other words, trying to move beyond fiction by writing fiction. But what he should have done, he believes, is to set out to "affirm what existed, affirm the state of things as they are, in other words, revel in the outside world instead of searching for a way out" (1.222, translation altered). He should have embraced the linguistically structured world and the idea that everything, like the medial death we are exposed to everywhere, is just fiction.[21] But he didn't. He didn't because he couldn't, he says, and because he believed that there was something else: a reality suppressed or hidden but that he wanted to reach with his writing.

The longing for such hidden reality recurs in all of Knausgård's books: from the very title of his first novel, *Out of the World* from 1998, to his book on Edvard Munch, *So Much Longing in So Little Space*, published in Norway in 2017 in concurrence with the opening of an exhibition he curated at the Munch Museum in Oslo.[22] But the longing can be traced even further back to his childhood and his formative reading of Ursula K. Le Guin's fantasy novel *A Wizard of Earthsea* (1968). This particular book, Knausgård writes in *Inadvertent* (2018), changed his world.[23] As a young boy, he would plow through endless piles of books that he forgot the second he put them down, but *A Wizard of Earthsea* was different. It was a book he "often thought about and read over and over again" because it gave his "feelings a form and direction."[24]

A Wizard of Earthsea is set in premodern times. It chronicles the transformational years of Ged, a young boy, from his first discovery of his talent for magic through wizard school, where he learns to master his skills. In *Inadvertent*, Knausgård summarizes the premise of the novel: "Every thing, every animal, and every human being has a true name, outside language, linked to what it really is. The art of magic is connected with these names: if only one knows the name one can control the thing, the animal, the person" (21).

Knowing the true name of things is in Le Guin's novel referred to as "True Speech," and the magician who speaks this language can be seen as the realization of Knausgård's authorial ambitions: he, too, wants to learn True Speech and link language to the actual reality beyond the linguistically structured surface, to be able to connect the signifier with the signified.

The link between fantasy and Knausgård's longing to write reality is not just the stuff of boyhood memories. The longing he describes in Book 1 of *My Struggle* for something beyond the linguistically structured world has a utopian element to it. He even writes at one point: "Literature has always been related to utopia" (1.222). Throughout *My Struggle*, he interchangeably describes a longing for reality and a longing for what he calls "the sacred." This explains his use of the mixed directions, when he interchangeably speaks of his longing for something either above, under, or beyond.[25] Whatever the location, he suggests attaining a kind of rapture beyond the existing world, as Dan Sinykin also has proposed, beyond

38 | Knausgård and the Autofictional Novel

the world as a superstructure.[26] Such rapture opens the world, creating a certain state that he names several times throughout the six volumes: "Everything was possible" (1.71).

This might be why Knausgård refers to his longing as "essentialist, that is, outmoded, and furthermore, romantic," driven by an enduring, even consuming, ethos (1.222). His insistence on the seriousness, the severity, and the scope of his longing is his best argument against a view of language that tells him that each linguistic sign, each signifier, only refers to other signifiers "with which," in the words of Paul de Man, "it can never coincide."[27] It is also his only defense against the contention that his longing should be rejected as nothing but reactionary and antiquated: I know it is there, damn it, because I have experienced it.[28] Ultimately, it makes his longing for something beyond the linguistically structured world a central endeavor in his overall novelistic ambition.

The complex and unusual relationship between fantasy and reality also plays an important role in Knausgård's second novel, *A Time for Everything* (2004). The novel starts out as a biography of the fictitious scholar of angels, Antinous Bellioris, which paves the way for a radical revision of the biblical stories of Cain, Abel, Noah, and the prophet Ezekiel. Toward the end of the novel, a present-day narrating I is introduced. It turns out to be to Henrik Vankel—the protagonist of Knausgård's first novel *Out of the World* (*Ute av verden*) from 1999—who has created the whole novel with its elements of fantasy based on a comment his father once made about seagulls being fallen angels. The story of the angels—an invisible and alternative history—is Vankel's attempt to recreate a moment of intimacy with his recently deceased father, whom he otherwise considered distant and authoritarian.[29] Fantasy, in that novel, does not necessarily bring Vankel closer to reality, but it helps him undo the narrative of his father as dominant and frightening. *The Morning Star* [*Morgenstjernen*], Knausgård's 2020 novel, also has a strong element of fantasy, as an enormous star suddenly appears in the sky. Animals start behaving in new and surprising ways, and the star brings out the core of each of the nine characters. As such, fantasy makes these characters confront their own reality.

In both *A Time for Everything* and *Out of the World*, Knausgård tried to manifest this longing within a fictional universe. But by the time he began writing *My Struggle*, that approach had come to seem insufficient. He came to see the fictional as a hinderance for an engagement with the world as it actually is, including the kind of death we go out of our way to hide.

A Commitment to Reality | 39

The earnestness of this endeavor has, with noticeable exceptions, been dismissed by scholars and critics alike.[30] Some do this by rejecting his thoughts on engaging with reality as banal or as "familiar educated talking points," as William Deresiewicz writes in his now-infamous critique of *My Struggle* in the *Nation*.[31] Others apply the very view of language to Knausgård that he seeks to move beyond. Such readings reject not only Knausgård's longing, but also his commitment to write about his own life as it is, as naïve or illusionary. But his longing for reality, and commitment to writing about his own life, is key to the work's urgency, appeal, and success.

Autobiography as Fiction

In an article from 2019, Timothy Bewes makes the bold claim that *My Struggle* is no different from any other fictional novel. The article is an extended version of a paper he gave at the conference for the Modern Language Association in 2018 in a session that I happened to attend. The fact that the first part of the article originated as a conference paper is an important point in Bewes's argument, as he uses it to make a forceful and illustrative case for the importance of separating direct and indirect discourse, direct and represented speech, and to distinguish a critical discourse from a fictional one. Bewes suggests that what we refer to when talking about fiction and fictionality is nothing but represented speech or thought. Using his own paper at the MLA as an example—a talk "I am going to read, here and now, in this space," though admitting that "the words I am speaking at this moment—right here, right now—were actually written on my computer seven days ago"—he claims that what separates his talk from indirect discourse, and establishes it "firmly and conceptionally in the realms of direct speech," is temporality.[32]

Soon after, when Bewes turns to literary examples, it becomes clear that the kind of temporality he is most interested in is temporality as a formal aspect of a novel. In a discussion of Knausgård, he seeks to counter what he refers to as claims of the "presence" of *My Struggle*, by which he means the notion that Knausgård seeks out reality and writes about himself.[33] He turns to a description from Book 2, where Knausgård talks about Geir Angell's book on boxing, which Bewes quotes in its entirety:

> Geir's book was not only about independence, it was also enacted within its terms of reference. He described only what

40 | Knausgård and the Autofictional Novel

> he saw with his own eyes, what he heard with his own ears, and when he tried to describe what he saw and heard, it was by becoming a part of it. It was also the form of reflection that came closest to the life he was describing. A boxer was never judged by what he said or thought but by what he did. (2.129)

Following this quote, Bewes writes:

> However, like every programmatic claim or moment of description in *My Struggle*, this passage is in free indirect discourse. Yes, the focalization is with Karl Ove himself, but Karl Ove, the recipient of Geir's book, is an object of representation, his thoughts removed in time and being from the moment of narration . . . Passages of description or reflection in Knausgaard do not betoken a special "presence" or quality of "attentiveness" so much as an irreducible fictionality inside all such notions of presence. This element radically differentiates practices of description in Knausgaard from those that take place in non-literary contexts, whatever the author himself may think. (546)

There is a lot at stake in this reading: Bewes makes the bold claim that all descriptions and passages of reflection in *My Struggle* should be seen as fictional because they use free indirect speech. He also asserts that any presence in the novel turns out to be an absence, because Knausgård employs free indirect discourse. Free indirect discourse exists only in literary texts that refer to the temporality between narrator and character, Bewes writes.[34] If that is the case, Bewes's conclusion stands and falls with his reading of the passage from *My Struggle* as an example of free indirect discourse.

Yet nothing in the block quote that Bewes cites suggests that it should be considered free indirect discourse, or FID, as it is often abbreviated. If a concept such as FID makes any sense, it is precisely because it "frees" the narration. Free indirect discourse creates what has been called a "third voice" in the narration where the novel—in the words of Anna Kornbluh—"can 'get inside a character's head' and propagate psychological ascriptions of subjectivity."[35] It creates an ambiguity, where we might ask: "Who is speaking?" And it also, as James Wood argues, opens a gap "between author and character, and the bridge—which is free indirect style itself—between them simultaneously closes that gap and draws attention

A Commitment to Reality | 41

to its distance."[36] But the passage singled out by Bewes in which Knausgård writes about his friend Geir Angell's book on boxing is a regular third-person account written in past tense. Not at any point is there any doubt who is speaking.[37] There is also no "free" in the passage that draws attention to the gap between author and character.[38] Consequently, the characterization of the passage as an instance of free indirect discourse seems to undermine the very notion of the term with the result that his reading makes us question his initial assertion: that temporality can help us distinguish between fictive and nonfictive discourses.[39]

The attempt to "disclose" that presence in *My Struggle* is in fact absence is Timothy Bewes's way of discrediting Knausgård's claim of reality. There is no difference, he asserts, between *My Struggle* and any other fictional account.[40] He ignores Knausgård's explicit and stated intention about writing honestly about his own life and suggests that any attempt to move beyond what Fredric Jameson famously called "the prison-house of language" is doomed to fail: we are once and for all caught in the linguistically structured world and there is no escape.

In a similar "disclosure" of *My Struggle*, Taylor Johnston avers that the structure of the novel "never really coheres into meaning" and concludes rather surprisingly—at least for anyone who has read *My Struggle*—that Knausgård does not succeed in narrating his own life story: "Rather than advancing the story of Knausgaard's life," the description of his own life "forms a sort of 'black hole' in the narrative."[41] Indeed, Dan Sinykin, in *Post45*'s slow burn on *My Struggle*, also writes that Knausgård's "transparency is an illusion" and that his "apparent simplicity, openness, innocence, and honesty have nothing to do with mimesis and everything to do with form."[42]

These claims—that Knausgård's commitment to reality becomes indistinguishable from fiction the second he sets pen to paper—come directly from the contention that a linguistically structured world also makes autobiographical writing impossible. It is an idea that can be traced back to Paul de Man's seminal essay "Autobiography as De-facement" (1979). In this essay, we find programmatically pronounced what Derek Attridge has referred to as the "necessarily fictional nature of autobiography," which provides the foundational logic behind both Bewes's and Johnston's very different rejections of *My Struggle*.[43] De Man's essay has already been cited in a remarkable number of readings of *My Struggle*, perhaps partly because Paul de Man himself figures rather prominently in the books.[44] In Book 5, for instance, Knausgård refers to him with the nickname used

42 | Knausgård and the Autofictional Novel

by many of de Man's devotees, "Paul *the* Man."[45] Knausgård also relates how, as a young literature student at the University of Bergen—known as the Scandinavian beachhead of deconstruction and critical theory—he wrote a song for his band with the lyrics: *"I'm a fan of Paul the Man"* (5.279, original italics).[46]

In his essay, de Man argues that autobiography cannot reveal "reliable self-knowledge" but instead only demonstrates the impossibility of referentiality. No doubt, this is why Linda Anderson, in her short book *Autobiography*, calls the essay radical and says that it "signaled the end of autobiography."[47] In this light, Knausgård's longing for something beyond the linguistically structured could be seen as specifically directed toward de Man, whose essay on autobiography Danish scholar Hans Hauge even claims Knausgård must have read, given his insistence upon autobiographical referentiality in *My Struggle*.[48] With or without direct knowledge of the essay, Knausgård does seek to discredit its central claim: that autobiographical writing is impossible.

De Man opens "Autobiography as De-facement" by claiming that contemporary theory of autobiography—which for him means the late 1970s—is "plagued by a recurrent series of questions and approaches" that take for granted assumptions about "autobiographical discourse that are in fact highly problematic."[49] Seemingly identifying the study of autobiography solely with the work of French scholar Philippe Lejeune, de Man ignores the work of scholars such as James Olney, Paul John Eakin, and Elizabeth W. Bruss, all of whom, in the decade leading up to de Man's essay, problematize the idea of autobiography as a literary genre in its own right.[50]

The first of the questions raised by de Man is whether autobiography should be treated as an independent literary genre. Asserting that the study of autobiography is dominated by attempts to come up with a generic definition, de Man claims that scholars working on autobiography simply focus on "questions that are both pointless and unanswerable" because "autobiography lends itself poorly to generic definition; each specific instance seems to be an exception to the norm" (68). Why autobiography needs a bullet-proof definition in order to be taken seriously never becomes clear. Surely, such definitions of the other genres he mentions—tragedy, lyric poetry, and the novel—do not meet this standard. In fact, one might argue that the very definition of a literary genre is that it escapes and challenges of any generic definition.[51] De Man asking for a generic definition of autobiography suggests a "craving for generality," as Toril Moi calls it in a critique of poststructuralism, adding that the belief "that all

A Commitment to Reality | 43

the instances that fall under a concept must have something in common is usually called essentialism."[52] To put it even more bluntly: through a pseudo-argument about the scholarship on autobiography, de Man creates a straw man to help him discredit the idea of treating autobiography as an independent genre.

The second question de Man takes up, and on which he spends the remainder of the essay, is how to distinguish between autobiography and fiction. Autobiography, he says, depends more on actual and potentially verifiable facts than does fiction. Because of that, it "seems to belong to a simpler mode of referentiality, of representation, and of diegesis," where his use of the word "simpler" suggests that he momentarily ranks literary works that claim reference to reality as inferior to those that do not (68). But, de Man goes on to inquire, is that the case? Does autobiography really depend on referentiality? "We assume that life produces the autobiography as an act *produces* its consequences, but can we not suggest, with equal justice, that the autobiographical project may itself produce and determine the life and that whatever the writer *does* is in fact governed by the technical demands of self-portraiture and thus determined, in all its aspects, by the resources of his medium?" (69, original italics). What de Man seems to be saying in this cryptic formulation is that autobiography is not a "pure" image of the author and that language is not simply a vessel that unproblematically communicates this image to the readers. He reverses realist causality, where literature is seen as a reflection of life, asserting instead that form and language have the potential to determine the content and therefore also the life portrayed in the autobiographical text.[53] De Man's mind is made up: autobiography produces and determines life.

Turning to Gérard Genette's reading of Proust, de Man further complicates the relationship between autobiography and fiction. While Genette argues that *Recherche* is simultaneously fiction *and* autobiography, de Man calls this a matter of undecidability and asks rhetorically if "it is possible to remain, as Genette would have it, *within* an undecidable situation?" (70, original italics). Answering his own question, de Man turns to metaphor: "As anyone who has ever been caught in a revolving door or on a revolving wheel can testify, it is certainly most uncomfortable" (70). The metaphor of the revolving door that de Man uses here originates in Genette's reading of Proust, as Genette, presumably in an allusion to the scene in *The Guermantes Way* in which Marcel gets stuck in the revolving door on his way into a café, argues that we in reading Proust should "remain *within* this whirligig" between fiction and autobiography (70). But extending the

44 | Knausgård and the Autofictional Novel

metaphor—a rather unusual move for de Man—simplifies the question to a point where it easily can be dismissed: none of us, of course, wants to be stuck in a revolving door or on a revolving wheel, especially when de Man adds that the "whirligig is capable of infinite acceleration" (70). Why the "whirligig is capable of infinite acceleration" never becomes clear, except that such imagined excess might make us hastier to leave the dizzy scene for the relative comfort and stability of de Man's insistence that, when reading autobiography, we reject undecidability.[54] Because of that, de Man says, a text that claims to be autobiographical can be read in one of two ways: either as autobiographical or as fiction, but not as both.

The strict ontological demand implied in de Man's reading is an important element in his rather complex line of argumentation, where he sees the two I's involved in autobiography—that is the "I" that is writing and the "I" that is being written—forming a "spectacular structure" that reflects the difficulty of closure within any system of tropes. And, as the structure of self-reading—the writing "I" writing about the written "I"—is the basis of all self-knowledge, it follows, in de Man's reasoning, that all self-knowledge depends on a system of tropes. In other words, what makes autobiography interesting is, according to de Man, "not that it reveals reliable self-knowledge—it does not," but that it demonstrates the impossibility of closure (71). With that, he concludes: "The spectacular system has been displaced but not overcome, and we reenter a system of tropes the very moment we claim to escape it" (72).[55] We are trapped—in a metaphor de Man invokes in his essay—in the prison house of language.

This is precisely the line of thinking that Knausgård seeks to challenge when asserting that there must be more to life and writing than just language. Familiar with poststructuralism, if not de Man's essay, Knausgård still insists on the possibility of something beyond a linguistically structured world. There is, he says, a reality beyond fictional superstructure. Yet scholars inspired by the kind of arguments put forth by Paul de Man easily reject this belief and seek to "prove" that Knausgård, despite his naïve desire, never manages to escape the linguistically structured world of signifiers as we saw in both Johnston's and Bewes's readings.[56] In truth, there is no need to point this out: Knausgård readily admits to it himself in the novel. So instead of continually pulling the rug out from under his project, I believe we should study its patterns and seek to better understand his meaning. A good place to start is with the genesis of Knausgård's novel.[57]

A Commitment to Reality | 45

As Close to Life as Possible

Knausgård recounts how *My Struggle* came into being in Book 2. What eventually became *My Struggle*, he says, grew from a frustration with fiction that had led to a bad case of writer's block. After writing two critically acclaimed novels, he had spent nearly four years trying to write about his father's death in the form of the novel. But everything he wrote spoke to his growing mistrust in literature: "Over recent years I had increasingly lost faith in literature. I read and thought, this is something someone has made up. Perhaps it was because we were totally inundated with fiction and stories. It had got out of hand. Wherever you turned you saw fiction" (2.561). In the passage, Knausgård moves from a loss of faith in literature writ large to a more specific loss of faith in fiction. In a world that is already pure fabrication, fiction merely adds more layers of unreality, as verisimilitude is so dominant that whether something is actually fictitious or real no longer matters. To Knausgård, this creates a feeling of sameness, where any claims of uniqueness are invalid. It all added up, he says, to "a crisis."

> I couldn't write like this, it wouldn't work, every single sentence was met with the thought: but you're just making this up. It has no value. Fictional writing has no value, documentary narrative has no value. The only genres I saw any value in, which still conferred meaning, were diaries and essays, the type of literature that did not deal with narrative, that were not about anything, but just consisted of a voice, the voice of your own personality, a life, a face, a gaze you could meet. (2.562)

While Knausgård's thoughts on being fed up with fiction correspond to his thoughts on death and longing for reality in Book 1, his further appreciation of diaries and essays makes it possible to read *My Struggle* as an attempt to write in those genres within the form of a novel. It also provides a reason for the many essayistic and diaristic passages throughout the six volumes. In *Inadvertent*, Knausgård writes that he wanted "to get close to reality, and the genre with which I felt the greatest affinity at the time was the diary."[58] And like a writer of diaries, he logs dates and place-names throughout *My Struggle*. The first of these—"Today is the twenty-seventh of February. The time is 11:43 p.m."—occurs early in

46 | Knausgård and the Autofictional Novel

Book 1, right after one of the most pivotal scenes in *My Struggle*, where Knausgård describes his face reflected in the window in front of him.[59] This particular scene, which Martin Hägglund refers to as "the degree zero of his project," reoccurs in Book 2, where it is contextualized as a central piece in the origin story of *My Struggle*.[60]

One night in late February 2008, Knausgård says, when he came home from a trip to his old hometown of Kristiansand in Norway, he went into his study and started writing that very scene. Though the descriptions of this scene diverge in the English translations of Book 1 and Book 2, they are identical in the original Norwegian, and I have translated here with that in mind:

> In the window before me I can vaguely make out the reflection of my face. Apart from one eye, which is glistening, and the area immediately beneath, which dimly reflects a little light, the whole of the left side is in shadow. Two deep furrows divide my forehead, one deep furrow intersects each cheek, all of them as if filled with darkness, and with the eyes staring and serious, and the corners of the mouth drooping, it is impossible not to consider this face gloomy. (1.25, 2.582, translation altered)

The scene—sitting alone late at night and writing about his own face as he sees it reflected in the window—creates a sense of confidentiality with the reader. We feel we are invited to witness the most intimate, private core of the creative process. The intimacy is similar to that of the diary, which in the words of Philippe Lejeune can be likened to "a dark room that you enter from a brightly lit exterior" and where you slowly "begin to see the outlines" and "silhouettes begin to emerge from the shadows."[61] Lejeune also suggests that the diary, due to the fact that it is "hooked on truth," can be considered what he somewhat ambiguously calls "antifiction."[62]

Written in the present tense, Knausgård's paragraph creates a contemporaneousness that mimics what Dorrit Cohn has called simultaneous narration, with the temporal distance, between the narrating and experiencing self, reduced to zero: "the moment of narration *is* the moment of experience, the narrating self *is* the experiencing self."[63] Invited to see, even to sit with, Knausgård at this innermost moment of creation, we feel privileged that we are the ones he chooses to confide in, that we are, as Arnaud Schmitt and Stefan Kjerkegaard write, "drawn into an intersubjective relation with the author."[64] We experience what Rita Felski, differentiating

A Commitment to Reality | 47

between four strands of identification in reading, has called alignment: "the formal means by which texts shape a reader's or viewer's access to character."[65] Though we might not always agree with Knausgård, perhaps even wanting to distance ourselves from him, we still sympathize with him because he has shown us trust, by writing honestly about himself.[66]

In Book 1, Knausgård goes on to describe his face as "stiff and mask-like and almost impossible to associate with myself whenever I happen to catch a glimpse of it in a shop window" (1.26). A similar scene of self-reflexivity can be found in his first novel *Out of the World* (*Ute av verden*): "In the window only the unclear glare of the room was reflected now. My own blurry face."[67] While both descriptions invoke a long modernist tradition of self-reflexivity, the description in Book 1 seems to push ever closer to the real because Knausgård is writing about his own face.[68] It is the realization of the qualities he sees in essays and diaries: "the voice of your own personality, a life, a face, a gaze" (2.562).

What Knausgård is seeking, then, is not realism as a literary practice but the intimacy and truth associated with the diary. Realism involves fiction and overarching narrative, while the diary, in his formulation, avoids both and, according to Knausgård, encompasses a physicality typically not found in realism. By imitating the diary, Knausgård endeavors to press beyond fiction and the linguistically structured world—"antifiction," in Lejeune's formulation—and to insist that what he is writing about is himself and his own life. It is, as he writes in Book 2, an attempt "to get as close as possible to my life" (2.582). Knausgård introduces the phrase when telling the story of how he, in the days after describing the reflection of his face in the window late at night, kept writing about his wife and three children, about his parents' divorce more than twenty years earlier, and about a New Year's Eve from when he was a teenager. Writing about his face sets off this writing that makes up *My Struggle*.

The phrase "to get as close as possible to my life" can mean almost anything. Any artistic movement worth its salt during the past 150 years or so has also claimed to get as close to life as possible, albeit with a variety of means and aims. For the naturalist writers of the late nineteenth century, for example, this meant describing the inner nature of human beings, our biology and psychological nature, and the effects of heredity and environment. For the surrealists, by contrast, it meant depicting our subconsciousness and how it affects our consciousness. And for a certain kind of postmodernist writer, it meant embracing the idea of a chaotic and fragmented world, characterized by a lack of depth, and the incapacity of

48 | Knausgård and the Autofictional Novel

language to fully capture it. In short: as Knausgård is far from the first to make such a claim, the claim itself becomes less important than the implications of what is at stake in his version.

The other key to the origin of *My Struggle*, as Knausgård describes it in Book 2, is his focus on process rather than product—and a pledge to write five pages a day. With this pattern in place, the writing starts to take control over him:

> Suddenly I was under the text, suddenly it had power over me, and it was only with the greatest effort of will that I managed to write the five pages a day I had set myself as a goal. But I managed, I managed that too. I hated every syllable, every word, every sentence, but not liking what I was doing didn't mean I shouldn't do it. One year and it would be over, and then I would be able to write about something else. (2.589)

Knausgård hating everything he wrote is part of what has created a narrative of *My Struggle* as essentially an antiliterary novel with Knausgård deciding to let go of any literary ambitions he might have.[69] It is a persuasive narrative but here it is countered by Knausgård's very deliberate attempt to push through the linguistic superstructure by force if he lets the text take charge.

Knausgård never reveals how this pledge came about or how the results became novelistic. Alexandra Kingston-Reese is undoubtedly correct when she claims that the "novel form is often happened upon by accident in the self-reflexive texts of the early twenty-first century," but it would be a mistake to extend this origin story to *My Struggle* as she does, since Knausgård refutes it in Book 6.[70] After explaining that his pledge to write five pages a day within a year had developed into a 1,200-page manuscript, he notes "the idea all along having been for a single novel, to be published in the autumn" (6.66).[71]

Consequently, *My Struggle* becomes a site of reflection on the tension between Knausgård's novelistic ambition and his longing for reality, his "reality hunger," to use David Shields's expression in the context of him writing about his own life.[72] The tension establishes the very compositional DNA of *My Struggle*. It is a complete rejection of the claims that, as Paul de Man and those in his wake would have it, such a duality is impossible because we always "reenter a system of tropes the very moment we claim to escape it."[73] Knausgård shows that it is not just possible to write while stuck in a revolving door but that it is possible to inhabit it, to stay within the whirligig, for a full six books.

Submitting to Form

Fueling a seemingly antiliterary project with novelistic ambition gives Knausgård the form he needs to proceed. Form is his alpha and omega. It is at the root of his explanation, in Book 1, for why his attempt to fictionalize his father's death failed. The story about his father, he writes, was "not so easy to fit into another form," with the implication that a fictional account of his father's death would necessitate both "condensation and drama" and the need to "decorate the language," as Knausgård states in an interview about being fed up with fiction.[74] To Knausgård, form is both a prerequisite for literature and its sole enforcer of law: as he puts it in Book 1, "everything has to submit to form" (1.197). But what does Knausgård actually mean when he talks about form? And how does it relate to his longing for reality and ambition of getting as close to life as possible?

In Book 6 of *My Struggle*, Knausgård writes about his literary idol and fellow countryman Knut Hamsun. Referring to Hamsun's influential 1890 manifesto, "From the Unconscious Life of the Mind," Knausgård describes Hamsun's literary project as if it were his own: "Literature as Hamsun saw it was simple, schematic, structural, cohesive, harmonious, explained, whereas the life he saw around him was complex, unsystematic, incohesive, arbitrary, unexplained. How could the writer transport the language out of the system into life as it was lived? This was the question Hamsun posed in Lillesand in the autumn of 1890" (6.439). Knausgård does not use the word "form" here, but he writes how Hamsun sought "a new, truer realism" and in doing so removed the categories that otherwise would create certain associations and expectations. He sought, Knausgård writes, to "move beyond the now" and to a "world prior to meaning, *prior to interpretation*" (6.440).

Both Hamsun and Knausgård seek to reconnect life and literature, thus creating a new literary language. This, Knausgård asserts, is precisely what form can do. In a 2007 essay, "Sjelens Amerika" ("America of the Soul"), from which he lifts most of his reading of Hamsun in *My Struggle*, he in fact uses the word "form" to describe this very process. Hamsun, he says, needed "a form that could open a language sensitive enough to move into the world prior to meaning."[75]

50 | Knausgård and the Autofictional Novel

Form, as Knausgård understands it, can be likened to a prism through which we see the world. The second that prism shifts, we see the world in a new light. Form is what enables a literary work to connect to the world it describes and show it anew. This view of form is similar to Victor Shklovsky's notion of "defamiliarization," which to Shklovsky means imparting "the sensation of things."[76] It is far cry from how literary scholars often think about form—that is, literary techniques both large and small: word choice, rhythm, syntax, imagery, narration, plot, composition, and so on, and it might not stand up to the scrutiny of those following in the footsteps of Paul de Man. But it is nevertheless how Knausgård consistently conceives of form.

In *Inadvertent*, Knausgård uses the *Seasons Quartet*—the four books written after *My Struggle* and dedicated to his newly born daughter—to illustrate what he means. With these books, he wanted to create unexpected connections and to make the previously hidden visible. This is what form can do, he says. Form makes it "possible to say certain things but not others" (29). With their short, phenomenological descriptions of mainly physical objects, the form revealed a new relationship between that particular form and reality. It made it possible for him to show the world anew. "It was form that allowed this insight to emerge, it was form that allowed it to be seen, it was form that made it possible to say. The rudiments of it already existed in my mind, but were neither articulated nor meaningful; meaning came with form."[77]

Prioritizing form as literature's sole law, Knausgård enters a debate that dates back to Aristotle's claim that all objects consist of a compound of form and matter. In the history of literary criticism, the dominant position has been to view form in a Hegelian light as "a fixed container, like a bottle, into which the 'content' or the 'subject matter' of a work is poured," as M. H. Abrams summarizes this position.[78] Paul de Man reversed the relationship, seeing form as determining the content, and rendering both the Aristotelian and Hegelian relationship, as he put it, "superficial and expendable."[79] But Knausgård debunks that view, insisting on form as that which makes certain things possible—including meaning. Extending the assessment of form in *Inadvertent* to *My Struggle*, we can see that the novelistic ambition and diarylike form of *My Struggle* do not cancel each other out. Rather, the combination of the two—the tension between them—establishes a new relationship and a new connection between writing and reality, literature and the world.

Knausgård's conception of form is right in line with what Caroline Levine describes in *Forms* (2015). Attempting to free form from the realm of aesthetics, where literary studies often, and proprietarily, tries to keep it, Levine, as I also mentioned in the introduction, borrows the term "affordance" from design theory to more accurately describe "the potential uses or actions latent in materials and designs."[80] This opens a new understanding of form, as we, instead of asking what forms do, can ask, "What potentialities lie latent—though not always obvious—in aesthetic and social arrangements?" The concept of affordance helps us see both the potential and the limits of forms and materials, and while different forms appropriate different affordances, all forms have in common that they are portable. Picked up and moved to new contexts, their "meanings and values might change," Levine writes, though the forms themselves remain "surprisingly stable" (7). That means when forms move they bring with them not only their possibilities, but also their limitations. Or as Jeremy Biles writes in connection with *My Struggle*: "Forms emerge and forms merge."[81]

The notion of affordance lets us see exactly how Knausgård's idea of form works. Using the form of the diary affords him intimacy, closeness, authenticity, singularity, immediacy, and secrecy, while it does not afford grand narrative, overarching plots, generalizations, or retrospective explanations. For those, Knausgård turns to the form of the novel (and to which chapter 2 is dedicated) that affords him what he is missing. It is a form of the novel that embraces a traditional understanding of the genre where Knausgård simultaneously employs what Philippe Lejeune calls an autobiographical and a fictional pact. Ultimately, incorporating the affordance of the diaristic form into that of the novel enables Knausgård a new engagement with the world, and shows a connection between fiction and reality that previously was unseen. And once again, death helps him get there.

The Dead Body

"I was almost thirty years old when I saw a dead body for the first time," Knausgård writes in Book 1 of *My Struggle* (1.226). He and his brother Yngve were visiting the chapel where their father's corpse was laid out on a table in the middle of the room. It was a July afternoon, Knausgård recalls, and

52 | Knausgård and the Autofictional Novel

"the sky was overcast, the light in the room dull, outside the window a lawn mower was slowly circling around the lawn" (1.226). Seeing his dead father caused two opposed feelings: it made him want keep his distance as it "felt like an act of violation," yet it created a sense of hunger, "an insatiability that demanded that I keep looking at him" (1.227). He notes:

> I was familiar with the facial features, I had grown up with this face. . . . I was familiar with the features, but not the expression they had assumed. The dark yellowy complexion, along with the lost elasticity of the skin, made his face seem as if it had been carved out of wood. The woodenness forbade any feelings of intimacy. I was no longer looking at a person but something that resembled a person. (1.227)

Knausgård's description of his deceased father's face contrasts with his description of his own face reflected in the window. In that earlier scene, his reflection gazed back, creating a sense of intimacy and authenticity, a promise of hidden secrets that could be understood and shared, if he only studied it enough. Now he tries to read his father's face similarly: "there were still traces of what I would only describe as determination," he says, realizing that he "had always tried to interpret the expression on his face" and never been "able to look at it without trying to read it at the same time" (1.228). Yet when he sees the corpse, he sees that there is nothing beyond the face. The person has become an object.

For the first time in his life, Knausgård is confronted with what he, in the essayistic passage on death that opens Book 1, calls "death as it actually turns out to be," death that is usually hidden away, death as the signified (1.5). Standing in the chapel, he realizes that such death is in fact very much a part of everyday life, as becomes evident when he raises his head and looks out the window. It is the embodiment of the reality he longs for:

> The gardener who was riding the lawn mower kept turning in his seat to check if he was following the line of the previous cut. The shorter blades of grass the bag didn't catch whirled through the air above him. Some must have gotten stuck to the underside of the machine because it regularly left behind damp clumps of compressed grass, darker than the lawn from which they came. On the gravel path behind him there was a small cortège of three persons, all with bowed heads, one in

a red cloak, resplendent against the green grass and gray sky. Behind them cars streamed past toward the town center. (1.227)

Knausgård's description of the world places death as part of—even the central point of—its surroundings. Beyond the dead body on the table, the world Karl Ove sees standing in the chapel extends through the walls to the gardener, the grass, the group of three people further away, and the cars passing by even further away. Expanding his gaze from part to whole, the narration suggests that these things are connected and conveys Karl Ove's vision to the reader as that of a modern-day romantic genius; he conveys an order, which nevertheless remains inaccessible to the rest of us. At the same time, the objectivity typically associated with the visions of the romantic genius is absent in *My Struggle*, as the insight only extends from Karl Ove to the reader and never pretends to be a neutral and impersonal description of the world as it actually is. Instead, it is a kind of form-making by way of which he shapes the world starting with himself and the body of his dead father in the chapel.[82]

At the center of this world are Knausgård and the body of his dead father. He situates the dead body as a natural part of what he himself creates, a world where everything has its right place: a narrative form based on a spatial metaphor of concentric circles. The common center is the chapel; the first circle is the gardener mowing the lawn; the second circle is the group walking across the gravel; the third circle is the cars passing by; and the fourth is the world beyond. It is the first time he can approach the world from the same vantage point as his father; the first time he can see his own place along with that of his dad. To that extent, it is the merging of father and son. And while his brother is still present in the chapel, he becomes increasingly absent in the narration as Knausgård trains his gaze outside the window.

Knausgård's description of his father's corpse directly follows the essayistic section, midway through Book 1, that has picked up on the idea from the opening pages: there are two kinds of death, death as fiction and reality. Standing in the chapel, Knausgård incorporates the dead body—the thing that we normally hide and keep out of sight, and by which he opens his novel—into a world that begins with him. That death is an integral part of the world—and that death, as Knausgård sees it in the wake of his father's death, indeed unites the two kinds of death described earlier—is reiterated in the very last sentence of Book 1, when Karl Ove claims he has returned to the chapel to see the body of his dead father for a second time, and, in a series of metaphors, figures death

54 | Knausgård and the Autofictional Novel

as an ordinary interruption: "And death, which I have always regarded as the greatest dimension of life, dark, compelling, was no more than a pipe that springs a leak, a branch that cracks in the wind, a jacket that slips off a clothes hanger and falls to the floor" (1.441). Here, Knausgård confirms what was merely implied when he was standing in the chapel with his brother a few hundred pages before: that death is part of life. Death, as he sees it now, integrates what the opening pages framed as two kinds of death. It is death as fiction—the images we constantly are exposed to in the media—and death as reality—the physical death as we conceal it—united in an affront to the notion of a linguistically structured world by the three metaphors used in the short description. This death is neither spectacular, like death depicted in the media, nor something we cover or hide in the basements of hospitals. Instead, death in this respect is prosaic, ordinary, and banal—the stuff not of novels, but of dutifully kept, mundane diaries.[83] Death is ever-present, natural, and daily.

It is also—as the metaphors of a pipe that springs a leak, a branch that cracks, and a jacket that slips off a hanger suggest—a disruption. It is a turn away from life, but not a turn into the great unknown.[84] It is, instead, a turn of the prism, which allows us to see life anew, creating a new connection between language and the world. When death is rendered in such simple and familiar terms, it ceases to be mysterious, and going to lengths to keep it out of sight begins to seem odd, even misguided. And even as Knausgård writes about death, he seems to be gesturing toward his larger project, of writing honestly about his own life. Though he merges the reality of the diary and the fictionality of the novel, his ambition is primarily novelistic: he wants to redefine the relation between fiction and reality in the novel.

Yet the veracity of this final scene, in terms of hard facts, is questionable. According to Book 1 of *My Struggle*, after seeing the body of his dead father in the Kristiansand chapel the first time, Knausgård keeps returning to the question of why there was blood on his body when he died. Staying in his grandmother's house where his father has died, he wakes up after a dream in which his father appeared and suddenly knows what he has to do: "I had to see him again," he writes, and he immediately calls the funeral home to arrange for a "final visit" to the chapel (1.440). He mentions this second visit again in Book 5: "Four days later I left the chapel in Kristiansand after seeing Dad, or what had once been him, and was now a corpse with his features, for a second time" (5.599). But in the essay on the future that contained so much of what became

Book 1's treatment of death, Knausgård writes nothing about a second visit. Instead, the essay suggests that, in fact, he only saw the dead body of his father in the chapel once, with his brother Yngve.

In an interview with the Norwegian public TV broadcast *NRK*, recorded before the publication of Book 1 of *My Struggle* and broadcast a month after, Knausgård clarifies that he in actuality only visited the chapel once: "He, who is the protagonist of the novel, sees his dead father twice. But in reality, I only saw him once. I needed to write it that way in terms of the novel's composition."[85] As such, he seems to operate with a notion of the novel as a whole but not in a way that suggests enclosure or containment. Rather, his need to add a second visit "in terms of the novel's composition" suggests something closer to Caroline Levine's understanding of wholes as "forms organized by their unfolding over time."[86] It means that the whole of the novel is not autotelic but that the end extends past the time represented in the text to both the next volumes of *My Struggle* and to the social world outside the text.[87]

After admitting that the description in *My Struggle* does not represent what actually happened in the wake of his father's death, Knausgård, in the interview with *NRK*, adds: "So it's not true, but yet it is true anyway." This cryptic admission seems to confirm that Knausgård, in *My Struggle*, operates with an understanding of what it means for a representation of an event to be true in a way that transcends a typical binary view of fact versus fiction. Where scholars in a deconstructive and poststructuralist tradition might argue that everything is fiction, or even, as David Shields would have it, that this fictionality should be celebrated, Knausgård goes in the opposite direction. He may have made up a second viewing of his father's body, but "it is true anyway," and so, by extension, is the overall factuality of *My Struggle*. Indeed, Knausgård's renewal of the novel can be seen in his very attempt to push past fiction and to break away from the prison house of language with a commitment to reality that challenges our notions of what a novel is.

Chapter 2

Reforming the Form

Knausgård and the Novel

In Book 2 of *My Struggle*, Knausgård describes attending a writer's retreat in June 1999 where he met his future wife, Linda, and—having declared his love for her on the last night, and meeting with rejection—returning to his room and methodically cutting his face with a piece of broken glass. He continued, he writes, until "there was hardly room for one more cut" (2.198). The following morning, when confronted by his own defaced face in the mirror, he felt more ashamed than he had ever been before: "I was marked, I had marked myself," he writes (2.199).[1]

In Book 5, Knausgård recounts another, earlier episode of cutting up his face. He recalls how he first introduced Tonja, the girlfriend who eventually becomes his first wife, to his brother, Yngve, at a local club, and was horrified by how well they were getting along. "They chatted away as though I didn't exist," he writes, with a fresh recollection of Yngve previously "stealing" Ingvild, the first great love of his life (5.535).[2] While his brother and girlfriend were immersed in conversation, he made periodic visits to the bathroom, placing a few cuts on his face each time, using a piece of broken glass he found on the floor:

> I did it for the rest of the evening, coldly and methodically, every part of my face was covered with cuts, and stung more and more, in the end, sitting beside them and drinking, it hurt so much I could have screamed, had it not been for the fact that, simultaneously, I enjoyed it. There was a joy in the pain, there was a joy in thinking that I could stand it, that I could stand everything, everything, everything." (5.536)

58 | Knausgård and the Autofictional Novel

In both scenes of self-mutilation, the character Karl Ove attempts to express his inner turmoil to the outer world by making his exterior align with the interior.[3] It is a kind of inscription, with his face as paper and the glass as pen, such that his words, as in the Gospel of John, are literally made flesh.[4] And it is a sign of his ambitions as a writer to make his "primitive" feelings visible in a literary form that preempts his objective in *My Struggle* of writing honestly about his life in the form of a novel—something he eventually learns to do not by writing on this face, but, in part, by writing about it.

In these episodes, as in the rest of *My Struggle*, Knausgård seems to be understanding himself in dualist terms, with the inner distinct from the outer. He tries—when self-mutilating, dramatically and violently—to turn the inner outward as he throughout the six volumes is "obsessed with the passage from interior to exterior," as Jeremy Biles puts it.[5] For more than a century, scholars have considered the tension between self and world as a defining feature of the novel. While dualism can be traced back Plato, its modern iteration originates with René Descartes, whose radical separation of mind and body is famously summarized in the phrase "Cogito, ergo sum," I think, therefore I am, which took center stage in numerous philosophical inquiries and debates on what the self is and how it is related to the mind and body. If, as in the case of Descartes, the inner is seen as a source of reliability, the outer is in principle unreliable. And vice versa: the inner becomes unreal, if the outer appearance is seen as the self.[6]

Today, we find a broad distrust of dualism in critical theory. Jacques Derrida, for instance, shows how Western philosophy is grounded in a dichotomy between inside and outside that without any logic has been used to "distinguish the closed, essential inside from the unnecessary outside."[7] And Judith Butler famously deconstructs the dichotomy in *Gender Trouble*, arguing that it reproduces a hierarchy and subordination in which the mind subjugates the body: when the mind has been historically associated with masculinity and the body with femininity, any "uncritical reproduction of the mind/body distinction ought to be rethought."[8]

The dramatic dualism, that in these two episodes in Knausgård's telling turns literal, drives the narration of *My Struggle*. Knausgård, I argue, turns dualism into a literary form. This formal dualism is an important aspect of *My Struggle* as Knausgård further employs what Philippe Lejeune called, some decades ago, an "autobiographical pact," at the same time that he employs a novelistic or fictional pact.

The Extensive Totality of Life

In his seminal *The Theory of the Novel*, Georg Lukács identifies the conflict between interior self and exterior world as central to any understanding of the novel. Lukács wrote his study of the novel at the dawn of World War I in 1914, before he became a Marxist, and it was not published in its entirety until 1920. It is a tonally and stylistically abstruse book with a Hegelian-inspired history of novels that, Jonathan Arc points out, has a "beginning, with *Don Quixote*, and an end, adumbrated by Dostoevsky."[9] It also remains one of the best studies of the genre, and it helps us see how *My Struggle* engages with novelistic form and expands it.

Lukács begins by holding up the age of the Homeric epic as a sort of Paradise where everything was connected and made sense: "Happy are those ages when the starry sky is the map of all possible paths—ages whose paths are illuminated by the light of the stars."[10] The novel came into being, Lukács writes, when it was no longer possible to perceive the world in such harmony: "The novel is the epic of an age in which the extensive totality of life is no longer directly given, in which the immanence of meaning of life has become a problem, yet which still thinks in terms of totality" (56). Longing for a totality, but knowing that it no longer exists, we experience a permanent feeling of homelessness or alienation. We cannot inhabit the world as we want it to be, but the world as it actually is, and this creates a conflict between inner and outer reality.[11] The novel aims to resolve this conflict, simulating a totality that our experience tells us has been lost. This aim is the will to art of the novel, or what Lukacs calls the *Kunstwollen*.

Knausgård's *Kunstwollen* is precisely the conflict between self and world. Early in Book 1, he writes, "I not want anyone to get close to me, I do not want anyone to see me, and this is the way things have developed: no one gets close and no one sees me" (1.25–26). Yet he wants to understand himself, and by extension invites us to see him too, as when he studies his own reflection in the window and writes: "What has engraved itself in my face?" (1.25). As readers, we experience what Peter Brooks calls a "desire *for* the end," where we keep reading in the hope of finding not just an answer to Knausgård's question, but relief for the larger tension between self and world.[12] As such, the dualism might explain why so many readers speak of "binge-reading" Knausgård's novel, as if it were the latest TV series on Netflix.

60 | Knausgård and the Autofictional Novel

In *The Theory of the Novel*, Lukács cannot explain why the novel seeks a totality that our experience otherwise tells us is lost. Instead, he provides a label for the result: irony. The kind of irony Lukács has in mind is not irony in the rhetorical sense—saying the opposite of what you mean—but an irony that is endemic to the genre's form. The protagonist searches for meaning in a world without meaning, and—however momentarily—the novel provides it. Novels reconcile the conflict between self and world, and their very form, in its totality, substitutes the missing totality of God in a secular world.

In *My Struggle*, Knausgård is engaged in what Lee Konstantinou calls "postirony" and sees as a response to postmodernism: a longing "to move beyond postmodern irony partly because irony has lost its critical power or because irony's mode of critique no longer adequately addresses contemporary reality."[13] Indeed, in a highly concrete and tangible display of postirony, Knausgård throughout the six volumes describes his difficulties with understanding irony. In Book 4, for instance, he recalls how, as a young man, he was reading Thomas Mann but did not understand the irony until it explicitly was pointed out to him by a friend: "So he doesn't really mean it. Is that what you are saying?" he asks the friend when he points out Mann is "famous for being ironic" (4.486). Elsewhere, he remembers a comment made by his father in his childhood, writing that "irony was plain, even I caught it" but also "complicated, because I didn't understand the reason for it" (1.39). Less concrete, his commitment to reality and to authenticity is at odds with the irony of postmodernism.

Still, Knausgård points to irony as a defining feature of his project. In the essay "Literature and Evil" ("Litteraturen og det onde"), published shortly after the last volume of *My Struggle*, he asserts that "the most important feature of the novel is that it is ironic."[14] Responding to a Swedish critic, who claimed that *My Struggle* gave evidence of how Knausgård's wife was oppressed in their relationship, he rejects the charge by saying that irony makes such a reading impossible: novelistic irony, he contends, is characterized by its ability "to establish distances throughout whereas the most important one is the one between 'I' and the one writing 'I'" (3.10).[15] Then he pulls the ace from his sleeve: "No one would dream of criticizing the opinions of Emma Bovary, condemn them, and say that they are wrong." Irony increases the complexity of the novel, he continues, and invalidates any attempt to make simplified readings: "This complexity is the most significant," he says, implicitly relating the irony of his novel not to the irony of postmodernism but to the irony that Lukács sees as defining for the novel as such (3.10).

Reforming the Form | 61

While Knausgård relates irony to the novelistic form, the same extends to the dualism at play in *My Struggle*.[16] Though Lukács points out that the "formal nature" of the novel "is less obvious than in other art," Knausgård's dualism provides him with a form that gives his diaristic ambitions a narrative progression.[17] The affordance of dualism as a form is that it allows Knausgård to pursue what Lukács calls "the extensive totality of life" across six volumes and more than 3,600 pages (Lukács, 56).[18] It is a crucial building block of the space and structure the novel constructs.[19]

In his ambitious *The Theory of the Novel* (2011), Guido Mazzoni embraces Lukács's notion of the "the extensive totality of life" and seeks to bring it into the twenty-first century. For Mazzoni, tracing the novel's history from antiquity to the present shows that "the extensive totality of life" is not a lost paradise but the "unlimited sum of multiple small, singular stories" that make up ordinary existence.[20] Other discursive modes have ignored such details, but for centuries the novel has been a genre of particularity, written in prose that Mazzoni several times refers to as "the mimesis of everyday life," with all the social structures that shape it.[21] Novels, he writes, tell the stories of individuals who are "moving in a predictable reality that is desacralized and organized according to the mechanism of the state and civil society" (225).

Mazzoni traces the genre's history by means of what it has abandoned: first it gave up allegory, then the adventurous hero, then the melodrama. Later, with high modernism at the beginning of the twentieth century, it gave up the storyline, shifting "the balance of narrative interest from the story to the meaning of the story" (294). Now that it has reached the twenty-first century, he argues, the only thing left for the novel to explore is the banality of everyday life—helped along, I would add, by having abandoned lyrical language and high style. Contemporary novels, Mazzoni writes, focus on ordinary people living ordinary lives, occupied with reaching their personal goals while trying to balance between desire and reality.[22] For the reader, he suggests, these stories are, to a large extent, interchangeable with other stories as well as their own lives. In this present state of the novel, everything becomes equally important and equally unimportant. And if everything is of equal importance, we end in a relativity where the only thing of value is lived life:

> Inside our small local worlds, everything at stake has an unquestionable value, as if there were no longer a sense, as if the word *sense* could no longer be in the singular, and instead, there were lots of little, regional meanings—all absolute in their

relativity. This is the form our life has taken today, this product of impersonal forces, this improper concretion that we cannot go beyond, because it is our only property, the sole layer of existence, that, for a certain span of time, distinguishes us from nothing. Nothing is important but life. (375–376)

Without mentioning capitalism, Mazzoni reads contemporary novels as a reaction to a commodification that puts value on everyone and everything. The only thing left is lived life. *My Struggle*, as Ben Parker suggests, functions as "an empirical confirmation" of Mazzoni's thesis.[23] In fact, Knausgård takes Mazzoni's series of abandonments one step further: he gives up on fiction and turns the "extensive totality of life" into an autobiographical creed.

Though Mazzoni borrows both his title and chief trope from Lukács, he is also updating another of the so-called grand theories of novel: Ian Watt's. In *The Rise of the Novel* (1957), Watt argues that the novel's focus on individual experiences reflects the rise of individuality that began with René Descartes.[24] He singles out the novel's depiction of particular people in particular circumstances, which he refers to as its formal realism.[25] But Watt's idea of formal realism turns out to be more about content than actual form; he claims that the novel is "under the obligation" to provide details and particulars of its characters, time, and place that are "presented through a more largely referential use of language than is common in other literary forms."[26] This "referential particularity" closely mirrors the extensive totality of life that Mazzoni speaks of. Both Mazzoni and Watt, in other words, see the novel as transparent realism, where the novel's "poverty of formal conventions" is, as Watt puts it, "the price it must pay for its realism."[27]

The trope, in Watt's words, of "the formlessness of the novel" has been repeated in numerous theories of realism and, more recently, in numerous accounts of *My Struggle*. It has often been considered a "novel without form," where Knausgård's narration supposedly creates a transparent and unstructured realism.[28] *My Struggle*, however, is anything but a formless novel. Dualism as a literary form and structuring principle gives the novel plot and creates a narrative desire. And when Knausgård further merges this dualism of the novelistic tradition envisioned by Lukács with the diaristic form, he has a formal frame to chronicle the extensive totality of his life. It leads to a "referential particularity" that does not cancel out the form he engages but is instead a direct result of it. It means giving up on fiction and writing honestly about his life, in the form of the novel.

A Double Pact

It is hard to imagine anyone beginning to read *My Struggle* without having a sense that its author, narrator, and main character are one. In an American context, the penetrating portrait of Knausgård on the cover of the FSG paperback of Book 1, the blurb on the back calling *My Struggle* a "provocative and brilliant six-volume autobiographical novel," the worldwide media frenzy around Knausgård, and the controversies surrounding his novel upon publication in Norway all render a "naïve" reading more or less impossible.[29] As Arnaud Schmitt and Stefan Kjerkegaard write, "Some readers already knew more than their reading of the actual and available work allowed them to."[30] The paratextual markers all "signal the author's willingness to engage with the real and to engage the reader in the real" (Schmitt and Kjerkegaard, 566).

But if a reader had somehow stumbled onto the novel without that knowledge, her first indication that the writer and protagonist may be identical would arrive five pages into Book 1, when an "I" enters the essay on death: "I stare at the surface of the sea without listening to what the reporter says, *and suddenly the outline of a face emerges*" (1.7, original italics).[31] That sense would be strengthened after she sees the eight-year-old "I" addressed by his father, using the author's first name: " 'And Karl Ove, remember,' he said . . . , 'No running this time' " (1.12). Not too long after, following the description of his face reflected in the window, Knausgård declares outright that he is indeed both the narrator and protagonist of his own novel (or what Genette calls an autodiegetic narrator): "Today is the twenty-seventh of February. The time is 11:43 p.m. I, Karl Ove Knausgaard, was born in December 1968, and at the time of writing I am thirty-nine years old. I have three children—Vanja, Heidi, and John—and I am in my second marriage, to Linda Boström Knausgaard" (1.25). With these four sentences, Knausgård provides a stamp of authenticity that applies to all six volumes of his novel. The accumulation of precise numbers—time, year, age, number of children, number of marriages—act as a kind of confirmation: the facts check out. Knausgård is the "I" of the narration.

64 | Knausgård and the Autofictional Novel

Names authenticate narration—or, as Knausgård reflects in Book 6 of *My Struggle*, "Great is the power of the name" (6.429). The name, he continues, is entwined with the inner self to such an extent that we often think of the name as belonging to that self. As such, it can almost be seen as the embodiment of the language Ursula K. Le Guin refers to as "True Speech" and that Knausgård encountered as a young boy when reading *A Wizard of Earthsea*. "I *am* my name, my name *is* me," he writes in Book 6 (6.432). When Knausgård introduces his name, establishing a homology between the character, narrator, and author, he is closing the gaps in what J. Hillis Miller calls "a chain of displacement—displacement of its author into the invented role of the narrator; further displacement of the narrator into the lives of imagined characters."[32] He also erects a bridge between external and internal, between language and what it represents.

In 1975, in a theoretical landscape in which the author was widely considered "dead," Philippe Lejeune argued that such a homology—between character, narrator, and author—is the most important aspect of what he called "the autobiographical pact."[33] Lejeune defines autobiography as a retrospective prose narration "*written by a real person concerning his own existence.*"[34] Any book or literary work that "fulfills all the conditions in each of the categories is an autobiography," he explains (4). But should any element of the definition change, we are no longer dealing with autobiographical writing. This means that if, for instance, there is identity between the narrator and protagonist, but not between these and the author, we are dealing with a novel narrated in first person; if the narrative is not mainly retrospective, we are dealing with a diary.[35] Lejeune's main focus, however, is on the homology between narrator, character, and author, which is the backbone of his notion of the autobiographical pact: "The autobiographical pact is the affirmation in the text of this identity, referring back in the final analysis to the *name* of the author on the cover" (14).

Lejeune envisions the autobiographical pact as an invisible contract between the reader and the author, signed paratextually by the author's name on the cover, by genre designations such as "Autobiography" or "The Story of My Life," and by the corresponding attitudes of readers. Homology or its absence, Lejeune writes, determines the reader's attitude: "if the identity is not positively stated (as in fiction), the reader will attempt to establish resemblances, in spite of the author; if it is positively stated (as in autobiography), the reader will want to look for differences (errors, deformation, etc.)" (14). In other words, when we read fiction, we tend to look for autobiographical traits in the narration, but when we read autobiographical narratives, we tend to look for details that seem to undermine the autobiographical pact. Lejeune's approach, as many critics have pointed out, seems usefully pragmatic: the question of homology between author, character, and narrator seems more important to him than any verification of autobiographical details, which could be hard to carry out.[36] Yet Lejeune still allows for a rigorous accounting of discrepancies and inconsistencies. A reader of autobiography, he writes, behaves "as a detective" on the lookout "for breaches of contract" (Lejeune, 14). If we spot too many "differences," we abandon reading the text as autobiographical.

My Struggle certainly invites readers to enter into an autobiographical pact. But given the numerous signs of unreliability that we find throughout the novel, including Knausgård's earnest admissions of having a faulty memory, might we also ask whether the contract holds up? If we are to follow Lejeune, signs of unreliability might prompt us to identify a breach of the autobiographical pact and to abandon the notion that My Struggle is autobiographical. But is that really what happens?

Early in Book 1, Knausgård writes about walking out into the yard, at age eight, having seen a face on the surface of the ocean during a newscast about a sunken fishing boat and wanting to tell his father. He is in the suburbs, in the late 1970s, and he describes the atmosphere outside the house in remarkably minute detail:

> The crack of the sledgehammer on rock resounded through the estate. A car came up the gentle slope from the main road and passed, its lights blazing. The door of the neighboring house opened. Prestbakmo paused on the doorstep, pulled on his work gloves, and seemed to sniff the clear night air before grabbing the wheelbarrow and trundling it across the lawn. There was a smell of gunpowder from the rock Dad was pounding, of pine from the logs behind the stone wall, freshly dug soil and forest, and in the gentle northerly breeze a whiff of salt. (1.11–12)

The description starts with the sound of the sledgehammer, turns to what is physically visible, and concludes with smell. It is a sensory description that moves from sound to vision to smell, with the "whiff of salt" of the northerly breeze concluding a metonymic chain of shifting odors.[37] The specificity is striking. On the one hand, the details create a poignant and

66 | Knausgård and the Autofictional Novel

persuasive realism. On the other, the same details make us question the accuracy of what is supposedly a recollection from Knausgård's childhood more than thirty years before the time of writing. It is an instance of what Dorrit Cohn, writing about the problem of credibility in self-quotation, refers to as "mnemonic overkill," and it raises the question of how anyone, Knausgård included, could remember so much and to such an extent.[38] Surely it is impossible for Knausgård to remember all of the details he recounts.[39]

Knausgård invites such skepticism outright. In Book 1, following a long, detailed description of a specific New Year's Eve from his childhood, he writes: "I remembered hardly anything from my childhood" (1.191). It is almost as though he is mocking readers, telling them not to trust him. Earlier, he writes he "spent a lot of time thinking about the past then, almost a morbid amount of time," but he claims that the same past "is now barely present in my thoughts" (1.29–30). Becoming a father, he explains, has made his memory worse than ever before: "Ask me what I did three days ago and I can't remember" (1.30). In Book 6, too, Knausgård writes at some length about his horrid memory. After talking to his high school crush Hanne for the first time in two decades, letting her know that he would send her the pages from *My Struggle* concerning her, he admits to the readers that he had made up most of their conversations from back then: "She had said she remembered that time very well. I didn't. Or rather, I remembered a few episodes very well. Others I recalled only faintly, shaping them in my writing, inventing dialogues, for example" (6.164–165). The accuracy of his memory becomes especially urgent when his Uncle Gunnar accuses him of not just fictionalizing but outright fabricating the story of his father's death in Book 1.[40] Readily admitting that he probably exaggerated some of the descriptions, Karl Ove begins to doubt the truthfulness of everything he has said on the subject: "In itself this was a crushing admission. But had I been unreliable in everything I had written? Did it in any way alter the fundamental truth of the novel? . . . Yes, it did" (6.176). The character of Uncle Gunnar (whose real name is Bjørke Knausgård) formalizes the trope of Knausgård's terrible memory.[41]

In interviews and features, Knausgård has also been candid about forgetting and making things up in his narration. Even before Book 1 was published, he had admitted that the second visit to see the body of his dead father never occurred. Later, when specifically asked by Sheila Heti whether another description from Book 1—of how his mother was scrubbing potatoes in the kitchen sink on a particular New Year's Eve in his youth—was a real memory, Knausgård said, "No, no, I made it up."[42]

All this suggests that in *My Struggle* the autobiographical pact exists side by side with what Lejeune refers to as the fictional or novelistic pact. Dorrit Cohn has proposed the possibility of such a double pact with regard to fictional autobiographies, but her account concerns seeming autobiographical pacts that are, in fact, fictional—one pact giving way to the other.[43] In *My Struggle*, though, the fictional pact exists in tandem with the autobiographical pact.[44] It is a specific trope of reading that encompasses two otherwise contradictory ways of reading *My Struggle*. Indeed, using a cognitive framework and empirical studies, recent work by scholars of autofiction confirms that such a trope of reading exists among actual readers.[45] These two modes do not undermine each other. Instead, they exist side by side. The result is a continual duality between fact and fiction, and we do not, as Philippe Lejeune claims in "The Autobiographical Pact," act as detectives in reading *My Struggle* because whatever there might be to detect is already made explicit in the narration.

As readers of *My Struggle*, we might find it implausible that Knausgård could remember his past with such a precise level of detail, but we also know that these details potentially *could* be true. Arnaud Schmitt reminds us that "the truth value of a single event, or of a single fact might be a complicated, multisided, holistic, much-debated issues."[46] Discussing James Frey's *A Million Little Pieces*, in her book *The Art of Memoir* Mary Karr also insists on complexity when it comes to a conception of truth, as the "line between *memory* and *fact* is blurry, between *interpretation* and *fact*." Yet she simultaneously maintains that what Frey did in *A Million Little Pieces* never was a matter of blurring the line between memory and fact: "He didn't really believe he was incarcerated for months, when he never served a day. He set out to fool people."[47]

There is no indication that Knausgård with *My Struggle* wants to fool us. On the contrary, his elaborate descriptions of what *potentially* could be true are attempts to evoke the feeling of childhood and make it palpable to the reader, though the improbability of the specificity of the memories makes them part of the fictional part. An example of Mazzoni's notion of "the mimesis of everyday life," they are markers of what Roland Barthes calls "reality effects": nonnarrative textual elements that "denote what is ordinarily called 'concrete reality'" with the caveat that, in Knausgård's case, these reality effects relate to both the autobiographical and the fictional pact.[48] Probably, everything Knausgård singles out in his

68 | Knausgård and the Autofictional Novel

sensory description of the spring evening happened at a certain point in his childhood. But every detail or action might not have happened that very night. Combining them in his description foregrounds the sensory impression—and shows the double pact at work in his novel.

Knausgård's narration works with the double pact of fiction and autobiography. Yet on the original cover of the Norwegian editions of *My Struggle*, the intended genre is clear, printed directly below the title: "Novel" (or *Roman*). Of course, that does not, in and of itself, make *My Struggle* a novel, and when Book 1 was first published in Norway, some of Knausgård's most skeptical critics insisted that the term was inaccurate, speculating that Knausgård and his publishers were motivated by profits. Each year, as part of the public support for the arts, the Norwegian state buys almost one thousand copies of a number of literary works that are distributed to libraries and cultural institutions throughout the country. By designating his autobiographical project a "novel," Knausgård and his publisher would ensure that what they considered a risky endeavor from the outset would sell, at the very least, about a thousand copies.[49]

In Book 6, Knausgård writes that the Norwegian purchasing program did play a role in some of the publication decisions. Originally, his editor suggested publishing *My Struggle* in twelve installments but ultimately opted for six. As Knausgård writes, "Six had been difficult too, but eventually he had managed to get them all covered by the State Purchasing Program, thereby minimizing the financial risk" (6.68). When Knausgård expresses amazement that his editor has convinced the purchasing program to buy copies of all six novels, since a rule states that they only buy one book a year per author, the editor explains: 'I had to present my case. It's a very unusual project. They listened and agreed" (6.68). Given how willing Knausgård is to admit that he restructured the novel's divisions because of the purchasing program, it seems safe to assume that he would have been just as willing to admit to a corresponding change in genre, had it happened. But he does not. And as this paratextual genre designation still exists in both the German and the French versions of *My Struggle*—though not in the English and Spanish—it suggests that Knausgård refers to *My Struggle* as a novel deliberately, and for his own, artistic reasons.[50] In Book 6, too, Knausgård refers to *My Struggle* as both "*six autobiographical* novels" and as "my autobiographical novel" (6.62, 6.241, original italics).

For Lejeune, the idea of an autobiographical novel—that a book, on one hand, expresses homology between author, narrator, and character and, on the other, is designated as a novel—is difficult to imagine. Stressing, in 1975, that nothing "would prevent such a thing from existing," and even noting that "it is perhaps an internal contradiction from which some interesting effects could be drawn," he nevertheless refers to the character of such a book as "the hero of the novel," implying that such a novel alone would activate the fictional pact and not the autobiographical (Lejeune, 18). Soon after, however, he goes on to reject such a construct. Writing that in these cases "the reader is under the impression that a mistake has been made," he suggests that he, for one, would consider an "autobiographical novel" a serious authorial error (Lejeune, 18).

Two years later, in 1977, such a book—with homology between narrator, character, and author, yet designated a novel—was published in France in a direct and open challenge to Lejeune's theory. The author was Lejeune's friend, Serge Doubrovsky, and the book was *Fils*, labeled a novel on the front cover but described, on the back, as "fiction, of strictly real events and fact; *autofiction*, if you like."[51] Over time, the term came to be applied to any literary works that play with the autobiographical pact, but Doubrovsky seems to have been up to something more pointed: not just naming a novel with autobiographical content but also debunking a theoretical assumption. In a letter to Lejeune, Doubrovsky noted how he, with *Fils*, "wanted very deeply to fill the 'box' that your analysis left empty," that is the empty box in Lejeune's chart in "The Autobiographical Pact" where the fictional pact is employed but the protagonist and the author are one and the same.[52] But designating *My Struggle* autofiction can only tell us so much—in the writing itself, however, we can see what is at stake in *My Struggle*'s double pact.[53]

Autofictionalization and Narrating a Past Self

Early in Book 1, after going out to the garden to tell his father about the face he has seen on the surface of the water in the news, eight-year-old Karl Ove is about to return inside. By this point, we learn that Karl Ove and his brother were "not allowed to run in the garden"; though Karl Ove runs around on his own, he slows down when heading outside to tell his father about the face in the water on the TV news, beginning to walk just before his father can see him. Yet somehow his father knows that he has been running. After their brief conversation, when Karl Ove turns and starts walking back inside, his father stops him:

70 | Knausgård and the Autofictional Novel

"And Karl Ove, remember," he said.
I paused, turned my head, puzzled.
"No running this time."
I stared at him. How could he know I had run? (1.12)

The question of how the father knew he had been running, despite slowing down before coming into his sight, keeps puzzling the eight-year-old. "How on earth did he know I had been running?" he ponders. And soon thereafter: "How could he possibly have known?" (1.13).[54] The repetition creates an image of the father as all-knowing, even Godlike, and the suspense extends to the reader: Yes, how did the father know that the eight-year-old Karl Ove had been running?[55]

Seven pages later, the mystery is solved. It is now early in the evening. The father is sitting in the living room, and Karl Ove is in the kitchen, eating dinner with his brother Yngve. When the smoke from the father's cigarette reaches the two brothers, Yngve leans forward and opens the window. The sounds from the outside drifting into the kitchen makes it feel as if the kitchen "was a part of the country outside" and creates an uncanny sensation in the young boy: "*It's like we're sitting on a shelf*, I thought. The thought caused the hairs on my forearm to stand on end" (1.18, original italics). (James Phelan has called such moments "synthetic character narration," describing times when literary characters know that they are constructs.)[56] With outside noises floating through the kitchen, Karl Ove suddenly realizes that the father must have heard him running on one side of the house through the open windows: "Of course. He had heard me! My feet running on the shingle" (1.19).

While the eight-year-old Karl Ove may have been fearful of his father's mysterious surveillance abilities, Knausgård, as the aging narrator retelling the story forty years later, knows all along why his father knew he had been running.[57] Knausgård keeps what Dorrit Cohn calls "the narrative consciousness" aligned with the experiencing character, not with the aging narrator.[58] There is no retrospective explanation or context for what the younger Karl Ove goes through. Unlike Proust, who can explain the actions of his self, situate them in a larger frame, and relate them as part of a pattern of occurrences—he does so within the very first sentence of *La Recherche*, "For a long time I used to go to bed early"—Knausgård presents the experiences of his eight-year-old self as though they were happening here and now.[59]

In another episode, this time from Book 2, we find a similar mode of narration. Now, it is 2004, and Linda, eight months pregnant with the

Reforming the Form | 71

couple's first child, is stuck in a bathroom at a party in Stockholm. The attention of the entire party turns to the heavily pregnant woman locked in the bathroom, and eventually someone calls for a locksmith:

> While we waited for him I stood by the door talking to Linda inside, unpleasantly aware of the fact that everyone could hear what I said and of my inability to act. Couldn't I just kick the door in and get her out? Easy and effective? (2.34, translation altered)

Focusing on how he believes he should have acted, Knausgård creates a dualist drama of self against world, with a contrast between Karl Ove's sense of his own weakness and a perceived masculine ideal based on action, decisiveness, and simplicity. When the locksmith arrives and cannot get the door open either, he suggests that the guests need to kick in the door to rescue the pregnant woman. Again, Karl Ove frets about whether he can fulfill his sense of manly duty:

> It had to be me. I was Linda's husband. It was my responsibility.
> My heart was pounding.
> Should I do it? Take a step back in full view of everyone and kick it with all my might? (2.34)

As the narrator, Knausgård knows very well what will follow: ultimately, he will not kick in the door. But, as with how he describes himself at eight, he keeps the narration close to the experience of his past self. The narrator knows the outcome, but the character seemingly does not. Yet, here the similarity ends and we are left with a key difference in how the two episodes are narrated. As readers, we wonder along with the eight-year-old Karl Ove about how the father could have known that he had been running, whereas we know that the adult Karl Ove will not kick in the door to that bathroom and save Linda—and not only because, one book in, we are alert to his personality. The reason is that, early in the scene, Knausgård introduces Chekov's gun in the narration—a gun that we know will eventually be fired.[60]

In this episode, Chekov's gun, or what we with Genette also could call prolepsis, is a boxer: Knausgård sees a man at a child's birthday party who reminds him of a boxer at a party he and Linda attended when she was pregnant, which leads to him to retell the story of the night Linda was stuck in the bathroom. The boxer's mere presence at the party, as

72 | Knausgård and the Autofictional Novel

he sits quietly in the kitchen at a party otherwise filled with writers and artists, gives Karl Ove "a distinct but unpleasant sensation of inferiority, a sensation that I was inferior to him" (2.32). So by the time we read of Linda being stuck in the bathroom, and of Karl Ove believing that it is his responsibility to get her out, we do so with the knowledge of the boxer's presence. When Karl Ove fails to act, it is not surprising that the boxer—whose name, we learn, is Micke—is called for. He kicks in the door and saves Linda. Soon thereafter, as the couple leaves the party, Karl Ove makes a point to fulfill his "last duty" and thank Micke, even as, he says, his "shame burned inside me" (2.35–36, translation altered).

Knausgård's use of prolepsis suggests that he is not writing in a kind of boilerplate stream of consciousness, where he, so to speak, lets his former self guide the narration.[61] Rather, he establishes the distance between narrator and experiencing character, long or short, to create intimacy, urgency, authenticity, and intensity, or what Hans Ulrich Gumbrecht calls "the presence effect," a concept several other scholars have connected with *My Struggle*.[62] In the episode with the boxer in Book 2, this is accompanied by a gentle but undeniably humorous aspect, as Knausgård the narrator mocks his former self. But that does not undermine the presence effect. Nor does it point to the sort of unreliability in the narration that Marta Figlerowicz claims when writing how it "eerily seems as if Karl Ove's relationship to his experiences were schizophrenic or as if the book's narrator and its implied author (or its represented world as such) were in silent conflict with each other."[63] Instead, it helps the narrator and subject exist side by side, in an extension of the two pacts—the autobiographical and the fictive—that also exist simultaneously in the novel.[64]

Several scholars and critics have pointed to the uniqueness of this kind of narration, which we do not usually find in autobiographical writing. Joshua Rothman, for instance, concludes in the *New Yorker* that Knausgård has invented a new kind of fiction as he "chronicles the minute details of his own existence, but not from the perspective of himself."[65] Martin Hägglund sees the mode of narration as "not simply an act of remembering but of reliving," which is echoed by Peter Sjølyst-Jackson, who argues that Knausgård "enacts and dramatizes" the episodes in which he writes about his former self.[66] Writing with Mads Bunch, Poul Behrendt, whose original analysis of Knausgård's narration has laid the foundation for mine, suggests that Knausgård writes "about himself and his life in first person in a way that you normally only write about fictitious characters in third person," while Anna Rühl, evoking Gérard Genette's narratological terminology, simply characterizes the technique as "internal focalization."[67]

By situating the narrative consciously with the experiencing character and not with the narrating agent, Knausgård treats his former self as what renowned autobiography scholar John Paul Eakin calls an extended self: "the self of memory and anticipation, the self existing outside the present moment."[68] Eakin borrows the term from cognitive psychology to categorize the different selves in autobiographical writing and to create "a more comprehensive model of the self, one that includes both the body of physiological process and the body of social, linguistic encounter" (22). Likewise, Arnaud Schmitt has introduced the term "self-narration"—a term various scholars, including Schmitt, also have applied to *My Struggle*—to describe how certain writers "tap into the intensity and the directness that the narrative of undisguised personal experience yields while enjoying the wide-ranging plasticity of the novel."[69] Stressing that self-narration is loosely referential, Schmitt asserts that it is a genre "born out of necessity" for autobiographies to describe the complexities of an everchanging self.[70] In *Transparent Minds*, Dorrit Cohn identifies a dual voice, analogous to Knausgård's, in a reading of Iris Murdoch's novel *A Severed Head* (1961).[71]

With a multitude of definitions and terms in play to characterize this kind of narration, it seems evident that what Knausgård is doing is both new and part of a longstanding tradition. Knausgård is certainly not the first writer to place the consciousness with the acting character rather than the narrator in an autobiographical account. In recent decades, for instance, Annie Ernaux has composed several of her novels using this very trope, which we also find sporadically in Proust's *La Recherche*.[72] But Knausgård's radical and abiding usage of it, as a dominant feature in all six books of *My Struggle*, is truly original. And the monumentality of *My Struggle* with its six volume is precisely that which affords such radicality.

Treating his former self as a fictional character, Knausgård's complex narration reinforces the notion of an autobiographical and fictional pact in *My Struggle*. But it also raises the question of how we are to evaluate fiction that claims not to be fictional in a more traditional sense. Turning to discussions of what fiction is, and how it functions, does not provide much help. Here, the dichotomy of referential fact and nonreferential fiction still permeates, whether as an attempt to uphold the distinction, as Dorrit Cohn vehemently aims to do in *The Distinction of Fiction*, or to show that any such distinction fails upon closer scrutiny, as proponents of panfictionality, such as Hayden White, Roland Barthes, and Paul de Man, argue.[73] Even in historical understandings of fictionality, such as Catherine Gallagher's "The Rise of Fictionality," this dichotomy still takes center stage.[74]

With newer rhetorical approaches to fictionality, however, it becomes possible to bypass the fiction/reality dichotomy altogether. In their much-debated "Ten Theses about Fictionality," Henrik Skov Nielsen, James Phelan, and Richard Walsh argue that "fictionality, far from being escapist or irrelevant for our real-world understanding, is a valuable, oft-employed means to affect our understanding of and reasoning about what is actual, factual, and real."[75] Indeed, fictionality in this understanding is neither a category nor a genre designation, but a textual quality and communicative strategy that exists in both fictional and nonfictional discourses. As a communicative strategy, it is characterized by a "communicative agent who intends to speak fictively," making communicative agency and intention "more significant than any a priori divide between fiction and nonfiction based solely on textual features" (64). The three authors refer to fictionality to as "a basic human ability to imagine" and liken it to irony, though stressing that a fictive discourse "is clearly distinct from lying" (62–63). Here, too, *A Million Little Pieces* can be a case in point, for James Frey certainly did more than just fictionalize his previous self as he made up parts of his drug abuse experiences, his life, and his critical record.

Where traditional approaches to fiction define fictional discourses in opposition to reality, fictionality, as defined by Nielsen, Phelan, and Walsh, is not a "means of constructing scenarios that are cut off from the actual world but rather a means for negotiating an engagement with that world" (63). Fictionality is always a means to an end. In fictional discourses, it invites the reader to imagine; in nonfictional discourse, it occurs in hypotheticals, speculations, counterfactuals, and other "deviations from the actual." Because of that, the three authors urge us to talk about degrees of fictionality instead of what distinguishes it, as fictionality is attached "to the communicative act, not the object of representation" (65).

In their ten theses, Nielsen, Phelan, and Walsh do not pay much attention to literature. Rather, they focus on a broader view of fictionality as ubiquitous as a cultural and communicative phenomenon. But in his book *The Rhetoric of Fictionality*—a title alluding to Wayne Booth's formative study *The Rhetoric of Fiction*—Walsh uses several literary examples in his discussion of fictionality. Taking his point of departure in relevance theory, Walsh argues that adopting fictionality in any kind of discourse is about maximizing relevance. That allows him to sidestep the question of truthfulness: "Relevance theory allows for inference, and the generation of implicatures, to proceed from an utterance that is clearly false in the same direct way as for one that is taken as true: evaluations of truth only come into play in consequence of that process."[76] In other words: as readers, we evaluate the relevance of an utterance before evaluating its truth value. Consequently, fictionality is not a textual marker but the result of a contextual assumption that appears as part of an interpretation.[77]

If fictionality is a communicative strategy that should be evaluated by its relevance, it becomes possible to see Knausgård's fictionalization of his former self as an engagement with the world of that former self. He uses a fictional discourse as a deliberate instrument to situate the description in the past and to foster readers' engagement with his text.[78] Fictionalization becomes Knausgård's method, or more distinctively, what I propose we call *autofictionalization*: a fictionalization of the self to affect the reader's understanding of the past. Where autofiction purports to define a literary genre, autofictionalization refers to a particular literary technique. It allows Knausgård to describe his life in concrete particularity. It lets him situate himself in a potential and possible past by placing the narrative consciousness in that past. Minimizing the type of retrospective narration we expect from a traditional life story, autofictionalization makes the past seem present by placing the literary consciousness with his past self.

Autofictionalization is a governing trope in *My Struggle*, used at various degrees throughout the six volumes to remarkable effect. It is what makes the young Karl Ove's belief in the omniscience of his father in Book 3 tangible; it is what makes the adolescent Karl Ove's early sexual experiences in Book 4 cringey; and it is what makes the effect of Uncle Gunnar's accusation that Book 1 is made up devastating and crushing to Karl Ove, as Knausgård recounts in Book 6. Autofictionalization is not merely a strategy Knausgård uses to enhance his own work but a vital tool for his attempt to renew the entire genre of the novel. It helps him deconstruct the traditional dichotomy between fiction and reality, as well as the perceived alignment of novels and fiction.[79] And it allows him to maintain the autobiographical and fictional pacts at the same time.

In their reading of *My Struggle*, Arnaud Schmitt and Stefan Kjerkegaard hint at a somewhat similar idea. Stressing that *My Struggle* should be read as a narrative of a self, not as a narrative of a life, they argue that Knausgård writes to remember and in doing so "recreates the past and fills the void of oblivion with narrative" (567). Schmitt and Kjerkegaard also identify what

76 | Knausgård and the Autofictional Novel

they call a "generic riddle" in the midst of *My Struggle*: Knausgård is trying to "combat fictional narratives with the fiction of remembering, the fiction of creating a narrative of a life, which is our common lot and very much real" (568). They argue that Knausgård never shows any interest in the difference between the name Karl Ove as it appears in the novel and the empirical identity behind the novelistic name, but instead aims at what they call "a 'higher' truth where the label 'novel' does not undermine the autobiographical 'quest' but supports it" (555). I would add that autofictionalization is how he gets there. It is what gives the novel its sense of authenticity and a way for Knausgård to evoke reality: an attempt to distance himself from postmodernism by insisting that his life is not fiction or a signifier, and give the novel a renewed relevance and depth.

Novel and Self

If Knausgård renews the novel by ignoring, challenging, or perhaps even trying to undo the work of postmodernism with its supposed depthlessness, he fails to convince Fredric Jameson.[80] In a review of Book 6 in the *London Review of Books*, Jameson places *My Struggle* within the boundaries of a postmodernity that he, more than anyone, has helped define. Postmodernism, he writes in his most famous book by the same name, is characterized by a lack of depth, a waning of affect, and a departure from an inside/outside dichotomy.[81] This puts any novelistic attempt at a disadvantage, let alone Knausgård's, since a central concern of the novel historically has been the conflict between the interior and the exterior. But readily admitting this—"My sense is that this [postmodernism] is essentially a visual culture, wired for sound" (298)—Jameson also sees postmodernism everywhere, such that there is no escaping it, except through utopian discourses. Since *My Struggle* is no such thing, it simply becomes the latest iteration of postmodernism. As he puts it in the *LRB*:

> We have, in postmodernity, given up on the attempt to "estrange" our daily life and see it in new, poetic or nightmarish, ways; we have given up analysis of it in terms of the commodity form, in a situation in which everything by now is a commodity; we have abandoned the quest for new languages to describe the stream of the self-same or new psychologies to diagnose its distressingly unoriginal reactions and psychic event. All that is left is to itemise them, to list the items that come by.[82]

To support this analysis, Jameson quotes a passage from Book 6, where Knausgård describes a trip to a local grocery store: "I . . . turned to the shelves of fresh-baked bread. They had seven rolls for ten kronor, so I took one of the paper bags meant for loaves and put seven rolls inside, scrunched the top end together and dropped it in the basket, then moved on to the milk and dairy, grabbing a packet of coffee and a one-and-a-half liter of Pepsi Max on the way" (6.299). Although Jameson is correct when asserting that itemization is a result of a general situation "in which everything by now is a commodity"—especially, one might add, at the grocery store—he misses an important aspect of what is at stake in *My Struggle* and in this passage.[83] Knausgård undoubtedly uses itemization as a literary technique in his mimesis of everyday life but it is also a strategy to support his project of writing about his own life honestly and without artifice.

Though Jameson acknowledges that the passage is both preceded and followed by a childhood memory, he pays scant attention to why that might matter. In the paragraph preceding the passage that Jameson cites, Karl Ove stands in the bakery department of the grocery store with its abundance of bread and baked goods, and he remembers the limited varieties of bread in the supermarkets of his childhood and how his parents, in contrast to many of his friends' parents, always kept their bread in a paper bag. Following the short sequence quoted by Jameson, Knausgård returns to his memory of the past:

> I also remembered the supermarket where we used to buy our bread. I remembered what it looked like outside, and what it looked like inside. I remembered when it was built, the enormous flat expanse of concrete they laid next to the road only a few hundred meters from our house, and the shop that rose up bit by bit on top of it, with its name proudly displayed on the side, like on a boat: B-MAX." (6.299)

At the level of story, these memories relate to the issue at hand: bread. But the repetition of "I remembered" three times also functions as a comment on the reliability of memory. It is Knausgård's attempt to reassure readers, and perhaps himself, too, that he certainly does remember the past, even if some of the details he has shared seem so detailed as to inspire doubt. To be sure, as readers, we also recognize the name B-MAX, the local supermarket, close to Knausgård's childhood home, that is mentioned numerous times throughout *My Struggle*, first in Book 1 and most frequently in

78 | Knausgård and the Autofictional Novel

Book 3—part of a bank of memories he has built up, that we share with him.[84] Now, he seems to authenticate his own, earlier accounts, and by implication, the overall truthfulness of his narration over six volumes that have built a bank of memories and experiences that we share with him.

What's more, the trip to the grocery store occurs at a time when Uncle Gunnar is threatening to sue. Uncle Gunnar's accusation—that major parts of Book 1 are made up—makes Karl Ove doubt the accuracy of everything he has written. A few pages before the passage Jameson cites, Karl Ove verbalizes his fear of a potential trial to his friend Geir Angell, asking, "But what if he really can demonstrate that what I've written isn't true?" (6.282). A few pages later, he receives another threatening email from the uncle. In this context, the detailed shopping description takes on additional significance. Surely, someone who notices and records the present with such attention and particularity that he tells us, for example, about grabbing milk and eggs, then heading "toward the checkout, along the deserted aisles, between the refrigerated counters, and the shelves of shampoo" can be trusted to remember things in similar detail (6.286). Knausgård's attention to the present becomes a verification of the detailed descriptions of the past that his uncle questions.

The description of the trip to the grocery store is unremarkable and matter-of-fact, lacking any of the sensory details that characterize so much of *My Struggle*. Despite Jameson's claim to the contrary, I would argue that the itemization in the passage does advance what Victor Shklovsky defined as defamiliarization. Simply by portraying the ordinary experience of grocery shopping in a style and tone that mimics the actual occurrence—a series of minor actions, separated by commas—Knausgård throws our attention on our own everyday acts, so that we notice what usually seems unremarkable.[85] At the same time, the description prompts us to consider anew the complexity of memory, as we notice how the autobiographical and fictional pacts interact: interdependently, boosting one another's credibility, and validating the entirety of the project. And the basis for the relationship between the two pacts are laid in the form of the novel and through the use of autofictionalization.

Knausgård embraces what Jameson says is impossible: he brings a new language to the novel by writing about himself in that very form. He responds to a crisis of fiction brought about by, among other things, the financial crisis in 2008 by turning to reality and bringing the novel into the twenty-first century.[86] According to a long critical history, the novel is necessarily fiction, but Knausgård rejects that requirement, using the novel to write about his own life.[87] What makes *My Struggle* stand out in the literary landscape of today is the fact that Knausgård claims that he writes about his life and that readers trust him.[88] He might use techniques associated with postmodernism—formal experiments, genre blending, and metafictional strategies—but the result gestures a departure.

Chapter 3

A Son of Shame

When asked in an interview why he burned his diaries as a young man, Knausgård responded, "It's one thing to be banal, stupid, and idiotic on the inside. It's another to have it captured in writing. . . . I just couldn't stand that bastard diarist-self, and I had to get rid of it."[1] But years later, when he worked on his first novel *Out of the World* (*Ute av verden*), the sections of the manuscript of which he was most ashamed were those his editor singled out for praise. This discovery led him to judge the quality of his work with what he calls his "shame-o-meter": "In a way, it was my shame-o-meter, the belief that the feeling of shame or guilt signified relevance, that finally made me write about myself, the most shameful act of all, trying to reach the innocence of the now burned diarist-self."[2] Shame, to Knausgård, signifies importance. Due to its emotional significance, it creates tension and substance. Writing toward that shame, rather than away from it, became a way for him to ensure the literary value of his work.[3]

Scholars and critics have been quick to point to shame as a central theme of *My Struggle*, and I agree. But I go further, arguing that Knausgård integrates shame into the novel's very form. Shame operates on two levels in *My Struggle*. One shame—explicit and named—occurs within the plot, where it is central to Karl Ove's experiences and allows him to enter narratives from his past. The other shame—unnamed—arises in the novel's form, resulting from the incommensurability between ethics and aesthetics. The novel's final sentence, where Knausgård proclaims that he no longer is a writer, makes that implicit shame explicit. And as a steady current through the book, shame is central feature of Knausgård's autofiction.

82 | Knausgård and the Autofictional Novel

Erasing the Self?

In Book 1, we learn how the eight-year-old Karl Ove is met by indifference when telling his father about a face he believes he has seen on the surface of the water in a news segment about a sunken fishing boat. Anxious about the face, and anxious to prove himself, Karl Ove devises a plan. Lying in bed waiting for his mother to come home from work, he decides that when both of his parents are sitting together he will sneak down and stand outside the living room. When the news report about the sunken fishing boat comes on, he will step into the living room and show them "so that Mom and Dad could see what I saw" (1.24).

At this point, the narration is structured by the fluorescent glow-in-the-dark arms of an alarm clock lighting up the dark bedroom. The image functions as a countdown while materializing Karl Ove's anticipation of what he imagines will happen. As his expectations intensify, he grows acutely aware of everything that happens around him: cars passing by in the distance, a door opening, a neighbor taking out the trash. The description is detailed and sensory, another example of how Knausgård's narration simultaneously engages the fictional and the autobiographical pacts, employing fictional techniques to dramatize certain moments in his life. It also alludes to Proust's *Swann's Way*, recalling the image of a young Marcel waiting for his mother to come and kiss him goodnight.

Finally, a few minutes before 11 p.m., Karl Ove gets in position outside the living room door. But the story that opens the news is different than the one he had watched earlier and does not include the images of the sea where the fishing boat supposedly had sunk. Knausgård writes: "After the item was over there was the sound of my father's voice, then laughter" (1.24, translation altered). Hearing his father's laugh, though without knowing why he laughs, fills Karl Ove with shame:

> The shame that suffused my body was so strong that I was unable to think. My innards seemed to blanch. The force of the sudden shame was the sole feeling from my childhood to measure in intensity against that of terror, next to sudden fury, of course, and common to all three was the sense that I *myself* was being erased. All that mattered was precisely *that* feeling. So as I turned and went back to my room, I noticed nothing. (1.24)

Shame, in Knausgård's telling, occurs when one's interior reality—in this case, his plan to show his parents the face he has seen—comes into conflict with the exterior reality—his father's laughter.[4] Knausgård seems to believe that we feel shame when the dam that typically separates the inner from the outer fails, and the inner spills over. Or, as Kim Adrian puts it in an open letter to Knausgård, shame functions as a semipermeable barrier meant to keep that which is undesirable and socially unacceptable from "leaking out of the self and into the social sphere."[5]

Shame enters *My Struggle* early in Book 1 and stays there—sometimes quiet, sometimes loud—for the remaining five volumes.[6] It often occurs in conjunction with the dualism that gives the novel a narrative drive. Shame adds depth and authenticity: by explicitly displaying what is typically concealed and considered embarrassing, Knausgård makes us feel that he bares his most private thoughts and feelings.

Shame, however, is also related to exclusion. When hearing his father's laughter in the living room, the eight-year-old Karl Ove feels left out. As he is about to step into the room and, so to speak, into character, the laughter signals that his notion of who he is is not valid in the world his parents inhabit, where the parents' tacit interactions are incommensurable with Karl Ove's experience. In another allusion to Marcel lying in bed and feeling excluded from his family downstairs, the scene makes Karl Ove aware that his parents have a life together that he is not part of, an intimate life that comes into existence after he has gone to bed.[7]

The shame manifests itself physically.[8] Karl Ove's bodily response—that his "innards seemed to blanch"—seems to precede any consciousness of the shame he is experiencing, emphasized while the narration, in yet another instance of autofictionalization, informs us that shame made him "unable to think." In the very next sentence, the narrative consciousness changes from that of the eight-year-old Karl Ove to that of Knausgård at the time of writing. In a rare instance of taking on the role as a Proustian narrator—a move that Dorrit Cohn refers to as a "dissonant self-narration"—Knausgård extends the bodily feeling of shame to a general sensation of his childhood feelings of shame, terror, and fury, and the notion "that I *myself* was being erased."[9] After this brief insertion, the narrative consciousness returns to the eight-year-old. Defeated, the eight-year-old returns to his room with shame overwhelming all other sensations. He takes several deep breaths and says that "it helped, in much the same way that vomiting helps when you are nauseous" (1.24).

84 | Knausgård and the Autofictional Novel

And shame, importantly, is also bound with subjecthood itself.[10] Knausgård's portrayal of shame as a feeling in which "I *myself* was being erased" and all "that mattered was precisely *that* feeling" is what Giorgio Agamben calls a "desubjectifying experience."[11] Desubjectification, Agamben argues, can only be understood in relation to the subjectification that happens simultaneously. He writes that shame makes the relationship between the two—the subjectification and the desubjectification—most discernable: "[Shame] is nothing less than the fundamental sentiment of being a subject, in the two apparently opposed senses of this phrase: to be subjected and to be sovereign. Shame is what is produced in the absolute concomitance of subjectification and desubjectification, self-loss and self-possession, servitude and sovereignty."[12] Shame, in Agamben's version, has more to do with ontology than psychology. It speaks to the core of who we are. While other contemporary critics frame subjectification as a domain of knowledge, Agamben urges us to see shame as grounded in our capacity to break away from ourselves.

In Knausgård's narration, the self-loss of desubjectification thematically relates to erasure and eradication, while he also instills the subjectification formally. In the four sentences that comprise the preceding quote from Book 1, we find nine personal pronouns (eight in the Norwegian original), including first-person singular and possessive pronouns. The numerous pronouns create an uncanny effect so that, while Knausgård establishes himself as a strong novelistic subject, at the same time Karl Ove feels as if "I *myself* was being erased." In other words, on the character level, shame becomes a desubjectifying experience, erasing Karl Ove, while his writing about it formalistically functions as subjectification, asserting his presence.

Knausgård often uses numerous pronouns in descriptions of desubjectifying shame in *My Struggle*. In Book 2, for instance, he writes self-deprecatingly about being interviewed by a Norwegian journalist at a café in Stockholm after his second novel, *A Time for Everything*, had been nominated for the Nordic Council Literature Prize. He writes with ironic distance: "Merely sitting there I had gone along with the premise, which was that the two books I had written were good and important and that I, the writer, was an unusual and interesting person" (2.515). The shame of accepting this premise increases when he walks home after the interview: "Oh, I could cut off my head with the bitterness and shame," he writes, adding that if there is anything he learned over the years "it is the following":

A Son of Shame | 85

Don't believe you are anybody.
Do not fucking believe you are somebody.
Because you are not. You're a smug, mediocre little shit.
Don't believe that you're anything special. Do not believe
that you're worth anything, because you aren't. You're just a
little shit.
So keep your head down and work, you little shit. Then,
at least, you'll get something out of it. Shut your mouth, keep
your head down, work, and know that you're not worth a
shit. (2.516)

With this, Karl Ove formulates a modern, personalized version of the
infamous Law of Jante, characterized by an underlying Protestant ethic and
originally coined by Aksel Sandemose, one of Knausgård's literary heroes.[13]
Formulated by Sandemose in his 1933 novel *En flyktning krysser sitt spor*
(*A Fugitive Crosses His Tracks*), the law speaks to the egalitarian nature
of the Scandinavian countries with its disdain and criticism of individual
achievements and self-aggrandizing. With a sharp shift in register, short
sentences, numerous paragraph breaks and repetitions, and dramatic use
of the second-person, Knausgård emphasizes the self-loathing that followed
self-assurance in his conversation with the journalist.

Karl Ove does not feel ashamed because he has spoken to the journalist about his novel and contemporary literature. Rather, he feels ashamed
because he has thrust himself into a situation based on the premise that
he, as an author, is worth listening to. Shame, in this instance, is mainly
related to Karl Ove's retrospective verbalizing, rationalizing, and discerning
the interview (what Dorrit Cohn calls "quoted monologue"), less than to
an inner versus outer dichotomy. The desubjectification, then, results from
a speech act—Karl Ove telling himself that he is a nobody—happening
in the wake of what he finds shameful. This speech act is made possible
by the numerous second-person pronouns (fourteen to be exact, in both
the Norwegian and the English translation). The second-person pronouns
engender the subjectification that shame then strips away.

As these examples convey, *My Struggle* portrays shame as complex
and paradoxical. Shame points to an erasure of the subject, but it also
firmly establishes that very subject as subject. Shame becomes a way for
Knausgård to insist on the existence of a subject, Karl Ove Knausgård,
whose experiences can be conveyed through the novel—in the first
example, through the use of autofictionalization; in the second, through a

86 | Knausgård and the Autofictional Novel

retrospective speech act.[14] In Knausgård's version of shame, self-negation coincides with self-assertion and is uniquely tied to his novelistic project.[15]

The American psychologist Silvan Tomkins considers shame one of nine affects and refers to it as "the shame-humiliation affect." Shame, he says, is "the affect of indignity, of defeat, of transgression, and of alienation." His analysis focuses on its facial manifestation.[16] While the child learns to cover her face with her hands early on, he argues, the adult responds to shame either by blushing or by "dropping his eyes, his eyelids, his head and sometimes the whole upper part of his body." But while the "aim of shame is to reduce facial communication" (352), blushing has "the effect of increasing facial communication, even though the response is instigated by the feeling of shame and the wish to reduce facial visibility" (352). As Timothy Bewes summarizes Tomkins's position, shame in this version becomes "an experience of simultaneous inclusion and exclusion; it marks us as both inside and outside the community."[17] In short: shame seeks to hide itself while trying to manifest itself at the same time.

While Tomkins emphasizes the paradoxical aspect of shame, the communicative or performative part of his theory has been embraced most vigorously by contemporary scholars such as Eve Sedgwick.[18] Yet there is no visible communicative or performative aspect of the shame the eight-year-old Karl Ove experiences standing alone in the hallway, outside the living room, listening to his father's laughter. There is no one watching him, no one who can see him while he feels as if the shame is erasing him. But even if there had been someone present, if his brother or parents had surprised him, they likely would not have been able to notice anything. As Knausgård describes the shame in his narration, it is an internal feeling, something that made the "innards" of his former self seem "to blanch." Nowhere does he write that the shame he felt that night also made its mark on his face by him blushing, dropping his eyes, or lowering his head. His shame is only visible to the readers of the novel because the older Knausgård chooses to show it to us. And what we get to see is not the performative aspect of Karl Ove's shame but the performative aspect instilled by Knausgård's narrative. To that extent, it showcases how uncanny it can be to read about anyone's private life, as our violation of the character's privacy blinds us to what D. A. Miller calls "our ontological privilege over them," namely that "they will never be reading about *us*."[19]

Throughout *My Struggle*, Knausgård frequently describes shame in similarly interior terms, as a bodily feeling without any physical markers that might communicate its existence to others. Time and time again he invokes the metaphor of "burning" to describe the internal feeling: the "shame burned in me from the moment I woke to the moment I fell asleep," he writes in Book 5, emphasizing the interiority of shame, while in Book 2 he writes about how "my shame burned inside" (5.461 and 2.36, translation altered).[20] In Book 1, he fights to make sure that the shame does not externalize in tears ("hot with shame, on the verge of tears" [1.343]), while in Book 6 he explicitly contrasts it to an external reaction that is different from the internal shame, as he "burned with shame as I laughed politely" (6.31). In these examples, Knausgård shows that shame can be invisible to others. Even though he responds to an imagined or real social situation, what makes Karl Ove ashamed is not his relation to others but his relation to himself. It is a shame where "the self is ashamed of itself," as Tomkins writes, and where "the judge and the offender are one and the same self."[21]

Yet the physically performative aspect of shame is also present in *My Struggle*. At times, Knausgård writes about blushing or looking away when experiencing shame, as in Book 2 when Linda asks him to send the soup back to the kitchen at a restaurant and he writes that his face "was red with shame and annoyance" (2.278). But by opening his novel with shame as a purely interior and explicitly named feeling, and by returning to that formulation throughout the project, Knausgård ensures that read-ers will not miss its importance. Shame helps us see the centrality of the conflict between the inner and the outer in the novel and foreshadows the novel's existential conflict.

A Gateway to the Past

In *My Struggle*, shame also governs memory and gives access to the past. Midway through Book 1, Knausgård tells the story of how on one of the first days of 2004, he sat in his office on the outskirts of Stockholm starring at his blank computer screen. Unable to get any work done, he looked at a poster on the wall from a Peter Greenaway exhibition in Barcelona, then out the window:

> The sky above the hospital on the other side of the road was cloudless and blue. The low sun glistened on the panes, signs, railings, car hoods. The frozen breath rising from passersby

88 | Knausgård and the Autofictional Novel

on the pavement made them look as if they were on fire. All tightly wrapped up in warm clothes. Hats, scarves, mittens, thick jackets. Hurried movements, set faces. My eyes wandered across the flooring. It was parquet and relatively new, the reddish-brown tone at odds with the flat's otherwise fin-de-siècle style. I noticed that the knots and grain, perhaps two meters from the chair where I was sitting, formed an image of Christ wearing a crown of thorns. (1.190)

The passage consists of several shorter main clauses, some of them fragments, each functioning as a point that Karl Ove notices as he lets his gaze wander. It hinges on contrasts: high sky versus low sun, frozen breath versus fire, hurried versus set. The coldness of the winter day penetrates the description, and the description's specificity creates a sense of objectivity. Though Knausgård mentions that the poster from the Greenaway exhibition consists of four pictures, one of which is "of a 1920s pilot," he does not mention that the picture is a close-up of a small part of the pilot's face, with only one eye, part of his nose, and the aviator goggles on his forehead visible.[22] Comparing his description to the actual poster for the exhibition, it becomes clear that a metonymical chain of faces drives the progression: from the face on the poster, to the faces of strangers walking by, to the face of Jesus in the floor. When we furthermore learn that Karl Ove "leaned back" to look at the poster, the three faces also embody three different vantage points: he looks up at the face on the wall, out at the faces walking by, and down at the face on the floor.

When he first sees the outline of the face in the floor in front of him, Karl Ove does not pay much attention, "for images like this are found in all buildings, created by the irregularities in the floors, walls, doors, and moldings" (1.190). It is an instance of the psychological phenomenon pareidolia, the ability to see faces or shapes in seemingly random patterns. Pareidolia has played an important role in literature and the arts from Aristophanes's The Clouds to Shakespeare's Hamlet, where Hamlet mocks Polonius pointing to a cloud, claiming that it at first resembles a camel, then a weasel, and finally a whale.[23] Knausgård merely glances at the face at first, but when he gets up ten minutes later to make a cup of tea, pareidolia becomes point of access to his past:[24] "I suddenly remembered something that had happened one evening a long time ago, deep in my childhood, when I had seen a similar image on the water in the news item about a missing fishing vessel. In the second it took to fill the pot, I saw our living room before me, the teak television cabinet, the shimmer of isolated snowflakes against the darkening hillside outside the window, the sea on the screen, the face that appeared in it" (1.190). As an instance of Proustian *mémoire involontaire*, the above episode has been seen as Knausgård's version of Marcel dipping a madeleine in lime blossom tea in the *Recherche*.[25] But though a certain object in both cases opens up the past, the differences matter too. While the sense of taste takes Marcel back to his childhood summers spent at his aunt's house in Combray, the sense of sight takes Karl Ove back to his childhood. And where we find a linear causality in Proust, with the taste of the cookie immediately leading to the past, there is a delay in Knausgård's version, from when he first sees the face on the floor until the face in the water of his childhood returns, as well as a reversed causality in the narrative chronology: the recollected episode with the face in the water is situated early in Book 1, almost two hundred pages before Karl Ove sees the face in the floor that opens the floodgates to his memory. The delay brings focus to the Proustian allusion and shows a difference in degree: Knausgård, endeavoring to create a novel from life, is brought back to the past while attempting to write. He positions himself as an author in his own right.

The allusion to Proust helps imbue the narrative with literary quality, as though Knausgård is assuring his readers that the recollections that comprise large parts of the novel are neither random nor formless, but inscribed in a very specific literary and autobiographical tradition in which Proust's *Recherche* is the pinnacle. Knausgård first mentions *Recherche* explicitly in Book 1 when he recalls a time when he "not only read Marcel Proust's *Á la recherche du temps perdu* but virtually imbibed it" (1.29). In Book 5, he recounts, "Whenever I dried up or thought it wasn't good enough I leafed through one of the books I had with me, particularly Proust" (1.578). And in Book 6, he even refers to himself as "Proustized" (6.243).[26] These mentions confirm the positive lens through which Knausgård sees *Recherche* and suggests that he also sees Proust as the author par excellence in whose footsteps he wants to follow.

Back in part 2 of Book 1, Knausgård presents the memories from childhood that overwhelmed Karl Ove while he makes a cup of tea as a string of isolated images: the living room, the TV set, the snowflakes, the sea, and the face. They do not carry any significance or narrative unity in themselves; rather, they only gain it from our memory of his earlier description of the face he sees in the water in the beginning Book 1. To that extent, the images shed light on the complexity of the relationship

90 | Knausgård and the Autofictional Novel

between past and present, as the episode where Karl Ove sees the face in the floor in his office is "memory within a memory," as Ane Farsethås refers to it, that actually takes place four years before Knausgård started writing *My Struggle*.[27]

The images, however, reveal an important discrepancy with the past as it is described on the first pages of Book 1. Sitting writing in his office in January 2004, the winter outside seems to be carried into his recollection of the past, as he describes the "shimmer of isolated snowflakes against the darkening hillside outside the window." But in the earlier description, where he writes about sitting in front of the TV and seeing the face on the surface of the water, there is no indication that it is winter. Instead, Knausgård emphasizes that "it is some time in spring," with the windows open, Karl Ove's father working in the yard, and children playing in the street.

The difference between the two descriptions suggests that the older Karl Ove does not recall the particular circumstances of that earlier time. Instead, he is triggered by the memory of the shame he felt when his father laughed at him. At that point, it was not only dark outside but also colder, as evidenced by his mother taking off her coat and scarf. In other words, it is not the precise recollection of time or season, but a visceral callback of the feeling of shame, in which "I *myself* was being erased," that governs the memory and imbues it with so much power decades later. Pareidolia reminds him of the shame that gives him access to the past.

In Knausgård's novel *A Time for Everything*, the narrator Henrik Vankel expresses a similar sentiment: "Sense of shame was a mechanism whose highly receptive sensors picked up everything—even the tiniest thing—that concerned me. These small things were then put through a kind of amplifier and magnified into events of huge proportions in order to assure me that everything that concerned me was of great, if not huge, significance."[28] Shame makes the past meaningful. And it brings meaning to Knausgård's novelistic subject. It confirms that he is indeed a subject. This interpretation is corroborated by the fact that the memory of the episode about the eight-year-old Karl Ove seeing the face in the water and wanting to tell his parents builds to, and concludes with, his shame. We do not learn what happens after he walks back to his room and lies breathing heavily in his bed until he falls asleep, and the narration changes to the present.

That pattern of a recollection—of memories that culminate and conclude with shame—recurs across *My Struggle*. We see it when Karl Ove goes to Baby Rhythm Time at the library with his oldest daughter in

Book 2; when, in Book 3, he realizes he hurt his brother's classmate when he bragged that he could read while the older boy could not; and when, in Books 2 and 5, he cuts up his face in acts of such jealous desperation that he "never experienced such shame before" (2.199). The power of shame helps Knausgård both access his past and discern—or shape—its structure. For shame also is reflected in the form of Knausgård's novel and the conflict between ethics and aesthetics.

Shame, or How to End a Novel

In Book 6, Knausgård writes about writing *My Struggle*. Part of that means writing about his love for his (then-)wife Linda and their three kids—and his regret for putting them through the ordeal the books have become. He writes: "I will never forgive myself for what I have exposed them to, but I did it, and I will have to live with it" (6.1115).[29] Knausgård's admission points to the guilt at the core of his novel, a guilt from causing pain to those he loves and from finding writing more important than them. It is a guilt that is related to, and functions like, the shame as we previously have seen it, though based in a feeling of having done something wrong instead of an inner reality coming into conflict with an outer world. It is, Knausgård reveals, a guilt that has followed him throughout the process, especially in Book 2, in which his frustration with Linda spilled over so that this volume became "too aggressive and in some parts almost slanderous," as his "frustration and anger had occasionally infused it in ways that would damage both me and those I had written about" (6.921).

In Book 6, Knausgård reveals that he removed what he calls "the worst" and most aggressive parts of Book 2 before publication. He also added a section to Book 2 about how he met Linda and instantly fell in love with her: "So one morning, only a week earlier, I had sat down and written the story of when we met and what happened between us. Almost exactly twenty-four hours later I had finished, the story had turned into fifty pages and exuded the light the novel needed so that all the rest would not be incomprehensible" (6.921). While confirming the incredible speed with which he wrote parts of *My Struggle*, Knausgård simultaneously makes the case that the change to Book 2 was an attempt to erase his guilt. This new section did not simply change the content but also his intended structure for the project. Originally he had planned Book 2 as a book about "my life such as it was now," followed by descriptions

92 | Knausgård and the Autofictional Novel

of his childhood in Book 3, his youth in Book 4, and first marriage in Book 5, which was supposed to "end with meeting Linda in Sweden, in such a way that our love story, which was so intense, would cast its light back on the events of the second book" (6.921). Knausgård's last-minute change, then, is an attempt to balance ethics (in this case, the imperative of respecting others and their privacy) with aesthetics (his desire to write truthfully about his life). And it is an attempt to obliterate any feeling of guilt and shame involved in the project of *My Struggle*.

Danish critic Poul Behrendt calls this addition to Book 2 the "main event" of *My Struggle* because the new section landed "as a meteor in the middle of Book 2."[30] In a complex reading that Nils Gunder Hansen has characterized as "labyrinthic," Behrendt asserts that Knausgård gave his six-volume novel a plot and chronology it otherwise would not have had by adding the fifty pages about his initial meeting with Linda.[31] These added pages, he argues, become "the turning point for the novel as such where the most important threads are gathered only to be spread again."[32] To Behrendt, the shame Knausgård describes in those fifty pages, particularly when showing up for breakfast at a writer's retreat after having cut up his face, both generate the rest of the plot and signal its core concerns.

Though I believe Behrendt overstates the way the additional pages restructure the rest of *My Struggle*, I do not want to dismiss their importance. They provide evidence of the novel's irresolvable conflict between writing about his life and respecting the privacy of friends and family, and they help us see how shame is related to this conflict. And it is in this light that the apology on the last page of Book 6 should be read: by offering an apology to Linda and their three children, Knausgård acknowledges that his novel, despite the alteration of Book 2, has not struck the balance between the two as the aesthetic side of writing truthfully has overweighed the ethical considerations. Because of that, shame and guilt remain.[33]

Knausgård admitting an ethical failure does not mean that he believes he achieved his aesthetic aims of writing about his life in the form of a novel. In fact, in Book 6, Knausgård also writes that he was never able to get as close to life as he had intended: "It has been an experiment, and it has failed because I have never even been close to saying what I really mean" (6.1007). Balancing ethics and aesthetics proved impossible, and he can only imagine one form of resolution: to stop writing and renounce his identity as a writer.

That is precisely what he does in the last sentence of *My Struggle*. Writing about what will happen after he finishes the series, how he will pick up Linda and tell her "that I will never do anything like this to her and our children again," Knausgård discloses that he will "revel, truly revel, in the thought that I am no longer a writer" (6.1152). He describes a world beyond the literary universe that is *My Struggle* and imagines a future in which the shame of writing no longer exists, simply because he is no longer a writer. With that, shame becomes more than a theme in his novel and more than a formal device to access the past. Writing might be equated with shame, but writing is also how he can access, relive, and reproduce his shame—and give significance to his writing. This is the shame that has been at the core of *My Struggle*, unnamed, for all six books. It is a shame produced through the writing itself, a bringing of the interior into the exterior, that becomes the novel itself. Shame in this context is constituted out of the incommensurability of ethics and aesthetics.

In *The Event of Postcolonial Shame*, Timothy Bewes connects such an unnamed shame to the novelistic form, and argues Lukács's *The Theory of the Novel* should be read as a "founding text for the new intimacy of shame and form in the twentieth century."[34] He also wonders whether shame can exist separately from the form in which it appears, whether there is ever "a shame that precedes the work, a shame that the work takes for its subject, a shame that the work seems to be attempting to process" (14). By identifying an inherent paradox in dealing with shame, namely that "the notion of shame is inadequate to the experience, which itself *is* one of inadequacy, or incommensurability," Bewes concludes that this is not possible (15). Not only is there no shame without form, but "there is no form without shame," for "form materializes shame by its inadequacy."[35] As such, shame cannot be separated from the novelistic form, as the form is the expression of that very shame due to the novel's incommensurability of ethics and aesthetics: a shame, to put it simply, that is the result of the content never "fitting" perfectly into the form of the novel.[36]

The unnamed shame at the heart of *My Struggle* is inseparable from the novel itself. It does not exist independently: it is produced by the novel that embodies it. Shame is the result of the struggle that has given the novel its title: the struggle between life and writing, between form and substance, and between ethics and aesthetics. It is a kind of shame that Knausgård can neither name nor avoid. Yet shame should be central to any critical reading of Knausgård, as it solidifies *My Struggle*'s position in the novelistic tradition of dualism outlined by Lukács (as I discussed it in chapter 2) and brings the novel's different levels of shame into a single discourse.

94 | Knausgård and the Autofictional Novel

Renouncing writing provides Knausgård an exit from the conflict between the two and a way to end his novel. To conclude his ethical conundrum, he suggests that he gives up writing for his wife and children. To conclude the aesthetic conundrum, he finishes a novel that otherwise has the potential to keep growing for the whole of his life. As these two strands merge in his final declaration, it becomes clear that Knausgård's conclusion is a kind of last resort, a response to the necessity created by the novelistic form. He does not, as Jon Helt Haarder has suggested, challenge the role of the author with this conclusion.[37] Instead, his renouncement is a known literary trope. Arne Melberg points out that it is a reversal of Proust's ending, and Ben Lerner notes that such a "gesture is conventional" and has "a long tradition" from Virgil to Jay-Z.[38] In fact, Knausgård went on to publish numerous books after *My Struggle*. His conclusion functions not as a guide for his own life outside the novel, but a way to accentuate the importance of shame in *My Struggle*. Shame governs the novel as form, composition, subjectivity, and as an access point to the past. It is a vital component in Knausgård's version of autofiction.

A Son of Shame

In Book 4, Knausgård recalls how he saw his father naked for the first time. He was a young student at the University of Bergen and traveled to northern Norway for the weekend, where his father had relocated with his new wife. They went to the local public pool, and his father started undressing as they entered the locker room. Knausgård recounts, "I felt myself getting hot and flustered, didn't know where to look or what to do with myself, because now he was taking off his underpants and for a few seconds he was completely naked" (4.304). But he could not help looking: "I had never seen him naked before, and a shudder went through me as I cast my eyes over him" (4.304). He looks down and away but cannot help looking when his father takes off his underwear. When he looks up, he meets the gaze of his father, who, he writes, "looked at me and smiled" (4.304). Karl Ove feels that everything else in the locker room has vanished, and his father's nakedness is burned into his memory. The experience is almost a textbook example of shame.[39]

The episode comes in a section of Book 4 filled with excerpts from the notebooks Knausgård's father left behind. Of the numerous entries in what is essentially a diary, Knausgård writes that there is one of his

A Son of Shame | 95

father's diary entries, and only one, that he has "a clear memory of," where the Norwegian phrase "et eksakt minne," more precisely than the English translation, suggests that he, in fact, has learned it by heart. That entry is from the day he saw his father naked in the locker room. He quotes it in full:

> Friday 6 March.
>> *With K.O. and Frederik in the swimming pool.*
>> *Nice to swim again. Home for fondue and slides of China.*
>> *Talk after. Too much to drink. Scenes. Unni fed up—broke*
> *clock.*
>> *Shame.* (4.305, original italics)

The stylistic difference between the two accounts is striking: where Knausgård's account of the incident in the public pool is detailed, affective, and three pages long, the father's account of the entire day is telegraphic, blunt, and consists of only eight sentences, most of them fragments. Yet the entries are linked: both of them deal with shame. The father's experience seems related to the broken clock. The word "Shame" dangles like the last line of a poem, suggesting that the shame he feels also could be directed to his overall behavior (the drunkenness, the scenes), and perhaps even more generally directed to himself—that he, in fact, may be ashamed of the life he leads.

The diary entry may help explain why Karl Ove's father "gave up his old life and started afresh," as Knausgård writes in Book 1 (1.38). Starting over, we might speculate, was an attempt to rid himself of shame. While Knausgård never says outright that he and his father share deep feelings of, and preoccupations with, their own shame, the narration continually suggests it. We learn, for instance, that during his childhood his father would spend most of his time in his office in the basement, shutting himself from the rest of the family. We also hear how every time he tried to step out of the role as the strict patriarch to bond with his son—and there are several attempts in *My Struggle*—he failed. In Book 3, Knausgård describes how his father once took him skiing in what turned out to be a disaster. In a country known by the popular saying "all Norwegians are born with skis on their feet," the father did not know how to ski, and instead of gliding he simply "walked as he normally walked, without skis, taking short plodding steps" (3.332).[40] Similarly, in Book 1, when Karl Ove has moved away from home, his father unexpectedly shows up at his

96 | Knausgård and the Autofictional Novel

apartment and cooks them dinner. Yet the dinner fails to bond father and son, and they sit in silence together while eating: "I didn't want him to think this was a failure, that he had a failed relationship with his son, so I sat wondering what I could say" (1.48). These instances can all be seen as shame-producing, as they reflect what Silke-Maria Weineck refers to as the essential "tragedy of fatherhood," where the trope of the patriarch has become an empty ideal. As such, they are also related to a notion of masculinity that lost its validity in the latter half of the twentieth century and that Knausgård describes in Book 2.[41]

The father's attempt to reinvent himself and rid himself of shame is perhaps most pronounced at the end of the first part of Book 1, when the sixteen-year-old Karl Ove, in the wake of his parents' divorce, comes home from a soccer tournament to find his father hosting a yard party.[42] Hearing music and laugher as he nears the house, Karl Ove finds his father unusually relaxed, sitting at a table in the yard: "He looked straight at me. When I met his gaze he got up and waved. . . . I had never seen him like this before. He was wearing a baggy white shirt with embroidery around the V-neck, blue jeans, and light-brown leather shoes. His face, tanned dark from the sun, had a radiant aura. His eyes shone" (1.173). This is not the father Karl Ove has known and feared all of his life. This new father greets Karl Ove cheerily, rests his hand on his shoulder in a friendly manner, and introduces him to the people around the table, most of whom are strangers to Karl Ove. As he sits at the table in the summer night, Karl Ove can't stop thinking about what he did at the soccer tournament he just returned from, where he one night had gotten so drunk that he threw a lit cigarette through a mail slot into the hallway of a random house: "I had succeeded in repressing it for several days, but now, sitting at the long table in the garden on my first evening home, fear reared up again" (1.175).

Karl Ove's fear used to be directed toward his father, whom he throughout his childhood had seen as an all-knowing patriarch, quick to condemn and punish, forever withholding acceptance or love. Now, his fear is directed toward himself, due to his own action of throwing the lit cigarette and putting the safety of a building and its inhabitants in jeopardy. As his father sits relaxed and friendly in a chair across from him, the world of his childhood, and his fundamental understanding of good and bad, have been turned inside out. Having laid out the reversal of the roles of himself and his father, Karl Ove soon realizes that he is more like his father than he has ever thought. The realization evolves throughout the party, as Karl Ove walks upstairs to his room and overlooks the garden, where he can observe how his "new" father acts. The scene disturbs him. It marks a contrast between his inner turmoil and the relaxed atmosphere outside, where the guests now have started dancing. He projects his unease onto his father's change:

> There was something undignified about the clothes Dad was wearing tonight. The white shirt or blouse or whatever the hell it was. He had always, as far as I could remember, dressed simply, appropriately, a touch conservatively. . . . When he suddenly started wearing arty embroidered blouses, or shirts with frills, as I had seen him wearing earlier this summer, or shapeless leather shoes in which a Sami would have been happy, an enormous contradiction arose between the person he was, the person I knew him to be, and the person he presented himself as. (1.180)

Referring to the father's new style as undignified (in the Norwegian original, the phrase for Sami-inspired style even reads as a racial slur), Karl Ove gives the impression he objects to his father's hippieish clothing, while it, along with the phrase "whatever the hell it was" adds a component of frustration and rage to his own realization. But as he continues to claim that his father's clothes presented "an enormous contradiction," he reveals that his objections are less about style than a sense that inner and outer should match: his father's style does not reflect who he truly is. Karl Ove prefers his father to keep dressing conservatively, as this best represented his idea of the tyrannical patriarch he feared.[43] He thinks that the tyrannical patriarch represents the father's "true" self and that the new side his father has shown after the divorce is a deception—a fiction. His father wears a disguise, performing as a nice, sensitive guy.

As Karl Ove observes the party, he directs his disgust toward himself as much as he directs it toward his father. Having thrown a burning cigarette into someone's house, he knows that he possesses what Kierkegaard calls the demonic (to which I return later in this chapter). It is a different image of him than the polite son who comes home from a soccer tournament and interacts with guests at a party. While he recognizes the conflict between the two sides of himself, he will not allow the same for his father. That would require both seeing his father in a more humane light and recognizing that he and his father are more alike than he wants to admit.

98 | Knausgård and the Autofictional Novel

Later that night, Karl Ove makes it back outdoors where the party is still going on. What happens next makes it impossible for him to ignore that his father is more than the man Karl Ove has known. At the table in the garden, his father suddenly raises his glass and proposes a toast for a woman named Helene, which immediately makes the father's cousin, Bodil, raise her glass, too:

> "*Skål* to Helene," Bodil said.
> They drank, looking into each other's eyes.
> Who the hell was Helene? (1.185)

Helene, it is soon revealed, is Bodil's deceased sister. The father continues: "Helene was . . . well, we were very close when I was growing up." He also tells Karl Ove that he adored his cousin and had sat at her deathbed, a revelation that shocks his son: "What was all this?" (1.186). As Karl Ove's father continues to talk about Helene and her death, he starts to cry. Here, too, father and son might have something in common: Karl Ove has always been ashamed of his own tendency to cry easily; in fact, his father has mocked him for it.

As Knausgård concludes his description of the evening, his father is still crying, a napkin blows across the lawn, and the beers Karl Ove has been drinking throughout the night begin to affect him: "I lifted my glass and drank, shuddered as the acidic taste hit my palate, and once again recognized that clear, pure sensation that arose with approaching intoxication, and the desire to pursue it that always follows" (1.186). Karl Ove wants to escape the difficult realization that he and his father are similar, but his desire to drown his troubles with drinking only adds to their similarities. In part 2 of Book 1, we learn that his father started drinking the same summer as this party, and that his ensuing alcoholism led to his death fifteen years later. Similarly, in Book 4, Karl Ove spends his last months of high school drinking to excess. "I was drunk almost all the time," he writes. "And there was little that beat starting the day with a beer and walking around drunk in the morning. What a life. . . . It was fantastic. I loved being drunk" (4.326).

Admitting, some thirty years after these events, that he and his father are alike inspires shame in Knausgård and relates to his current-day struggle of managing literary ambitions and domestic life. Early in Book 1, he writes, "When my father was the same age as I am now, he gave up his old life and started afresh" (1.38). Knausgård also feels the pull of starting afresh and fantasizes about leaving his family so he can focus on writing. He already did it five years before, when he left his first wife and moved to Sweden. Now, the duties of being a husband and father are taking a toll: "I was almost suffocated by the thought of dishes, the rooms that look as if they had been systematically ransacked, as though someone had tipped everything from the drawers and cupboards across the floor, by the dirt and sand everywhere, and the pile of dirty laundry in the bathroom" (2.537). From the subsequent descriptions of everyday life in his household, Karl Ove makes it seem as if he does most of the chores. As he writes, "I took care of the children, I cleaned the floors, I washed the clothes, I did the shopping, I cooked, and I earned all the money" (2.539). Knausgård uses paratactical syntax to suggest a piling up of exasperating tasks. The descriptions contrast sharply with those of Linda as a passive mother who sits in the living room and expects him to take care of everything. This is, of course, Karl Ove's view of the situation, and his autofictionalization takes place much closer to the time of writing than many other uses of the technique, increasing the drama. He comes off as a martyr, that is, sacrificing himself for his wife and family.[44] And even as this aligns Knausgård with the responsible, modern Scandinavian fathers who, he writes, "made me feel a little uncomfortable" (2.74)—he is also aligned with his father, who, as Poul Behrendt has pointed out, did most of the household chores in Knausgård's family of origin.[45]

Amid the feeling of domestic suffocation, all that matters to Karl Ove is that he still has time to write. To him, writing is more important than Linda, their three children, and everything that has to do with them. He considers leaving her because of this: "If I couldn't write because of her and her demands, I would leave her, it was as simple as that. And somewhere she knew. She stretched my limits, according to what she needed in her life, but never so far that I reached my snapping point. I was close" (2.539). Where his father at the same point in his life "gave up his old life and started afresh," Karl Ove stays in it, partly because he recognizes himself in his father's story and is afraid to repeat it. He embraces the conflict between writing and family by staying, and he uses the ensuing struggle as material. In fact, by taking on the task of writing *My Struggle* in just one year, he deliberately intensifies and dramatizes the conflict between writing and family life. He does what would seem impossible to most of us while also distancing himself from his father, declaring that he is not like him, that he has got the stamina and the determination to endure the difficulties of marriage even as he does what he most wants to do: write.

100 | Knausgård and the Autofictional Novel

Knausgård makes his endeavor seem heroic, even superhuman. But it is a staged and self-inflicted heroism: he gets the material for a novel, but he could easily have chosen not to write it. He creates a loop in which his decision to write six books in one year leads to a constant struggle for more time to write. What other people might see as a matter of establishing a healthy work/life balance is, in the novel, presented as a mission, an impossible test, if not a matter of life and death.

To Fasten the Gaze

The existential aspect of *My Struggle* is clear from the outset of Book 1. In that vital scene where Knausgård sees his face reflected in the window, he writes, "What has engraved itself in my face?" (1.25). To Poul Behrendt, "the plot of the novel is formulated" with this question, while Martin Hägglund argues that "all of *My Struggle* can be seen as an attempt to answer the question he asks here."[46] Knausgård provides a tentative answer a page after he poses the question. "This is what must have engraved itself in my face," he says, referring to his choice to live in isolation, a self-imposed mental exile, such that "no one gets close to me and no one sees me" (1.26).

Ostensibly finding his own answer unsatisfactory, he rephrases it a few pages later with a narrow focus on his situation as a Norwegian expat living with his wife and children in southern Sweden: "How did I end up here? Why did things turn out like this?" (1.32). He continues:

> Time is slipping away from me, running through my fingers like sand while I. . . . do what? Clean floors, wash clothes, make dinner, wash up, go shopping, play with the children in the play areas, bring them home, undress them, bathe them, look after them until its bedtime, tuck them in, hang some clothes to dry, fold others, and put them away, tidy up, wipe tables, chairs, and cupboards. It is a struggle, and even though it is not heroic, I am up against a superior force, for no matter how much housework I do at home the rooms are littered with mess and junk, and the children, who are taken care of every waking minute, are more stubborn than I have ever known children to be. (1.32)

This is the first time Knausgård uses the word "struggle" in *My Struggle*, and it refers specifically to him trying to take control of his life by writing something great while also keeping up with the unending household chores. Writing that this struggle is not "heroic," even though he is up against a "superior force," suggests that it at least could be seen that way. Some imagined other could even see him as the martyr that, in Book 2, he makes himself out to be.

Knausgård turns the struggle between writing and family into the raw material for his novel. That means writing about his struggle with family life, his struggle getting through the daily chores, his struggle in finding time to write, and ultimately, his struggle to make these daily challenges into a novel. He writes that he does not "stand a chance." The following sentence, which James Wood has called attention to, shows exactly that, as it dramatizes the hectic morning routine with a piling-on of tasks and exasperation:

> It is a question of getting through the morning, the three hours of diapers that have to be changed, clothes that have to be put on, breakfast that has to be served, faces that have to be washed, hair that has to be combed and pinned up, teeth that have to be brushed, arguments that have to be prevented, slaps that have to be averted, sweaters and boots that have to be wriggled into, before I, with the collapsible double stroller in one hand and nudging the two small girls forward with the other, step into the elevator, which as often as not resounds to the noise of shoving and shouting on its descent, and into the hall where I ease them into the stroller, put on their hats and mittens and emerge onto the street already crowded with people heading for work and deliver them to the daycare ten minutes later, whereupon I have the next five hours for writing until the mandatory routines for the children resume. (1.32)

Written as one long sentence consisting of numerous subclauses and inserts, the passage could easily be read as a plea for domestic labor to be adequately valued. But Knausgård attempts to makes a different emphasis. Ignoring the political implication, suggesting that he, for one, is above the political, he evokes a nominal distinction between fathering and literature on the one hand and politics on the other that is steeped in male privilege.

102 | Knausgård and the Autofictional Novel

Within this problematic distinction, and ignoring an important tenet in Scandinavian literature of making the personal political, his thoughts about the work of fathering solely becomes a literary response to the existential quest at the heart of *My Struggle*.[47]

At eight o'clock in the morning on March 4, five days after writing about the reflection of his face (2008 was, in fact, a leap year), Knausgård's questions reflect geographic and existential concerns: "How did I end up here? Why did things turn out like this?" (1.29). The two oldest kids have already been dropped off at daycare, and Linda and the youngest child are still asleep. Looking out the window, it is no longer his own face Knausgård sees, but the neighboring houses in central Malmö: "Having lived here for a year and a half, I know this view and all its nuances over the days and the years, but I feel no attachment to it. Nothing of what I see here means anything to me. Perhaps that is precisely what I have been searching for, because there is something about this lack of attachment that I like, may even need" (1.28). Knausgård's lack of attachment to his surroundings aligns with the broader lack of attachment in his life. "I do not want anyone to get close to me, I do not want anyone to see me," he writes (1.25). Yet he still envies those who manage to fill their lives with meaning from family life, and he wonders why he can't do the same: "Why should the fact that I am a writer exclude me from that world?" (1.36). To Knausgård, the families around him represent the good life: a simpler, less complicated life in which parents have regular jobs and manage to organize their days in a way that makes them avoid chaos. But he rejects the possibility that his life could look similar because it would detract from his writing. "The family," he writes, "is not my goal" (1.36).

In *The Concept of Anxiety*, Søren Kierkegaard calls such a sentiment demonic, writing that "the demonic is anxiety about the good."[48] By "good," Kierkegaard, writing under the name Vigilius Haufniensis (literally, the alert or watchful Copenhagener), refers mostly to the freedom and salvation of Christianity but stresses that it can signify "whatever one wants to call it." Traditionally, Kierkegaard explains, there have been three ways of approaching the demonic—the aesthetic-metaphysical, the ethical, and the medical. But, he suggests, the three approaches fail to encompass the complexity of the concept, as "the demonic has a much larger compass than is commonly assumed" (147). Instead, the demonic should be thought of more widely as a state, an "unfreedom that wants to close itself off," or "the *reserved and involuntarily disclosed*."[49]

A Son of Shame | 103

Kierkegaard's understanding seems to be a precise diagnosis of Karl Ove's state when he starts writing *My Struggle. My Struggle*, as one commentator notes, "depicts a human being in a deep existential crisis."[50] It should not be a surprise, then, that Kierkegaard's remedy is equally appropriate. The Danish philosopher, whose work Knausgård writes he early felt attracted to, is mostly known for his interest in modes of existence. He writes: "Of a person there is in common speech a very suggestive saying: 'He won't come out with it.' Reserve is precisely muteness. Language, the work, is precisely what saves, saves from the empty abstraction of reserve. . . . For language implies communication" (150). Language and communication, including writing, are the key. They, Kierkegaard writes, free people from the "unfreedom" of the demonic.

This, I assert, is what Knausgård attempts. By writing about his own life, he endeavors to escape the state of the demonic, the "unfreedom" of the life he leads, and embrace what Kierkegaard calls the good. Writing allows him to do what his father failed to do when he was the same age as Knausgård at the time of writing. Knausgård holds on—as a father, as a husband—because he writes about his life as a father and husband, or as Martin Hägglund phrases it: it is "a project of owning his life."[51] As such, in a phrase that Knausgård turns over at some length, he fastens his gaze on himself and on his family.

Knausgård introduces the phrase "to fasten the gaze" in Book 5. When he first meets the minister, who was to conduct his father's funeral, he writes that he "didn't have much confidence in Norwegian priests." Still, he tells the priest about his fear of his father as well as his sense that his father was a tormented soul. At the funeral, the priest surprises Knausgård by addressing his father's failures. The priest "said it was vital to fasten your gaze. If you don't fasten your gaze, you fall. It was vital to fasten your gaze on your children, on your nearest and dearest, on what is important in our lives" (5.613, translation altered).[52] Repeating "fasten your gaze" three times fastens our gaze, as readers, on that particular phrase. At this point in the narration, Knausgård does not explain what the priest meant or how he interprets it; he just repeats the phrase.

In Book 6, however, he extends the phrase to his own life. The section in which he returns to it starts with the diary his father left behind, which included an assessment of what his father called "the solitary individual" (6.400). In Knausgård's summary, his father wrote that he "could tell solitary individuals apart from others" and expressed a longing for inclusive and

104 | Knausgård and the Autofictional Novel

social cultures as he knew them from Southern Europe. Knausgård writes: "the fact that he started drinking must have had something to do with that. Freedom, independence, community" (6.400). Further, Knausgård writes that his father's life became more social after he left the family, and that he developed new friendships and romantic relationships before his alcoholism became unmanageable. But the drinking, which at first seemed bound up with his hope of a new beginning, ended in self-destruction. Feeling trapped and turning inward, he died, drunk and alone, in his mother's house.

This is where Knausgård reintroduces the phrase from Book 5:

> The priest who held the funeral service said something I'll always remember. One must fasten one's gaze, he said. One must fasten one's gaze.
>
> One must fasten one's gaze.
>
> He could have said the little things are important; but he didn't. He could have said that loving thy neighbor is most important of all; but he didn't. Nor did he say what that gaze must be fastened upon. All he said was that it must be fastened. (6.401)[53]

The phrase, repeated four times, almost becomes a mantra. After employing short sentences and repeated syntax to stress the importance of his material, Knausgård changes the phrase from a sober description, as in Book 5, to an existential metaphor. In order for this change to come about, Knausgård conveniently forgets that when he introduced the phrase in Book 5, it did have an object—"your children, on your nearest and dearest"—whereas in Book 6 he recalls the priest using the phrase without any object at all: "Nor did he say what that gaze must be fastened upon." He interprets the phrase to mean that it does not matter *what* you fasten your gaze upon or what you see when you fasten it "because nothing means anything on its own. Only when an object is seen does it become. All meaning comes from the eye seeing" (6.400).[54]

Knausgård writes that the phrase made sense to him back then and that "it makes sense to me today, as I sit here writing these words." He claims he knows "what it means to see something without fastening one's gaze. Everything is there, the houses, the trees, the cars, the people, the sky, the earth and yet something is missing because their being there means nothing" (6.401).

I believe that he knows this from experience. The Knausgård who sits alone in his office in Book 1, writing about his detachment from the world, where nothing "of what I see here means anything to me," is not fastening his gaze (1.28). He is "someone who can barely recognize himself," Martin Hägglund asserts in his reading of the existential aspect of the novel.[55] But the Knausgård in Book 6 who reflects on writing the previous volumes of his novel is, as Toril Moi writes, "simply not the same writer as in Book One."[56] He has gone from being an impoverished writer, longing for recognition, to a literary sensation and celebrity. More importantly, though, he has made an existential change: through his writing, he has fastened his gaze on his own life and on his family.

This is the difference between Karl Ove and his father. By writing about his life and his family, Knausgård makes them the solution to his struggle, not just the cause. Earlier it was his ability to write that suffered from their presence, but in a chiastic turnaround, it is now the family who suffers from his writing, since he discloses the most private details from their lives. While the reversal creates an ethical dilemma, it resolves the existential crisis that, in combination with his feeling of being fed up with fiction, made Knausgård start writing *My Struggle* in the first place. Knausgård no longer feels trapped between life and writing, for, as Sebastian Köhler argues, the writing of *My Struggle* "is in fact just as much an attempt by Karl Ove to fasten his gaze on something as an attempt to fight the nihilistic in fiction."[57] The existential becomes intrinsically linked with, and works hand-in-hand with, novelistic ambition.

Kierkegaard, too, argues that the novelistic and existential are intrinsically linked in his first book, an extended review of Hans Christian Andersen's *Only a Fiddle*. The book, *From the Papers of One Still Living*, has often been considered an early precursor to Kierkegaard's "real" authorship, and its Hegelian language and complex criticism have earned it a reputation of being enigmatic, or even, as one writer put it, "unreadable."[58] Indeed, Kierkegaard's book is both dense and perplexing, not least because he rejects Andersen's novel based on its lack of a so-called "Livs-Anskuelse," or life-view. As he writes, "A life-view is more than the quintessence or a sum of propositions maintained in its abstract neutrality; it is more than experience, which as such is always fragmentary. It is, namely, the transubstantiation of experience; it is the unshakable certainty in oneself won from all experience."[59] Kierkegaard seems to suggest, however cryptically, that since a life-view is more than words, we should think of it as a commitment to understanding life "backward through the idea" while living it forward to the future (54).[60]

A life-view, Kierkegaard asserts, is more than a theme in a novel in which the protagonist reflects upon her life. Rather, it is integrated into,

106 | Knausgård and the Autofictional Novel

plausibly even identical to, the novelistic form: "A life-view is really providence in the novel [*egentlig Forsynet i Romanen*]; it is its deeper unity [*dybere Eenhed*], which makes the novel have the center of gravity in itself. A life-view frees it from being arbitrary or purposeless, since the purpose is immanently present everywhere in the work of art (*Konstværket*)" (81). A novel without a life-view, such as Andersen's *Only a Fiddler*, fails to convince its readers of its necessity and formal unity. Kierkegaard sees Andersen's book as a failure because the author seeks to locate meaning in the life of his protagonists, Christian and Naomi, by way of the plot points and storytelling, rather than by the novel's totality. In his portrayal of Christian, for instance, Kierkegaard raises the question if he in the novel "actually is presented as a genius by the author," as Andersen otherwise claims he is (95). Andersen is "depicting not a genius in his struggle but rather a sniveler who is declared to be a genius," Kierkegaard writes, suggesting that form and content are at odds with each other in Andersen's novel.

Where Andersen fails, Knausgård succeeds. His final declaration that he is no longer a writer allows his novel to embody Kierkegaard's idea of living life forward. From the pivotal scene in Book 1, when he sits in his office late at night asking what has engraved itself in his face, everything serves a narrative and formalistic purpose on the novelistic journey toward this end. Karl Ove's renouncement gives the novel what Kierkegaard calls a "center of gravity" and gives the life story told in the books between these two points a unity. Knausgård's declaration also distances him from what he has written. This move mirrors that of Kierkegaard, who by giving his review of Andersen's novel the full title of *From the Papers of One Still Living, Published against His Will*, suggests that any novel, as Yi-Ping Ong accurately observes, must "appear to be rendered independently of any existing beholder's relation to it." By signaling that there is an endpoint to his life's narrative, followed by a future vastly different from the present and past, Knausgård accomplishes Kierkegaard's idea of a successful novel and does what Ong refers to as "volatilizing the author figure into a character."[61] That change happens because he has turned from his stated intention, the realist credo to "get as close to my life as possible," and toward a potential future that only exists as a fictional possibility. At the same time, he resolves the struggle between writing and family life that has given his novel a name. He fulfills the novelistic promise of his narrative by giving it providence and a center of gravity. And he seems to relieve himself of the guilt and shame at the core of his novel—even if, back in the outside world, he professed a desire to burn all the copies of *My Struggle* if he could.

Chapter 4

Fiction and Trust

Fourteen days after the publication of Book 1 of *My Struggle*, the regional newspaper *Bergens Tidende* ran a long critical article of Knausgård's novel.[1] In the article, there was an interview with an unnamed "representative for the family," who lambasted Knausgård for calling his book a novel. What Knausgård had written, the family member said, was not fiction, but nonfiction, contorted by lies:

> He harasses both the living and the dead, and exposes us in an inappropriate way, without us being able to defend ourselves. Because when we do, he says that it is just a novel, and that he has taken our objections into account. But then he continues to say that this is as close to the reality of his own life as he can get. And in that life, we are his exposed family, who do not recognize the serious things the author claims have occurred. It should be evident that we are considering legal action.[2]

The article in *Bergens Tidende* also included an interview with Knausgård, who defended what he had done. He had, he noted, in order to accommodate the family's concerns, changed characters' "occupations, geographical names, and everything else that can identify individuals."[3]

The threat of legal action quickly made headlines in Norway and neighboring countries, helping to turn *My Struggle* into a literary phenomenon.[4] Indeed, as *My Struggle* made its way around the world, most introductions to Knausgård included the story of how the family had threatened to sue the author for libel and defamation, with some even asserting, incorrectly, that the family already had done so.[5] But where the

108 | Knausgård and the Autofictional Novel

threat could be seen as a sign of a legal process yet to come, it was rather, as Poul Behrendt points out, the conclusion of the negotiations between Knausgård, his publisher, and the novel's uncle Gunnar, whose real name is Bjørge Knausgård.[6]

Knausgård confirms this when he writes in Book 6 that he sent copies of the manuscript of Book 1 to family members and others who were mentioned. Before publication, he and his publisher met to finalize a letter to the uncle in which they "itemized all the changes we had made in the novel on his insistence," in order to prevent a future lawsuit (6.430). They agreed to all but one of the uncle's demands: they did not change the name of Knausgård's father. "I could change the names of everyone else," Knausgård writes in Book 6, "but not his" (6.390).

The family's accusations raised several ethical and legal questions that were heavily debated in the Norwegian media and that also made their way into scholarly discussions of *My Struggle*: Does a novel about real people violate their right to privacy? Who "owns" someone's story? And who is allow to tell it? Inside these ethical questions of the effects of the novel on the people named in it, the criticism evokes a number of questions that concern the status of the novel: What is the relationship between the novel and fiction? When is a novel fictional? And why do we trust Knausgård, even identify with him, when the family tells us his story is all made up?

Book 6 encourages readers to tackle these very questions. I argue that Knausgård's attempt to expunge fiction from the novels leads readers to emphasize absorption and identification with Karl Ove, ultimately engendering a feeling of intimacy and trust.

Uncle Gunnar

Book 6 narrates Knausgård's uncle Gunnar's angry response to *My Struggle*. In a string of emails to both Knausgård and his publisher, including one with the subject "Verbal Rape," Gunnar accuses Knausgård of making up parts of what he has written. Gunnar writes that the manuscript is "full of mistakes" and "harassing descriptions," and he characterizes his nephew as "dishonest" and "evil." While the accusation at first seems broad and unspecified, later emails make it clear that Gunnar objects specifically to how Knausgård describes the circumstances of his father's death, the despair and dirt and drinking:

Only there was no mess, Gunnar claimed. He had gone to the house shortly after the ambulance had been there and his brother's body had been removed from the chair in which he had died. All that day, and the one after that, he had stayed there in order to help and be with his mother. During that time he had quite naturally cleaned the place up where it was most urgent. What I had written, that the house had been littered with bottles from the front door all the way up the staircase, was utter nonsense. It was simply not true. By the time Yngve and I turned up a couple of days later, he [Uncle Gunnar] had already taken care of most of what needed doing . . . The work I had put in at Grandma's he reduced to nothing. It was his wife who had done the bulk of the cleaning up, changed the curtains, helped Grandma in the bath. I, the writer with his head in the clouds, had merely swanned about, bucket in hand, incapable of making a difference. (6.168)

Uncle Gunnar faults the second part of Book 1, in which Knausgård describes in detail how he spent days scrubbing and cleaning his grandmother's house, using the money earned from recycling the empty bottles to buy new cleaning supplies. His accusation shakes the foundation of the project: Knausgård's truth claim that underlies everything we read in *My Struggle*.

Knausgård reacts physiologically to Uncle Gunnar's accusation with shame once again taking over.[7] He does not defend himself or insist that he has been truthful. He repeatedly describes the emails' bodily effects on him: how they paralyzed him, made him unable to think, and how, after reading one of them, he had to "lay down on the bed and remained there motionless" (6.99). Surprisingly, he does not address the obvious contradictions in Gunnar's emails: If the house was normal when he arrived, why did he have to clean? And was it Gunnar or his wife that did the cleaning? Instead, Gunnar's accusation makes him question his own memory, as well as implications for his own literary project:

Had there been bottles? The way I remembered it, there had been empties all the way up the staircase from the living room to the top floor, there were shopping bags of them dumped underneath and on the top of the piano, and the kitchen had been crammed too. But what about the staircase leading up

110 | Knausgård and the Autofictional Novel

> to the living room? I had no recollection at all. I must have
> exaggerated. Unreliable, again . . . If he was right about what
> he was implying, that the sight that confronted us in the house
> had been quite normal, and that my depiction was grotesquely
> exaggerated, then everything fell apart. It bore down on some-
> thing fundamental, first and foremost of course the very premise
> of the novel, that it was describing reality. (6.177)

Knausgård's investigation of memory, truth, and reliability becomes the
basis of Book 6 of *My Struggle*, which eventually makes us doubt the
trustworthiness of all six volumes. The unease intensifies when Knausgård
contacts other central characters in his novel, most of them remembering the past better than him. Hanne, with whom he was in love in high
school, tells him that she remembers a lot from back then and that she
still thinks about it. After reading the manuscript he sent her, Knausgård
writes, she "said she remembered that time very well. I didn't. Or rather,
I remembered a few episodes very well. Others I recalled only faintly,
shaping them in my writing, inventing dialogue, for example" (6.165).

Most astonishing, however, is how Knausgård frames his own narration about Gunnar's accusations. He claims that, a year and a half after
receiving the emails from his uncle, it is impossible for him to describe
the feelings they raised:

> I can't recall its exact nature or how it felt, eighteen months
> having passed since, and I am no longer in the grip of its
> explosive alarm. I can comprehend it, and even comprehend
> it well, but I can't resurrect it. Reading those messages again
> now, I am filled with the most unpleasant emotions, and they
> confirm to me something I've always known, always felt, but
> compared to the force by which it became apparent to me at
> that time, this is merely a shadow. (6.99)

Well into the sixth volume of *My Struggle*, we are accustomed to seeing
Knausgård engage in autofictionalization, placing the narrative consciousness with his former self, and providing precise details about his memories,
as with the shame he felt when he, at the age of eight, heard his parents
laugh in the living room or the anticlimax of a New Year's Eve when he
was a teenager. His new account of doubt in Book 6, then, raises ques-

Fiction and Trust | 111

tions, especially since the subsequent pages attempt to do what he claims he cannot: make the "explosive alarm" of how he felt palpable to readers.

One could read Knausgård's admission in the context of a post-structural understanding of language as always already "merely a shadow," as Knausgård writes, of the world it supposedly designates. Yet there is more at stake here than that. While Knausgård's admission that he cannot recreate his feelings seemingly only is of thematic importance, it turns out that it, in fact, is a formal problem for the novel: how does the novel go about describing a feeling that Knausgård says he cannot resurrect and now is only a shadow to him? With the feeling that he no longer feels exceeding him as a subject, it is instead objectified and amplified in the narration of what happened eighteen months earlier.

That a certain feeling is perceived in a text, rather than felt, is what Sianne Ngai characterizes as tone in *Ugly Feelings* from 2005. Tone, she argues, stands out as a formal aspect of a literary work that "makes it possible for critics to describes a text as, say, 'euphoric' or 'melancholic,'" as the category that "makes these affective values meaningful with regard to how one understands the texts as a totality within an equally holistic matrix of social relations."[8] Tone is our response to a literary text that we place back at the book where we perceive it as "a literary or cultural artifact's feeling tone: its global or organizing affect, its general disposition or orientation toward its audience and the world" (28).[9] As such, tone blurs the line between subjectivity and objectivity, which is the reason Ngai also suggests that when talking about tone, we should shift our focus from the effects a certain text has on its reader to the "powerful question of 'objectified emotion,' or unfelt but perceived feeling" (28).

In an exhaustive and complex reading of Melville's *Confidence Man*, Ngai shows how the novel's governing tone of confidence allows it to become a negative model of affective/aesthetic engagement. She argues that the "ugly feeling" about Melville's novel is about *not* feeling bad about not feeling confidence. The novel, she claims, allegorizes, theorizes, and performs the absence of feeling—meaning that tone becomes the event, or dominant element, of the novel: "Put simply, the novel conscripts its own affective ambiguity to ensure that which we cannot *not* care about *without* feeling, well, *bad*" (84, original italics).[10] Referring to this novelistic maneuver as aggressive, Ngai also notes that, through this negative model of aesthetic engagement, the novel problematizes the status of literature in a capitalist world.[11]

112 | Knausgård and the Autofictional Novel

Through her reading of Melville and her notion of tone, Ngai offers a model for how to understand what is at stake in Book 6 of *My Struggle*.[12] The feeling perceived in *My Struggle*, but not felt, is that of distrust. That distrust is not reducible to how one particular reader might feel but hovers around the object, making it impossible to say whether it originates in the book or in the reader. The hovering of the mistrust makes it the governing tone of that particular part of Book 6 and, in a kind of retrospective implication, of *My Struggle* as a whole. With Gunnar claiming we cannot trust Knausgård, the narration suggesting that we cannot trust Gunnar, and Knausgård suggesting that we cannot trust him and that he does not trust himself, the feeling of distrust penetrates every aspect of the novel in a complex relationship that involves the characters in the novel, the author, and the readers. The novel tacitly invites us *not* to trust the narration—and we don't. Instead, thanks to the novel's tone of distrust, we learn to engage with it aesthetically.

This reading practice, guided by distrust and aesthetic disengagement, is personified by Knausgård's friend, the character of Geir Angell. Physically or ideologically, Geir Angell is a constant presence in *My Struggle*, a kind of Sancho Panza to Knausgård's Don Quixote.[13] As Knausgård writes in Book 6, it is Geir who originally suggested *My Struggle* as the title for the novel, and it is Geir Angell whom Knausgård calls several times every day to read what he has written for critique. Knausgård even admits that *My Struggle* "would have been unthinkable without him" (6.241). It is thus understandable that, upon receiving the emails from Uncle Gunnar, Knausgård immediately forwards them to Geir, whose response to them is very different than Knausgård's.

After reading the email with the subject line "Verbal Rape," Geir Angell calls up Karl Ove and pretends to be Uncle Gunnar: "Is this my despicable, friendless nephew?" he says as Karl Ove picks up the phone (6.100). While the uncle's email pained Karl Ove, Geir says that he, after reading it, "couldn't stop laughing." And contrary to Knausgård, who is terrified by the thought, Geir suggests that the threat of a lawsuit is a dream scenario: "You should hope he does, it'd be the stupidest thing he could do [i.e., take the case to court]. You'll be rolling in money! Everyone'll be wanting your books if it comes to a court case. This is literary history in the making. And you'll be a millionaire. There's no better scenario" (6.100). What is at issue here is not, according to Geir, a question of whether to trust or distrust what Knausgård has written. Instead, it is an issue of exploiting the capitalistic system that the novel inevitably is part of, as a

Fiction and Trust | 113

public scandal only would increase its market visibility and the ensuing profits for Knausgård. In the market, the only thing that counts is sales: truth or its absence will always be secondary. In fact, the tone of distrust might help increase sale of the novel. While the novel might formulate an implied critique of capitalism, Geir asks Karl Ove to embrace what his very novel seeks to counter.

Geir's cynical reading of what a potential lawsuit would mean stands as a kind of exemplary counterpoint to the way most readers would likely frame their engagement with *My Struggle*. Agreeing with Geir would mean that we are nothing but consumers who pick up whatever books happen to make the headlines. Even though, to some extent, this seems to be the case, as hardly any readers outside Knausgård's Norway picked up *My Struggle* without having read about it in media accounts, few people would be proud to admit that their reading habits are driven more by the market's famously invisible hand than by their own individual tastes.[14] Rejecting the tone of distrust means buying into the novel's aesthetic premise. Or to paraphrase Ngai: we do not *not* want to trust Knausgård. We want to believe him, and we want to believe that it is possible to engage aesthetically with the novel. Luckily, Knausgård guides us through this very practice and offers a model of what an aesthetic engagement could look like.

An Imaginary Lawsuit

In the wake of the accusatory emails from Gunnar, and in one of those mundane instances that lend credibility to the narration, Knausgård stands in the laundry room of his apartment building. With piles of laundry spread out around him on the floor, he watches the revolving drums of the washing machines, which transport him, like a transition via close-up in an old movie, to an imaginary trial against him. He sees himself arriving at the courthouse and leaving in "a blitz of photographers." He envisions salacious newspaper headlines, such as "Knausgård the Liar," and "Admits Lying" (6.190).

Knausgård imagines the scandal of a potential trial—it would be "dirty and sensational," he writes, and "all kinds of shit would be dug up about me"—with self-loathing that is tinged with a sense of remove, implying that we would not be interested in the attention of such a hypothetical trial because it most likely would be negative (6.190).[15] But this seems, at best, an instance of false modesty. He has already informed us, some

114 | Knausgård and the Autofictional Novel

ninety pages earlier, that what we are reading was written eighteen months after the events described took place. That means the media frenzy, interviews with the novel's "real" characters, and journalists' investigations into the accuracy of what he had written had already taken place. And what is missing in his account of the potential fallout is what was correctly prophesied by Geir: that *My Struggle* would become a major, international commercial success.

Knausgård pictures himself on the witness stand, defending his novel in a long, abstract monologue about how he sought to write about "the particular," which "in this case happens to me." After presenting his defense, it is his uncle's lawyer's turn to make his case. Listing several of what he refers to as "lies" in the novel, he turns to Karl Ove, who is still sitting on the witness stand:

> And therefore my question to you is this: Why are you lying about these matters? You, who wish to write about the world the way it is, why should you, of all people, depict a world that never existed? That is the issue facing us today. You can try to hide behind as much existential intellectualism as you like, to my mind it's pretentious gibberish, so pompous it makes me feel sick just standing here listening to it. However, that is not the issue at hand, at least not today, but from what I can deduce from your self-exalting and conceited claptrap, you consider what you have written to be the truth, this is to your mind the whole point of your despicable and duplicitous novel. Only it turns out not to be the truth at all. Can you explain that to me? (6.193)

As the lawyer presents a tirade of rhetorical questions, he serves not only as a representative of Gunnar but also as a cipher for us readers. He asks the critical, uncomfortable questions that we should ask, albeit more harshly and directly than an "ordinary" reader might. To an extent, the lawyer (and by implication Uncle Gunnar) embodies the notion of "that 'ideal reader' of whom great critics have talked so much," as Fredric Jameson suggests.[16] The lawyer's questioning also becomes a way to preempt any future criticism, because that criticism has already been included in the novel: the questions have been asked, the confrontation has taken place, and the uncle's accusations have been tried at court, even if only in an imagined scenario.

Fiction and Trust | 115

After halfheartedly defending himself, Knausgård returns to his seat to "await the testimony of the first witness" whom he has chosen to help his defense. Surprisingly, he has not asked his brother Yngve or anyone else who could corroborate his accounts to come to the stand. Instead, the witness is Horace Engdahl, "the man who for many years had announced the winner of the Nobel Prize, known for his literary elegance and incomparable style" to defend his literary, not legal, merit (6.194). Engdahl served as the Swedish Academy's permanent secretary and is to this day often seen as a kind of cultural aristocrat, the living and breathing embodiment of literary quality. Before the scandal that shook the Swedish Academy in 2018, he was considered the most influential member in deciding who would win the Nobel Prize in Literature. Knausgård writes that he remembered seeing Engdahl at a seminar in Bergen years earlier. During his talk, Engdahl had "veered off the theme" and started talking about the Swedish novelist Carina Rydberg's *Den högsta kasta* (*The Highest Caste*), which created quite a stir when it was published in 1997 for vengefully exposing living people by name. To Engdahl, Knausgård recalls, the "book was first and foremost a brilliant work of literature." Knausgård explains that is why he wanted Engdahl on the witness stand: "I supposed I was hoping he would say the same about my own book" (6.195).[17]

By focusing on his novel's literary merits, rather than defending its truthfulness, Knausgård seems to tacitly acknowledge the difficulty in separating truth from lies. As J. Hillis Miller notes in an essay on Proust, both truth and lies "employ the same syntax, the same grammar, the same semantic resources."[18] Nothing separates a lie from truth in a novel, and no linguistic marker tells us if we are dealing with one or the other. At the same time, meeting accusations of lying with a defense of literary quality becomes a way to avoid a game of "your word against mine," and to suggest that the literary aspect of a work is more important than any notion of truth. Furthermore, Knausgård knows that we know that what he has written is probably true. By the time of his own writing, and of readers making it to Book 6, journalists largely had verified the novel's accuracy, and the family's early accusations had been drowned out.

All the more reason, then, for Knausgård to suggest we assess the novel on the basis of its literary qualities. By imagining he will ask Horace Engdahl to vouch for the literary quality of *My Struggle* instead of asking witnesses to verify his account of what happened, he encourages a mode of aesthetic engagement but never tells us explicitly why we should read his novel as "a brilliant work of literature." The absence of an explanation,

116 | Knausgård and the Autofictional Novel

and of Knausgård never telling us why we should read his novel aesthetically, leaves us with an all-important question: Why should we read *My Struggle* as a fiction and as a "brilliant work of literature" when Knausgård has previously focused on convincing us of its truth-value?

The importance of this question only increases when we realize that, in this imaginary trial, Knausgård does precisely what he has claimed he was trying to avoid from the outset of *My Struggle*: writing fiction (in the traditional sense of the term), in that the trial never took place.[19] In his fictional trial, Knausgård dramatizes the tone of distrust, turning the novel into a site for exploring a feeling no one actually feels. The fictionalization culminates later in Book 6, when we realize that the manuscript Uncle Gunnar objects to actually is not Book 1 of *My Struggle*—at least not the version that has been published and that we have read. Rather, we have read a version that already has received the uncle's approval, as Knausgård and his publisher agreed to most of the demanded changes. This contradiction creates what Fredric Jameson in a different context refers to as "a utopian hole or absence at the centre of the work, a transcendence that can only be imagined." In Book 6 of *My Struggle*, we are left to imagine how the manuscript Knausgård sent his uncle differs from the novel we have been allowed to read.[20]

The fictional trial becomes, paradoxically, a testament to the novel's truth-value. While fiction and lies may be synonymous for Gunnar, Knausgård's narration suggests that fictionalization accurately represents his own anxiety in the wake of his uncle's accusation. The six-page trial scene also makes autofictionalization—the dominant narrative trait of *My Struggle* as a whole—into an explicit theme and formal concern. As such, it speaks to a larger relationship between fiction and truth: the only way for Knausgård to move beyond fiction, he suggests, is through the very fiction he seeks to reject. This relationship between fiction and truth is one that Catherine Gallagher informs us is uniquely tied to the novel as a genre: "The widespread acceptance of verisimilitude as a form of truth, rather than a form of lying, founded the novel as a genre."[21] In other words, *My Struggle* works to lay, all over again, the cornerstone of what a novel is.

Fiction and the Novel

Gallagher's influential article "The Rise of Fictionality" argues that the notion of fiction changed drastically in the "mid-eighteenth-century novel

Fiction and Trust | 117

in England, in which an explicit and ongoing discourse of fictionality developed" (336).[22] Realism and fictionality, she writes, have a paradoxical relationship:

> The historical connection between the terms *novel* and *fiction* is intimate; they were mutually constitutive. And yet the novel has also been widely regarded as a form that tried, for at least two centuries, to hide its fictionality behind verisimilitude or realism, insisting on certain kinds of referentiality and even making extensive truth claims. If a genre can be thought of as having an attitude, the novel has seemed ambivalent toward its fictionality—at once inventing it as an ontological ground and placing severer constraints upon it. (337, original italics)

By claiming that "the novel discovered fiction," Gallagher positions her study in contrast to universalist accounts of fiction. She distinguishes a notion of fiction that "stands on its own" as a separate concept from fantasy, for "plausible stories are thus the real test or the progress of fictional sophistication in a culture" (337, 339).[23] An all-important development in the novel from Daniel Defoe to Henry Fielding came when the names in the novel no longer laid claim to refer to actual people, fictional or not. While Defoe "asserted the existence" of an individual by the name of Robinson Crusoe, the belief in a correspondence between a proper name and "an embodied individual in the actual world" changed in the span of just a few decades with Fielding, where "proper names do not take specific individuals as their referents" (341). Gallagher singles out *Joseph Andrews* as the novel where the lacking referentiality of the proper name early becomes evident, arguing that the narrator "explicates the superiority of the new dispensation" by describing how he is interested in manners and species, not men and individuals. As the "key mode of nonreferentiality in the novel was, and still is, that of proper names," this change from Defoe to Fielding is simply what defines the novel moving forward, Gallagher asserts. This, she argues, is the birth of the modern novel: "The founding claim of the form, therefore, was a nonreferentiality that could be seen as a greater referentiality" (341, 342). In short: the fact that readers know that novelistic characters are fictional and they do not refer to actual people is what makes the novels relevant to our lives.

While the first part of "The Rise of Fictionality" has been widely cited and subject to extensive critical engagement, the second part, in

118 | Knausgård and the Autofictional Novel

which Gallagher moves from bold claims about fiction and the novel to an exploration of fictional characters, has received surprisingly little attention.[24] In her discussion there, she turns to what Dorrit Cohn calls "signposts of fictionality," those distinctive marks that inform us whether we are dealing with a fictional or nonfictional text.[25] Such signposts occur in third-person narratives when "the narrator depicts the subjectivity, or consciousness, of a character" and when, Gallagher writes, readerly affect is generated by "the mutual implication of their unreal knowability and their apparent depth, the link between their real nonexistence and the reader's experience of them as deeply and impossibly familiar" (356).[26] Gallagher evokes Cohn again when discussing first-person narrators who, she argues, "reveal their fictionality primarily through the techniques that indicate the difference between the narrator and an implied author" (357). Yet, as if Gallagher is stuck at an ontological and epistemological dead-end, she does not single out any such specific techniques.

She does, however, add that both homodiegetic and intradiegetic narrators "must sustain the illusion of opacity of the characters surrounding them," pointing to Proust, whose narrator never "really knows Albertine," and Marlowe, who in Joseph Conrad's *Heart of Darkness* never understands Kurtz. She continues: "In these cases, sharing the narrator-character's doomed hermeneutic struggle, often read as an allegory of reading, gives rise to an even more intense sense of the fictionality of such intimacy as well as a melancholy recognition of its discontents" (357). With this, Gallagher suggests that when we encounter a first-person narrator who expresses her or his frustration with their limited knowledge—when a narrator comments on his or her own narration, their lack of knowledge, or their failure in relaying to the reader what they intended—the narrator's frustration becomes an allegory of reading. Such metacommentary makes the marker of fiction more evident, and Gallagher seems to propose that they add a melancholy that makes us more intimately connected to the narrative.[27]

By insisting that the only indication of fictionality in a first-person narration is a narrator's comments on their own inadequacy, Gallagher contradicts her earlier claim that the nonreferentiality of proper names is the "key mode of nonreferentiality in the novel."[28] In fact, when it comes to the "doomed hermeneutical struggles" of first-person narrations that Gallagher writes about, she makes no effort to separate novels with referential and nonreferential proper names. The logical consequence, then, seems to be that books like *My Struggle*, whose proper names are referential, should

Fiction and Trust | 119

still be classified as novels. To be sure, when Knausgård says in Book 6 that he "can't recall its exact nature or how it felt" to be accused by his uncle Gunnar, and that he "can't resurrect it," he embodies what Gallagher refers to as a "narrator-character's doomed hermeneutic struggle" (6.99).

While the crack in Gallagher's argument makes room for Knausgård to be deemed a novelist, it does not follow that *My Struggle* is a work of fiction. Indeed, we can surmise that Gallagher, with her insistence on nonreferentiality as a key feature of a novel's use of proper names, would reject the notion that *My Struggle* should be seen as a novel. But the numerous instances of Knausgård's explicit hermeneutic struggle resonate with her approach to the novel. Book 3, for example, bares his shortcomings in a way similar to Book 6. It opens with what Anna Rühl has called an "impossible memory," as Knausgård uses a third-person narrator to narrate an instance from when he was a baby: "Of course, I don't remember any of this time," he writes, as it becomes clear that he is describing an old photo of his parents with he and his older brother, who were eighteen months and four and a half years old, respectively (3.7).[29]

It would be foolish to claim that *My Struggle* becomes a novel merely by virtue of these explicit instances of narrative reflection. Rather, they should be seen in conjunction with my previous discussions of how Knausgård invokes novelistic and fictional features throughout *My Struggle*. This is the very essence of the contemporary autofictional novel. The autofictional novel of today confirms Bakhtin's notion of the novel as a "developing genre" where the novel in many respects "has anticipated, and continues to anticipate, the future development of literature as a whole," while insisting that referentiality *is* possible.[30] As such, autofiction is an attempt to make the novel relevant, engaging, and vital by rejecting fiction. It asserts that the novel, indeed, is best suited to interpret the condition of modernity and give readers the opportunity to mirror their lives—not through imagined lives but the lives of the real people they read about.

Knausgård's insistence on referentiality contrasts with Gallagher's argument that it is easiest to relate to or identify with nonreferential characters who hold proper names. This development, she argues, points to the contradictory relation between truth and fiction, which included "a nonreferentiality that could be seen as a greater referentiality" where readers as early as the eighteenth century would "attach themselves to characters because of, not despite, their fictionality" (342, 351). Speaking more generally about the novel, and not only the novel of the eighteenth century, Gallagher concludes: "Character's peculiar affective force, I pro-

120 | Knausgård and the Autofictional Novel

pose, is generated by the mutual implication of their unreal knowability and their apparent depth, the link between their real nonexistence and the reader's experience of them as deeply and impossibly familiar. Because we know their accessibility means fictionality, we are included to surrender to the other side of their double impact: their seductive familiarity, immediacy, and intimacy" (356). What Gallagher is proposing is that we simply identify with, and are seduced by, the familiarity of fictional characters because we know that they are not real but only characters in a novel. Consequently, identifying with referential, nonfictional characters seemingly should be difficult, if not straight out impossible.

Scrolling through the many reader reviews of *My Struggle* on Amazon. com, however, quickly shows that readers respond differently than Gallagher expects. As one fairly typical reviewer puts it, Knausgård's writing "related to my life and made my own experiences more meaningful and vivid." Another speaks about relating emotionally to *My Struggle*, as the reader realized "that I was not alone with my thoughts growing up, that Karl Ove also felt things I thought were only true to me."[31] Professional readers—both critics and scholars—have also spoken about the relatability of *My Struggle*. Writing in the *New York Review of Books*, Zadie Smith says that when reading Knausgård you "live your life with him," a sentiment echoed by Toril Moi in an article in *The Point*: "I was absorbed. Transfixed. I identified. I suffered. I struggled alongside Karl Ove."[32]

In an essay from 2010, the Swedish author Stig Larsson was one of the very first to describe relatability and identification as important elements of *My Struggle*. Larsson—one of the most influential Swedish writers, not to be mistaken for his namesake, the deceased crime author Stieg Larsson—has often been mentioned in connection with *My Struggle*. Stefan Kjerkegaard, for instance, has referred to Larsson as "Knausgård's Godfather," while Knausgård himself has praised Larsson, even suggesting that *My Struggle* would not have been possible without Larsson's 1997 book *Natta de mina* (*Goodnight My Dear Ones*), a book, as he writes in Book 2 of *My Struggle*, that "hit me like a clenched fist" (2.92).[33] Larsson's essay focuses on how Knausgård hit him.

Larsson focuses his attention on Book 2, explaining how starting to read that volume gave him a shock and made him think that Knausgård was out of his mind. "The guy must be mad" ("Karln måst va´ galen"), he writes colloquially with a phrase that rhymes in the original Swedish and emphasizes the causality.[34] What truly shook him, Larsson writes, was how writing and living seem to coincide in *My Struggle*: "Apparently, he is just

Fiction and Trust | 121

writing about what is happening to him right now. How does he dare!"
But, he continues, seemingly somewhat embarrassed by saying it straight
out, he felt, "yes, how should I put it, a sense of togetherness, based on
complete identification with the protagonist of the book."

Stig Larsson's embarrassment is understandable, considering how
identification and absorption have been looked at suspiciously ever since
Plato warned against them in *The Republic*. Indeed, Cervantes's *Don
Quixote* and Flaubert's *Madame Bovary*, two of the most celebrated novels
in literary history, warn readers of the dangers of textual absorption and
identification.[35] Yet, in recent years, scholars such a Rita Felski have tried
to take identification and absorption seriously in the study of literature.
In a defense of identification, she argues that to "rethink identification is
also to rethink character" and makes the case for thinking of characters
as "being like persons without scanting or shortchanging their aesthetic
abilities."[36] Our "acts of identifying," she asserts, "drive various kinds of
engagement with fiction." Indeed, it is not that "naïve readers or viewers
identify and that dispassionate critics don't but that they find different
points of connection—affective, ethical, political, philosophical, or a mix
of all of these," Felski writes (119–120).

With *My Struggle*, identification happens not despite the referentiality
of proper names, to use Gallagher's terminology, but because of it. Reading Knausgård's novel with a homology between character, narrator, and
protagonist means that we do not have to choose between "identification"
and "aesthetics," because when we identify, we identify simultaneously with
the character and the author. One reason for the widespread identification
with *My Struggle* is, as I will show, because of a contemporaneousness in
the narration, which not only Larsson speaks to when linking identification
to the notion that Knausgård is "writing about what is happening to him
right now" but that also Zadie Smith notes, when she writes that it is "as if
the writing and living are happening simultaneously." Another reason is that
Knausgård himself provides an example of the kind of literary absorption
literary scholars traditionally frown upon but that Felski and Moi, among
others, nevertheless embrace and that is intimately related to identification.

Modes of Reading

Book 2 of *My Struggle* opens with the date written in the top corner—"July
29, 2008"—one of just a few times, throughout the 3,600-some pages that

122 | Knausgård and the Autofictional Novel

make up all six volumes, that Knausgård dates his writing. The strategy, what Philippe Lejeune would call "a pact of truth," suggests that the narration unfolds authentically at the same time as the events it narrates and adds a diaristic quality to the writing. (Other instances of such narrative contemporaneousness occur too, some with and some without precise dates.) Book 2, which describes Knausgård's challenges of being a father while living as an expat in Sweden, was published a little over a year after this date, underscoring the short distance between writing and reading, between the narrator and his audience. Book 2's first readers may well have been able to recall what they did on this same date while they read Knausgård's opening lines: "The summer has been long, and it still isn't over. I finished the first part of the novel on June 26, and since then, for more than a month, the nursery has been closed, and we have had Vanja and Heidi at home with all the extra work that involves. I have never understood the point of holidays, have never felt the need for them and have always wanted to do more work. But if I must, I must" (2.3). The ordinariness of Knausgård's summer holidays, his seeming assumption that we know the names of his children, the rhythms of his family life, and the minor personal conflict he feels, suggests an intimacy with the reader. Knausgård invites us into his life, and this bolsters our trust in his truthfulness. Why else, we might ask, would anyone write about how everyday life has become intensified because the kids are home for the summer, if not to be honest? By writing that he has never understood the point of vacation, Knausgård reaffirms the central conflict in *My Struggle*, between writing and family life. But he adds an ethical stance to this struggle—"if I must, I must"—suggesting that, at least for the summer, he has chosen to sacrifice his ambition for the good of his family.

After this diarylike opening, Knausgård's narration moves back in time with a retrospective investigation into how he, a Norwegian, ended up in Malmö, Sweden, as a father of three. The chain of events he describes leads us progressively further back in time. First, he provides an account of that summer's vacation with the family: a stay with some friends in their summer house and a visit to a small amusement park. Then Knausgård describes a children's birthday party a year or two earlier, and then, the party in Stockholm he and his wife Linda attended when she was pregnant with their first child. After a short return to the present, Book 2 backtracks even further, to when Knausgård first arrived in Sweden as a Norwegian expat, then further still, to when he first met Linda at a creative writing seminar almost a decade earlier.

Fiction and Trust | 123

In this retrospective narration, singular associations lead from one event to another. The kids riding a pony in the amusement park leads to the oldest daughter's horseback riding lessons; sending the kids to a parent-run daycare leads to a children's birthday party with the other children from the daycare and their parents; a father sitting quietly by the kitchen table at that same birthday party leads to a boxer who also sat in the kitchen at the party in Stockholm. This retrospective technique gives an impression of arbitrariness, as if the novel were formed without any clear organization or order. That's certainly how some critics have seen it: *My Struggle* has been called everything from a flat record of "superficial detail, unenlivened by the touch of literary art . . . by beauty, density or form" to—and many times over—a "formless novel."[37]

Poul Behrendt calls the inverted chronology that Knausgård uses to structure Book 2 a "V-form." The composition chronologically moves back in time (or down the V) until Knausgård's first meeting with Linda, at which the narrative line pivots forward again (which is to say, up the V), until it reaches the present.[38] I would add that metonymy constitutes this inverted chronology, so that one part of an episode—say, the quiet man in the kitchen—becomes the point of departure for the next episode—that with the boxer at the party in Stockholm. A continual metonymical chain becomes the structural principle that guides the book's composition.

As cognitive linguistics has taught us, metonymy is not just a rhetorical figure, but it is also a cognitive process in which one conceptual entity (also referred to as the vehicle) serves as a reference point that provides mental access to another entity (also referred to as the target).[39] Metonymy helps organizes our everyday thoughts and actions in a way that, when rendered narratively, seems casual and familiar. Interjections, explanations, and additions are part of how we tell someone a story, metonymically, with each vehicle leading to a new target and expanding our telling. In *My Struggle*, metonymy works alongside relaxed diction to further the readers' sense of intimacy with Knausgård, as though we are listening to him confide in us. And since the metonymic composition imitates our everyday thinking, it invites identification.

Knausgård's use of metonymy is not only limited to Book 2. Metonymy also structures the narration in Book 1, where Knausgård describes a disastrous New Year's Eve when he was a teenager, and functions off and on throughout all six volumes that make up *My Struggle*.[40] But Book 2 is a particularly fruitful place to examine how it suggests authenticity and encourages identification, because it is so tied to the contemporane-

124 | Knausgård and the Autofictional Novel

ousness of the narration. Indeed, the casualness of the narration, made through metonymy and easily mistaken as formlessness, is part of what leads readers to be absorbed by the narrative and identify. So too does the example of readerly engagement and absorption that Knausgård provides in his own reading, as narrated in his novel.

Two modes of reading dominate in *My Struggle*.[41] One is on display in the essayistic passages throughout the six volumes where Knausgård engages in readings of mainly canonical male authors such as Hölderlin, James Joyce, Rainer Maria Rilke, Marcel Proust, Knut Hamsun, and Peter Handke.[42] The other is as an integral part of the story of the novel, when Knausgård dramatizes how he reads. This is what we see, for example, in Book 2, when he describes becoming a stay-at-home dad after he and Linda have had their first child, moving through daily routines and taking endless walks through Stockholm with his daughter in a stroller: "Little by little, I mastered everything with regards to small children, there wasn't a single thing I couldn't do with her, we were everywhere, but no matter how well it went, and irrespective of the great tenderness I felt for her, my boredom and apathy were greater" (2.72).

Quickly, reading becomes an antidote to his boredom, a way for Knausgård to make it through the long days spent with his infant daughter. He writes that "there was hardly a park bench I had not sat on, at some time or other, with a book in one hand and a stroller in the other" (2.72). (The book he was holding, he lets us know, was often by Dostoyevsky, in whom he says he finally had found a light he had searched for.)[43] But then the novel pulls us back to the time of narration, as Knausgård as the novel's narrator explains these were not thoughts he had back then as he was sitting on a bench reading: "As usual I didn't think as I read, just engrossed myself in it, and after a few hundred pages, which took me several days to read, something suddenly happened, all the details that had been painstakingly built up slowly began to interact, and the intensity was so great that I was carried along, totally enthralled, until Vanja opened her eyes from the depths of the stroller, almost suspicious, it seemed: Where have you taken me now?" (2.73). Reading, Knausgård claims, is what made him forget the world around him. As he immerses himself in Dostoyevsky, reading becomes an inner sanctuary that he unambiguously valorizes as preferable to the outside world. Here, he can find refuge; here, he can forget the duties of everyday life. With that, the last question—"Where have you taken me?"—takes on a double meaning: it can refer to his daughter waking up and her eyes asking where he has

Fiction and Trust | 125

taken her, but it can also be read as a rhetorical question, with Karl Ove asking where what he has read has taken him. In short, that Knausgård's being "enthralled" in his reading and "carried along" suggests an immersive reading experience associated with identification.

Later in Book 2, his immersed reading returns with renewed urgency. We learn how Karl Ove has agreed with his wife that if he stays home all day with their infant daughter, he can go to a coffee shop in the afternoon to sit and read for an hour. One day, he heads to the café in a nearby department store. After ordering his coffee, he sits down by one of the tables, once again with Dostoyevsky, though the sight of the book "was not exactly tempting" as the "threshold for reading became higher the less I read" (2.96).

And with that, the novel changes from one mode of reading to another: from reading as part of the storyline to reading as part of the essayistic passages in the novel. The shift is marked by a blank line before a new paragraph, which implies that the following six-page essay on Dostoyevsky reflects Karl Ove's thoughts as he sits reads in the department store café (though the comparisons with Tolstoy, Freud, and Munch, and quotations by Ernst Jünger may suggest otherwise). Nevertheless, the impression that these are his actual thoughts as he sits reading furthers when the essay abruptly comes to an end and we find ourselves back in the café:

> I had a sense the crowds around me were thinning and that the streets outside were dark, but not until I put the book down to go and get a refill of coffee did it strike me that this was a sign that time was passing.
> It was ten minutes to six.
> Jesus Christ.
> I should have been home at five. (2.100)

Karl Ove's absorption, which causes him to lose track of time and place while reading, is an emblematic example of literary immersion. It is the kind of immersion that is intimately connected to identification, where you, in Rita Felski's words, "are transfixed and immobilized by the work and rendered unable to frame, contextualize or judge."[44] Yet Knausgård distinguishes himself from a naïve reader lost in the plot of a novel, for the writing suggests that, while reading, he has engaged in heady, critical reflections on Dostoyevsky. With that, Knausgård proposes a mode of

126 | Knausgård and the Autofictional Novel

reading that absorbs and transfixes yet becomes critically viable. This kind of reading that is both absorbing and critical is continually promoted in his discussions of literature in the essayistic parts throughout *My Struggle*.

And here, I believe, we find the reason why critics and scholars are compelled to share their stories of identification and absorption with *My Struggle*. Knausgård offers a model for a mode of reading that takes its point of departure in a personal, engaged aesthetic experience. But in Knausgård's case—as is the case of critics and scholars—the stories of absorption and identification are followed by critical reflections and engagement. As such, it is an illustration of what Rita Felski in *Uses of Literature* refers to as both "double consciousness" and "bifurcation of perception": that even "as we are bewitched, possessed, emotionally overwhelmed, we know ourselves to be immersed in an imaginary spectacle."[45] Or, more accurate when dealing with *My Struggle*, we know we are reading a novel.

The story of literary immersion does not end here. Knausgård's own absorption in Dostoyevsky curiously affects the form of *My Struggle*. This is what happens: after leaving the café in the department store, Knausgård tells us how he hurried to a nearby supermarket, picked up a few groceries, and started heading home, planning to spend a relaxing Friday night with his wife. From the second he enters their apartment building and meets their nosy Russian downstairs neighbor, it takes him 243 pages to climb the remaining stairs to their apartment. These 243 pages (229 in the Norwegian original) justify exactly why he needs to seek refuge from family life by immersing himself in literature. On these pages, which make up roughly half of Book 2, Knausgård tells the story of how the tedium of family life, with its fighting over daily chores, has taken precedence over his own needs and desires, and how the beautiful love story with which it all began—and that Knausgård also tells in these pages—has lost its momentum. It is the story of why literature and reading have become a necessary escape.

Two hundred and forty-three pages later we are back in the apartment building as he makes his way up the stairs: "Such was the situation on that evening in February 2005 when, with a book by Dostoyevsky in one hand and a NK carrier bag in the other, I passed the Russian on the stairs" (2.349). Thus, we might propose that his reading of Dostoyevsky—his absorption, identification, forgetting time and place as he has been sitting in the café in the department store—spills into the narrative structure of the novel, even with a metonymical link from the Russian author to his Russian neighbor. It shows how reading has thematic, compositional,

Fiction and Trust | 127

and formal implications for *My Struggle* as it models a certain readerly response. Losing himself in a book reflects how Knausgård loses himself in his own narration, forgetting both time and place.

Narrating or Describing?

To speak of two modes of reading in *My Struggle*—reading as part of the storyline and reading as part of the numerous essayistic passages—is also to speak of two modes of writing in the six-volume novel. The first of these is characterized by closeness, immediacy, and progress; the second by distance, reflection, and stillness. The first mirrors Knausgård's stated antiliterary intention of wanting "to get as close as possible to my life" (2.582), while the other reflects his ambition of writing literature of the highest quality. These two modes also correspond to the distinction between narration and description that has been a pivotal point of contention in literary studies since Aristotle privileged the former above the latter.[46]

In his influential essay "Narrate or Describe?" from 1936—written almost two decades after *The Theory of the Novel*—Georg Lukács privileges narration over description. He opens his essay by contrasting two horse racing scenes from two classic novels, Emile Zola's *Nana* and Leo Tolstoy's *Anna Karenina*. Lukács argues that where Zola describes, Tolstoy narrates. This means that Zola's description—"*described* from the standpoint of an observer"—is "a mere filler in the novel," while Tolstoy's—"*narrated* from the standpoint of a participant"—is "integrated into the total action in the novel."[47] To Lukács, the distinction between narration and description is more than a question of different approaches to writing. Instead, it is first and foremost a result of the historical and social development in which the function of description in the novel after 1848—by which Lukács refers to Flaubert and Zola—"underwent a fundamental transformation." After the June Days uprising in France, when the liberals crushed the radicals and any hope of a socialist republic was ruined, the bourgeois society became firmly established. But these naturalist writers did not participate in that bourgeois society. In fact, "they refused to do so," Lukács contends, and therein lay their tragedy: "For them the only solution to the tragic contradiction in their situation was to stand aloof as observers and critics of capitalist society."[48]

This is where a new understanding of description comes into existence. But these new descriptions, in which the author becomes a passive observer describing the capitalist society of which he is still part, turns the novel into "an artificial product of the artist's virtuosity" as opposed to "something that emerges and grows naturally, as something not invented, but simply discovered." In this environment, the book becomes "a merchandise" and the writer "a salesman of this merchandise" (119). The result, as Dora Zhang formulates it, is that the dominance of description "turns the novel into a simple succession of sketches rather than a work organized by a narrative logic that can establish causal relationships and make of it an organic unity."[49] This creates an undue pressure on and interest in the end of the novel, because, Lukács writes, the "complexity of patterns of life is clarified only at the conclusion."[50] This interest in the end of the novel is what Fredric Jameson half a century later would continue to pursue in his understanding of the changes to the novelistic form.[51]

When scholars today invoke Lukács's essay on narration versus description, it is often because they disagree. Suggesting that Lukács's view of description still dominates literary studies, Sharon Marcus, Heather Love, and Stephen Best, in their much-debated article "Building a Better Description," ignore the historical arguments in Lukács's essay. They claim that he rejects description because he finds it aimless, pointless, and deadening: "Aimless: without a thesis, a describer has no way to focus attention and guide observation. Pointless: on its own, description has no meaning; what matters are the larger forces, mechanisms, and values it serves to illustrate. Deadening: descriptions are just one damn thing after another."[52] While this account might hold some truth, it also shows an unwillingness to engage with the complexity of Lukács's argument because there is, as Toril Moi points out, "more to Lukács than this."[53] Instead, their swift rejection of Lukács becomes as much an illustration of how critics oftentimes simplify the distinction between narration and description to make it seem starker than it actually is.

In her discussion of Lukács, Toril Moi also sustains the distinction between the two modes of writing. But as she qualifies the reading of Lukács by Marcus, Love, and Best, she focuses on how Lukács rejects the description in the novels of Flaubert and Zola because they are not related to "lives which express themselves in action and passion, doing and suffering."[54] Arguing that Knausgård does precisely that with his description in *My Struggle*—writing "as a person fully immersed in the actions described, however insignificant they may appear"—she implies that *My Struggle* challenges any attempt to prioritize narration at the expense of description. While I am tempted to agree with Moi, I also believe her

Fiction and Trust | 129

reversal of the dichotomy between narration and description misses an opportunity to see how Knausgård is challenging this dichotomy altogether. For evidence, we do not have to look any further than the opening essay on death in Book 1.

At first, the essay on death that opens *My Struggle* seems to confirm the status of description in *My Struggle* as a site for Knausgård's literary ambition—a feature also observed by Moi.[55] Knausgård has on several occasions confirmed that he insisted on including the opening, even when his editor suggested cutting it, because it "represented quality to me" with their "sentences of the highest quality I could produce," as he writes.[56] But if we take another look at the opening of Book 1, this time with a focus on the relation between description and narration, a different story emerges—a story that is important if we want to understand how Knausgård connects the anti-aesthetic and aesthetic agendas.

After describing death as a physiological phenomenon, Knausgård turns to the two kinds of death he sees dominating contemporary society. While one of these is physical death—"death as it actually turns out to be"—the other is our concept of death, or the images of death portrayed in media. Asserting that these images of death "have no weight, no depth, no time," Knausgård lists examples of such images—presumably real incidents as portrayed by media: an off-piste skier falling and dying, an airplane exploding during takeoff, and a fishing boat mysteriously disappearing off the coast in northern Norway. He writes:

> A fishing smack sinks off the coast of northern Norway one night, the crew of seven drown, next morning the event is described in all the newspapers, it is a so-called mystery, the weather was calm and no mayday call was sent from the boat, it just disappeared, a fact which the TV stations underline that evening by flying over the scene of the drama in a helicopter and showing pictures of the empty sea. The sky is overcast, the gray-green swell heavy but calm, as though possessing a different temperament from the choppy, white-flecked waves that burst forth here and there. I am sitting alone watching, it is some time in the spring, I suppose, for my father is working in the garden. (1.7)

With the use of present tense and the sequence of events connected by commas, the description of death in *My Struggle* becomes concrete, indi-

130 | Knausgård and the Autofictional Novel

vidual, personable, and integrated into the novel's unfolding storyline. It shifts from reflection to immediacy, from an objective description without a defined subject to a narrated and personal account by an identifiable narrator, writing about his former self. The transition from absence to presence happens gradually, as specific details accrue. We understand that these TV reports have been seen by the narrator, who notices the dramatic contrast between the calm sky and choppy waves. Finally, in the third sentence, as Knausgård moves from what Lukács calls description to narration, that narrator is identified: an eight-year-old version of the narrator, sitting and watching this scene unfold on TV.

While we might question the accuracy of Knausgård's memory—the only case of a missing fishing boat in Norway that fully fits his description happened in 1970 when he was less than two years old—what is important is that the narration and the autobiographical storyline grow out of the one description in the novel whose literary quality Knausgård has insisted upon.[57] As such, the passage can be read as an allegory of Knausgård's literary project. It is an allegory that shows that the autobiographical narration in *My Struggle* is not at odds with the literary and the novelistic, as it is presented in the novel's descriptions. Rather, the allegory tells the story of how narration is embedded in and grows out of the descriptions. In Knausgård's version, narration and description live side by side, depend on each other, and in many cases can be hard to tell apart.

Consider, a few pages later, how description and narration run together inside Knausgård's autofictionalization in a passage I discussed at length in chapter 2. The young Karl Ove has just seen a face on the surface of the water where the fishing boat supposedly has sunken and is now stepping outside to tell his dad about it. It is a description of a time long lost, of the atmosphere outside his childhood sometime in the late 1970s:

> The crack of the sledgehammer on rock resounded through the estate. A car came up the gentle slope from the main road and passed, its light blazing. The door of the neighboring house opened. Prestbakmo paused on the doorstep, pulled on his work gloves, and seemed to sniff the clear night air before grabbing the wheelbarrow and trundling it across the lawn. There was a smell of gunpowder from the rock Dad was pounding, of pine from the logs behind the stone wall, freshly dug soil and forest, and in the gentle northerly breeze a whiff of salt. (1.12)

Everything in this description could be characterized as "mere filler," to use Lukács's description of Zola. It is a *stilleben* of suburban life taken in through the senses: the sounds, the sights, the smells. One might conclude, as Lukács claims is the case with Zola's description, that these seemingly random details—the car in the distance, the name of the neighbor—"could easily be eliminated." But this description is not, like Zola's, "*described* from the standpoint of an observer." Instead, it is focalized through the eight-year-old Karl Ove as a narration: what he sees that evening is what we get to see. Taking in the evening with all of his senses is a part of the narration, where he, after being rejected by his dad as he told him about the face on the surface of the ocean, experiences how the face changes in his mind as he is standing in the evening. "I thought of the face I had seen in the sea," we read in the sentence following the preceding description: "Now it was Dad's face I saw" (1.12). Descriptions in *My Struggle* thus not only give way to narration but become integrated and embedded into those same narrations.

Knausgård's descriptions cannot be separated from the action, as they always reflect the consciousness of the protagonist. This is precisely the kind of description Lukács champions as historically justifiable. Arguing that "good" descriptions "elevate chance [by which he seems to mean randomness] to the inevitable," he asks: "Is it thoroughness of description that renders something artistically 'inevitable'? Or does inevitability arise out of the relationship of characters to objects and events, a dynamic interaction in which characters act and suffer?"[58] Never explicitly answering his own questions, Lukács implies the answer: inevitability in description, and what elevates it to narration, is that it is "*narrated* from the standpoint of a participant." While all of the examples in Lukács's essay are written in the third person, the consequence of his argument seems to be that first-person writing, by definition, is narrated, not described—and that first-person writing inherently carries a sense of inevitability.[59]

Such a reading lets us see *My Struggle* in a flattering light—as a superior form of narration—but in order to fully appreciate and understand its work, we must challenge the dichotomy of narration and description altogether. Indeed, in *Narrative Discourse*, Gérard Genette shows how Proust, despite being "viewed as a novelist lavish in descriptions," "never brings about a pause in the narrative, a suspension of the story or of (according to the traditional term) the action," as the descriptive aspect "never evades the temporality of the story."[60] To Genette, the action of

132 | Knausgård and the Autofictional Novel

Proust's descriptions lies in their very perception, where the description becomes "absorbed into the narration" with the result that "description is everything *except* a pause in the narrative."[61] Accordingly, Genette suggests that description becomes indistinguishable from narration: that any description always carries an element of narration—an argument that, as Dora Zhang suggests, easily can be pushed "in the other direction, to say that narration is just the description of action."[62] Zhang further argues that our view of description often "depends on a spatialized idea of a novel's form as a bounded container viewed from above," and shows the difficulty in singling out description as an isolated feature if not as part of a larger scale analysis of a paragraph, scene, or page. "Only in larger units does it make sense to call a passage 'narrative' rather than 'descriptive'; on a smaller scale the distinction is impossible to maintain" (46).[63]

In those early pages of Book 1, it is the perception of the eight-year-old Karl Ove that guides the description of the atmosphere outside the family's house. By listing each part of the description in separate main clauses, Knausgård creates the illusion that he literally is standing outside the house—and we with him—while he slowly breathes in and looks around. It gives the description a direction and a narrative quality, as if the description were embedded in his eight-year-old self. And the description does seem to do anything but pause the narration, precisely as is the case in the *Recherche* according to Genette. Instead, it advances it and invites us to see the world the eight-year-old Karl Ove—and by extension Knausgård—sees.

In *My Struggle*, description always contains an aspect of narrative. Indeed, even the description of death that opens Book 1 also contains an element of narration with Knausgård describing death dramatically as an "invasion" of bacteria that moves through the different parts of the body. And, conversely, that otherwise clear instance, when Knausgård writes about how he is watching the news as an eight-year-old, is imbued in description. Writing that "I am sitting alone watching, it is some time in the spring, I suppose, for my father is working in the garden" is where the writing mode changes from description to narration. But the descriptive aspect is still present in the contextualization: that it probably is in the spring and that his father is working in the yard.

I do not mean to suggest that description and narration are indistinguishable in *My Struggle*, but rather that they are coconstitutive. Each description contains a narrative element, and every narrated action (to use Lukács's term) contains a descriptive element. In any analysis of *My*

Struggle, then, these techniques should be considered to exist in tandem. One may be foregrounded as a matter of stylistic choice, but that does not erase the traces of the other. To be sure, the narrative aspect of the descriptions in Knausgård's novel makes them engaging, specific, and personal, while the description inherent in the narrated parts materializes and establishes the narrated always locating it in both time and place.

This duality of narration and description should not be neglected when we try to discern Knausgård's claim to intimacy in the novel. When descriptions always contain narration, we read these—whether it is a description of suburbia in the 1970s or a description of the associations while reading Dostoyevsky at a café in Stockholm—as expressions of Knausgård's thoughts. And when the narration carries a hint of description, we are constantly reminded that the novel is about specific and real characters, and that the storyline is an account of something that has happened in real life. As such, the interplay between narration and description mirrors and corresponds to the two pacts of autobiography and fiction. It is also what enables an intimacy that leads to what Arnaud Schmidt and Stefan Kjerkegaard call "the reciprocity stage": the novel becomes contagious, and we begin to see our own lives in Knausgård's.[64]

Chapter 5

The Very Edge of Fiction

In *Kudos*, the third installment in what has become known as Rachel Cusk's *Outline* trilogy, the narrator, Faye, attends a conference for writers in an unnamed European suburb by the sea. She meets an acquaintance, Sophia, who introduces her to Luís, whom we learn is tall, speaks slowly and sonorously, has "an impassive expression on his great moody face," and is passionate about soccer.[1] We also learn that Luís is his native country's "most important novelist at the moment," and that his latest book "has been a sensation" because he writes about subjects most "other male writers would not deign to touch"—namely domesticity and ordinary life—things "most writers would consider to be beneath them" (138).

In his writing, he has been "honest about his own life" and written about "his family, his parents and his childhood home in a way that makes them completely recognisable" (146). At a dinner with other writers, Luís first chooses to sit at a table alone because, as Sophia explains, his "success was painful for him and caused him to suffer from intense guilt" (146). Cusk's portrayal of Luís, whom Katy Waldman refers to as a "doofy Karl Ove Knausgaard doppelgänger," is filled with an unmistakable irony that seems to mock as much as praise the author of *My Struggle*.[2] By renaming him Luís and switching his nationality, Cusk suggests that an allegiance to proper nouns, which to Knausgård is so important, is less of an issue for her novelistic project.[3]

When Luís eventually joins Sophia, Faye, and the other writers at their table, he tells a story his mother has shared with him from her childhood. He follows it with the declaration that he started writing because of his mother and because he "felt the pressure of her sensitivity" (153).

136 | Knausgård and the Autofictional Novel

Writing was a task "she had bequeathed to me that I had to fulfill." In his own life, he says, he has not fulfilled that task but has instead "been doomed to repetition as anyone else." Sophia interjects that what he is saying "is completely untrue":

> Your life has been completely transformed by your talents and what you have made of them—you can go anywhere and meet anyone, your praises are sung all over the world . . . If you were a woman you would certainly find your mother's life hanging over your head like a sword and you would be asking yourself what progress you had made, other than to double for yourself the work she had been expected to do and receive three times the blame for it. (153)

While praising Luís—and by implication, Knausgård—for his honesty, Cusk simultaneously seems to criticize him, and his critics, for having a blind spot when it comes to gender. Even though he might bring domesticity into literature, his experience of it is very different from that of a woman, who inevitably will be judged on how she manages family and household life. "Though of course if he were a woman," Sophia whispers to Faye before Luís joins them, "he would be scorned for his honesty, or at the very least no one would care" (147).

Talking to Luís, Sophia continues her criticism of his gender blindness by asserting that while he travels the world, his wife is staying at home, "devoted to bringing up your children" (153). This state of affairs contrasts with Faye's, who continues to mother her children whether she is with them or apart. Even when she is traveling abroad, her two sons decide to call her when lost on their way home from school or failing to find a missing sock instead of consulting their father with whom they live. The message to Luís is clear: you might write about it, but you still live it as a man. Knausgård's version of autofiction, as well as its reception, Cusk seems to be saying, are steeped in male privilege. At the same time, she seems to acknowledge his influence on the reception, and possibly the creation, of her own project, which, since *Outline*'s publication in 2014, has been frequently compared to *My Struggle*.

In that, Cusk is not alone. Together with a Sheila Heti and Ben Lerner, she has repeatedly been lumped together with Knausgård in discussions of autofiction and, as such, helped shape the public perception of what autofiction is. It is their names that appear most frequently in connection with Knausgård's, based on the presumed formal and thematic proximities of their work to *My Struggle*. And it is their names that are invoked, along with Knausgård's, when critics try to describe how contemporary literature, in the words of Megan O'Grady, showcases "an increasing dissatisfaction with the conventions of fiction."[45] To study them in the context of Knausgård is to get a better understanding not just of their relationship to his work but also of what contemporary autofiction actually is. But it is also a study of a group of writers whose formal experimentation with autobiographical writing seems genre defining because they are white, as Tope Folarin notes.

The three writers I discuss in this chapter—Heti, Cusk, and Lerner—have all expressed their admiration for *My Struggle* in criticism and interviews. All three have reviewed singular volumes of *My Struggle*, for the *London Review of Books* and the *Guardian*. And all three, I argue, share with Knausgård a feeling of exhaustion with fiction that is the foundation of *My Struggle*, but in different ways, with different results.

My reading focuses on Heti's *How Should a Person Be?* (2010), Cusk's *Outline* trilogy (2014–2018), and Lerner's *10:04* (2014). While the first two might share the concerns that motivate *My Struggle* and add to the renewal of the novel, they also add a deliberate exploration of gender, as they explore what it means to write autofiction as a woman in the twenty-first century. Lerner, I argue, complicates any distinction between fiction and reality by embracing a Knausgårdian autofictionalization, but it applies to the future instead of the past. Together, the three novels help us understand the complexity of a contemporary autofiction and its different iterations, as they reveal a broader unease with fiction that gives credibility to Knausgård's project. And along with *My Struggle*, these novels are early harbingers of autofictions to come.

Sheila Heti: Imitating Reality

In a 2014 *London Review of Books* piece on Book 2 of *My Struggle*, Sheila Heti recounts the first time she met Knausgård in real life.[6] When she asked him if a scene from Book 1, in which his mother was scrubbing potatoes in the kitchen sink on a particular New Year's Eve in his youth, was a real memory, Knausgård professed that it was not: "No, no, I made it up." His admission, she writes, left her so shocked and disappointed that she was "unable to pick up his books for another year."[7] Now, writing the review, she reconsiders Knausgård's answer to her question.

138 | Knausgård and the Autofictional Novel

"But if the scrubbing of the potatoes was made up, are the books true, in the way we understand true to be? If they don't have a faithful relationship with "what happened," does it matter? Might they even in some ways be better?"

To answer these questions, Heti turns to the passage in Book 2 where Knausgård writes that the very thought of a fabricated character or plot made him nauseous. She argues that the question of whether something is fiction or reality is inadequate to the task of interpreting *My Struggle*. Rather, she writes, Knausgård rejects fiction because the fictional "has become too fictional" and turned into an "imitation of fiction, not of life."[8] The result is a literature that depicts life as we want it to be or think it is—not as lived, actual life: "Life as it is lived is humiliating, a banal series of errands interrupted every few years (if you're lucky) by experiences that shoot up like a great flare—falling in love, the birth of one's child—but (unfortunately for the novelist) it's mostly not worth writing about."[9]

Heti circumvents her previous disappointment through this understanding of Knausgård. It is not, she argues, Knausgård's adherence to the truth that makes *My Struggle* remarkable, but the novel's rejection of fictional convention in order to engage with the banality of everyday life. She cites a *Paris Review* interview in which Knausgård says that writing about diapers and daily life is writing "without dignity." Writing "without dignity," as Heti interprets Knausgård's statement, is a commitment to reality, and to being uncompromising as an artist. It does not necessarily mean writing something truthful, where details and facts can be verified. Instead, it involves being honest about who you are as an artist, and about what you think and feel. And that means that "one must avoid dignity."

To avoid dignity is precisely what Heti does in her 2010 novel *How Should a Person Be?* where she pushes the form of the novel even further than Knausgård, using imitation as a thematic and formal strategy to write what Jennifer Cooke calls "her ugly self."[10] This avoidance, she makes clear, has different implications for a female writer than a male. Indeed, in the prologue, Sheila—the narrator and protagonist—states that while every era has its art form, and the nineteenth century "was tops for the novel," today we "live in an age of some really great blow-job artists."[11] This is a historical categorization with a punchline. The fictional, realist novel, she suggests, is no longer sufficient to understand the present day; honest descriptions of lived life, however crass the past might have found them, are all there is left to write about. At the same time, she is

The Very Edge of Fiction | 139

denying the value of writing literature in itself. She goes on to consider her abilities as one of the artists of our era: "I just do what I can not to gag too much. . . . At these times, I just try to breathe through my nose and not throw up on their cock" (3).[12]

Heti's detailed and explicit descriptions of fellatio challenge how readers might otherwise perceive her, based on her previous books: a young, serious author who flouts the status quo with casual and thoughtful pragmatism. She removes what she calls, in her review of *My Struggle*, "the frame, which lends so much importance to what we do."[13] It is a frame that Heti continues to undo throughout the novel, though it is particularly evident in the descriptions of her sexually explicit relationship with Israel, who is described as a terrible artist but "a genius at fucking."[14]

Referring to herself as a one of "the really great blow-job artists" of our time, Sheila is also suggesting that gender is inseparable from art. This "art form," she makes clear, is focused on satisfying the needs of men: "I know boyfriends get really excited when they can touch the soft flesh at the back of your throat." Myra Bloom writes about the novel's "acts of extreme sexual domination" as examples of "Sheila's 'messy feminism,'" which involves "exercising her choice to make decisions that she knows are ultimately disempowering."[15] That seems at least partly a result of the fact that she as a female artist doesn't have "too many examples yet of what a genius looks like" (4). Then again, Sheila says, "It could be me," paving the way for us to understand *How Should a Person Be?* as an attempt to rewrite the *Künstlerroman* from a woman's perspective.

How Should a Person Be? tells the story of a group of young artists in Toronto. The homology between author, narrator, and protagonist suggests an autobiographical pact, which is furthered paratextually by Heti's dedication of the novel "for Margaux," the name of Sheila's best friend in the novel. A short biographical blurb on the inner sleeve mentions that Heti previously published a book with a Misha Glouberman, who is also one of the characters in the novel, and that Heti, like Sheila in the novel, lives in Toronto.[16] On the bright red cover of the first edition, *How Should a Person Be?* is designated "A NOVEL FROM LIFE."[17] The novel follows Sheila in the wake of a recent divorce, as she struggles to finish a play she has been commissioned to write by a local feminist theater group.[18] Her two crises—one existential, related to the divorce, and the other artistic, related to her unfinished writing—unfold alongside the novel's ongoing consideration of the value of imitation versus authenticity.

140 | Knausgård and the Autofictional Novel

Initially, Sheila navigates the world through imitation, in both life and writing. She treats this tendency with casual humor, as when, for instance, we read, "Responsibility looks so good on Misha, and irresponsibility looks so good on Margaux. How could I know which would look best on me?" (1). Her attempts to handle her crises can suggest, along with the title, a mockery of self-help books. How should a person be? Do what I do, Heti seems to joke, and you too will also become rich, happy, or find love.[19] Yet the novel takes seriously the struggle for authenticity in a world where so much involves repetition and imitation, including situations that might drive readers to self-help. Indeed, the imitation of others, and especially imitation of women, is a serious point in the novel. But imitation also, I argue, especially imitation of her friend Margaux, paradoxically leads to a new authenticity both for Sheila as a character in the novel and for the novel itself.

Early on, when Sheila tries to find a reason for why her marriage did not last, she tells the story of how, on a stroll with her fiancé through a park, she had witnessed a wedding where the bride, to the scorn of Sheila and her fiancé, shed a tear while saying "for richer and poorer." Months later, at her own wedding, Sheila recalled the bride in the park as she repeated the wedding vows: "Tears welled in my eyes, just as they had welled up in hers. My voice cracked with the same emotion that had cracked her voice, but I felt none of it. It was a copy, a possession, canned. The bride inhabited me at the exact moment I should have been most present. It was like I was not there at all—it was not me" (23). The passage is about a feeling expressed but not felt. The display of emotion—the tears, the cracked voice—is an enactment, a signifier without any signified. Like the fiction whose falseness Knausgård laments, Sheila's actions are removed from reality; it is as though Sheila has become a literary character attending her own wedding. The episode makes her wonder "whether my marriage could truly be called *mine*" (23). How, for instance, does Sheila know if the first bride's tears were authentic or if she, too, had been imitating a received form? And how would the guests attending Sheila's wedding—"an audience of a dozen people"—know that the tears, in fact, were not authentic? Her uncertainty opens up the possibility that marriage itself may be a kind of imitation.

The problem of imitation is a central concern in the novel. It comes up, too, in an Ugly Painting Competition that Sheila's friends stage, and that helps provide a structure for the novel as a whole. Early on, the friends decide "that Margaux and Sholem would compete to see who could make the uglier painting" (12). Their goal sits in sharp contrast to the striving for perfection that is the root of Sheila's artistic and existential crisis. But it also becomes a roadmap for her own aspiration as she sees that embracing ugliness can lead to new and interesting forms.

When Sheila and her friends get together to choose the winner of the Ugly Painting Competition, Sholem reveals his painting first, and the friends all agree that it is indeed ugly.[20] But when Margaux reveals her painting—a painting she named *Woman Time*—she immediately undermines the notion of ugliness in her painting: "Well, it's confusing, because ugly's a confusing word for me," she starts (291). She further tells her friends how she while painting had tried to think of something ugly that she didn't like, but couldn't: "Well, everything I like is ugly-beautiful" (291). Throughout the scene, Margaux's painting remains conspicuously unaccounted for. The narrator makes no attempt to describe it. We learn about it only from what Margaux says while showing it to her friends and from their responses.[21] Yet there is no doubt that it is in a different category than Sholem's painting, which is just deemed ugly: not only does Sheila say that she wants to hang Margaux's painting in her kitchen, Sholem also notes that while the color and shapes might be ugly, it is still evidently painted by a master: "But see, the saving grace is your touch. . . . And that's one of the greatest strengths of your painting. You haven't obligated your hand" (295).

Like Margaux's painting, the novel Sheila writes can be characterized as "Woman Time." Sheila strives to find a female role model that she as an artist can mirror and a form to write in as a woman. In that endeavor, her imitation of Margaux becomes a central tenet in the novel, where Sheila imitates Margaux as a person and as an artist, as she embraces an "ugly-beautiful" aesthetics similar to that of Margaux.[22]

Traditionally, critics exploring imitation in literature have focused on the concept of mimesis. But for Sheila, imitation is not a matter of suggesting reality but of copying and emulating—and specifically, copying and emulating a female artist: her friend Margaux. When she buys a tape recorder (and yes, in a novel from 2010, she does, in fact, buy a tape recorder), she starts recording and transcribing her conversations with Margaux. Then, she uses the transcriptions verbatim to create a play. Excitedly, she tells Margaux what she has done, giving her some pages from the play to read, but Margaux responds with an "expression of aversion" that takes Sheila by surprise (174).

A week later, Sheila goes to Margaux's place, where she is met by Margaux "glancing at me with the unblinking eyes of an animal." The

142 | Knausgård and the Autofictional Novel

look makes her realize that she has crossed a line by using the transcripts of their conversation verbatim in her play: "Instead of sitting down and writing my play with *my* words—using *my* imagination, pulling up the words from the solitude and privacy of my soul—I had used *her* words, stolen what was *hers*. I had plagiarized her being and messed it up with the ugliness that was mine. . . . Unwilling to be naked, I had made her naked instead. I had not worked hard or at all" (179–180). The passage opens up ethical questions of ownership in life versus artistic freedom, questions that were also raised in the wake of the publication of *My Struggle*. Can a story by owned? By whom? Who is allowed to tell it? How far can you go in implicating someone in your story?

The passage also shows the difficulty of female writers seeking other artists in whom they can mirror themselves: there simply aren't "too many examples yet of what a [female] genius looks like," as Sheila puts it early in the novel" (4). It is very different from Knausgård, who also emulates and imitates but from a canon of male authors that he readily invokes. Writing how his "literary I" is "Gombrowiczized," "Larssonized," "Proustized," and "Hamsunified," as if he had physically absorbed Witold Gombrowicz, Stig Larsson, Marcel Proust, and Knut Hamsun, he can easily identify a tradition of male writers who seek to challenge conventional literary forms to more accurately describe the world they inhabit (6.254). Sheila, however, only has Margaux, whom she is imitating in both art and life. Margaux is both an artist and a friend, making it easier for Sheila to emulate her every move. But in *How Should a Person Be?* Sheila clearly goes too far: instead of finding the ugliness in her own being, she tries to shield herself behind an imitation of Margaux, even buying the exact same yellow dress as her.

After a period apart, the two friends reconcile when Sheila wants to make a sacrifice for Margaux to fix what she calls "a real imbalance" in their friendship (261). Asking Margaux what she wants her to do for her, Margaux replies: "I want you to finish your play" (262). Taken aback by her friend's request, Sheila asks if it has "to be a play," to which Margaux simply replies "No" (262). With that, the path is paved for Sheila to transform her play into a novel that, in striking ways, imitates a play. It consists of a prologue, five acts, and even an intermission following act 4.[23] The form of the play affords a scenic structure, with dialogue and stage directions, while the novelistic form integrates several plotlines into one and affords metafictional comments and reflections.[24] As such, as Jennifer Cooke observes, "the mistakes she makes in her friendship with

Margaux are metaphors for the missteps on her journey to writing *How Should a Person Be?*"[25]

Shortly after Margaux commands Sheila to finish her play, *How Should a Person Be?* changes to a new act, by far the shortest in the novel. The novel's penultimate act 4, only half a page long, is simply titled "Sheila Throws Her Shit." It begins: "Now it was time to write. I went straight into my studio and thought about everything I had, all the trash and the shit inside me. And I started throwing the trash and throwing the shit, and the castle began to emerge" (277). By referring to her office as a studio, Heti sees herself more like a sculptor than someone working with paper and pen (and aligns her form not just with theater but also with the visual art that Margaux creates). The castle that she creates is, of course, the very novel we read, which can be seen as the concretization of the novel "built from scraps" that David Shields writes about in *Reality Hunger*.[26]

According to Freytag's famous description of drama, the fourth act functions as a resolution. Heti's novel certainly follows that formula. Sheila discovers that ugliness makes beauty, a modern-day epiphany that clears the way for her artistic expression: "I'd never before wanted to uncover all the molecules of shit that were such a part of my deepest being," Sheila says, but the process "began to light up my soul with scenes." Her understanding is not unlike Knausgård's, in its concern with shame, but here too, she emphasizes gender. Making "what I could with what I had," she writes, "I finally became a real girl" (277). While the fairytale association of the phrase "real girl" offers some comic relief, its implications should not be underestimated. Sheila has found an answer to the titular question of the novel of how she should be: how she simultaneously can be a woman and a writer. She has figured out a way in which her personal and artistic imitation of Margaux can lead to freedom and authenticity *by writing about that very imitation* in a new female version of the *Künstlerroman*. She resolves to write about the innermost embarrassing parts of her life: the emulating, the artistic insecurity, the humiliating sexual games she plays with Israel, and everything else. The key is that it is *her* story, written in *her* language. That is the difference—her "hand," as Sholem put it when referring to Margaux's painting—that makes the ugly beautiful.

With *How Should a Person Be?* Heti deliberately pushes the form of the novel further than most other writers in what Alexandra Kingston-Reese calls "a formalistic attempt to formalize be*ing*," by which she emphasizes the importance of form in autofiction.[27] The novel's theatrical structure, narrative arc, and metafictional account of its own composition all help

144 | Knausgård and the Autofictional Novel

us see that the "feces" Sheila "throws"—the transcriptions, emails, quotes, and details of her private life, or what James Wood calls "the novel as a kind of collection box"—have become a castle.[28] The titular, existential question, then, is not only personal. Behind it, like a shadow, is a question about writing novels in the twenty-first century: How should a novel be? Or more precisely: How should an autofictional novel written by a woman be? The answer, according to Sheila Heti, is the book at hand.[29]

How Should a Person Be? is Heti's version of the "no dignity" paradigm she identifies in *My Struggle*—the literary equivalent of the Ugly Painting Competition. But her hand, her touch, is the language and the novelistic form and the fact that it is her story. The book is not inspired by Knausgård per se—in all likelihood, Heti did not read *My Struggle* before finishing her novel—but both authors are responding to a world where everything is fiction, and their responses are in sync. Both are formally omnivorous, letting their novels eat up other genres. Both write about the banality of life and their innermost thoughts in the form of a novel, challenging the notion that novels must be, or even should be, fiction. Heti shows that these tasks are different, and more difficult, for a woman than for a man. But taken together, she and Knausgård help lay the foundation of the autofictional novel in the twenty-first century.

Rachel Cusk: A Human Lie Detector?

For confirmation that Philippe Lejeune is correct when asserting that, if the autobiographical pact is not stated positively, readers try to find resemblances between the author and her characters, one need only to look at the reception of Rachel Cusk's *Outline* trilogy. Faye is often seen as a veiled version of Cusk because, as one article puts it, she "shares biographical data with Cusk and appears to present and process events from Cusk's actual life."[30] But Cusk divulges relatively few details about Faye, who is decidedly *not* a self-revelatory autobiographical narrator, coming to terms with her life through writing.[31] Instead, Cusk uses Faye's scarcity—or, one might say, Cusk experiments with self-effacement—in order to focus on stories and storytelling in a way that reflects her commitment to reality and truth, as her novel seeks a literary form that describes the lived experience of women.

In *Outline*, the first installment of the trilogy, we meet Faye as she travels to Athens to teach a weeklong writing course. Athens is still recov-

The Very Edge of Fiction | 145

ering from the aftermath of the debt crisis that ravaged the country to the brink of bankruptcy, with signs of the massive protests still visible in the city; the novel quite literally can be seen as a response to the financial crisis.[32] Broken and desolate, this background also reflects Faye's feelings in the wake of a recent divorce. Her life, too, has been ravaged, emotionally and financially. Indeed, the only time the name Faye appears in *Outline* is when her bank in England calls her to tell her that her application for a mortgage increase has been denied: "Is that Faye?" the banker asks in a phrase that simultaneously situates her an as object, "that," and a subject, "Faye."[33] As an object, she is a commodity in a neoliberal economy—an economical system that by creating a reality on its own can be seen as fiction—that nearly ruined Greece.[34] As a subject, she is a woman still dealing with the aftermath of leaving a marriage that came to be a fiction.

The interplay between capitalism and feelings is on display from the very outset of *Outline*: "Before the flight I was invited for lunch at a London club with a billionaire I'd been promised had liberal credentials" (3). Opening the novel in medias res with the unspecified mention of "the flight"—which flight, we might ask?—the novel thrusts Faye into an encounter with the billionaire, the embodiment of capitalism in the twenty-first century, with the paradoxical notion that he, indeed, "had liberal credentials." It is also an encounter between a man and a woman, where he, in the span of their lunch, gives Faye "the outline of his life story" while she listens quietly. As such, the short description of their lunch becomes indicative of what is to come: Faye, a woman, listening, while others, often men, speak.

Faye lunches with the billionaire to discuss "a literary magazine he was thinking of starting up." But she has to leave before they ever get to that topic. Hearing his life story, she starts wondering if the reason for him funding a literary magazine is that he wanted to be a writer, using "the literary magazine as his entrée." In her narration, she comments: "A lot of people want to be writers: there was no reason to think you couldn't buy your way into it" (3). Perhaps, the novel suggests, but that doesn't mean you can write good literature.

The billionaire functions as a stock character of sorts. Nothing sets his story apart—"which had begun unprepossessingly and ended—obviously—with him being the relaxed, well-heeled man who sat across the table from me today"—and it seems easily exchangeable with that of any other billionaire (3).[35] Admitting that she found "it difficult to assimilate everything I was being told," Faye confirms what the narration already

146 | Knausgård and the Autofictional Novel

has suggested: that the story of his life, where he constantly takes on new challenges and endeavors—buys his way "in, and out, of a great many things"—has taken precedence over who he is, and that the fiction has become more important than the reality. And when self-deception and the fictional dominate, narrative suffers. Finding the truth, in contrast, requires the kind of sustained attention that Faye displays.

Faye's own view of literature is unsnobbish, utilitarian, and arguably democratic; she repeats it in different reiterations throughout *Outline*, and more or less instructs us in it, by proxy, when recounting the course she teaches in Athens. Faye meets her writing class for the first time a little more than halfway through the novel. Referring to the students as "a curious group," she asks them to "tell [her] something they had noticed on their way" to the class (132). After the first student briefly talks about a man "standing on the platform [where she got off the train] with a small white dog on his shoulder," the second tells a story of finding a women's handbag on his way (134). With each student, the stories get longer, as the stories also reveal something about the storyteller as a person. Their stories are interspersed with their short discussions about the assignment, storytelling, and if there is such a thing as a "story of life" (137).

Faye's assignment is an exercise in observation and awareness, urging us to connect to, and find meaning in, the environment that surrounds us. It calls for a closeness with what we can see, feel, hear, and experience, on an everyday basis, similar to Knausgård's longing for the closeness of "a life, a face, a gaze you could meet."[36] In *Outline*, too, looking closely helps people cultivate self-understanding and get closer to truth. The assignment also suggests an aesthetic ideal: an attempt to minimize the distance between language and world, and a way to insist that language can describe. Cusk seems to be working to restore faith in the novel after postmodernism.

While most of the students in the class embrace Faye's assignment in one way or another, one of them—"a woman whose name was Cassandra and whose expression I had watched grow sourer and sourer as the hour passed"—refuses to take part in the assignment. She gets up, says she will ask for a refund, and insults Faye, calling her "a lousy teacher" (158). She declares that "learning to write" is about "using your imagination" and storms out the door. To her, it seems, literature equals fiction. Her anger suggests that the exercise itself is a radical departure from traditional notions of literature.

The Very Edge of Fiction | 147

Faye's narration of the exercise becomes a metacommentary on the poetics of *Outline*. Having instructed them to tell what they noticed, she writes down their observations, all of them simple and unplotted. This is writing with a commitment to seeing reality anew, and as a consequence with a rejection of fictionalization. Significantly, Faye also understands fiction to be more than the elaborate plots and made-up stories that Cassandra thought she was signing up for. Instead, she sees fiction as a force that operates in daily life, the product of self-deception and a desire for a protective shield between ourselves and the world.

Consider *Transit*, the second installment in the trilogy, where Faye, now home in England, meets with one of her students, who wants to become a novelist. Jane sits in her "jewel-coloured clothing amid the white landscapes of dust sheets" that cover Faye's house, which is in the midst of a renovation, and tells Faye about her identification with the painter Marsden Hartley. She had first seen his work at a retrospective in Paris and, during the course of the exhibition, "had undergone a complete personal revolution" (133, 130). Jane had realized that she is Marsden Hartley: she saw his paintings as thoughts, and believed "that those thoughts were her own" (135). After studying his life, which had nothing in common with her own, she realized that instead of "mirroring the literal facts of her own life," Marsden Hartley "was dramatizing them" in his paintings (138). And now she wants to write a novel about him.

Faye seems to dismiss Jane's plans, letting her know that she, too, remembers seeing one of Hartley's paintings and understands how it "was perfectly possible to become a prisoner of an artist's vision" (143). Jane responds defensively: "I've got three hundred thousand words of notes, she said coldly. I can't just throw them away" (143). Faye asks Jane to tell her about the time she spent in Paris *before* "her discovery of Marsden Hartley." Jane was in Paris to teach. She was instructing part of a course on photography, and the job brought her into contact with a famous photojournalist whose work she admired. On the last day, after a party where, catching his eye across the room, she had "felt elated, filled with certainty, like a bride in her white dress," the two of them had walked for hours through the streets of Paris, returning to their hotel at 3 a.m. (145).[37] Telling Jane that he and his wife at one point were separated, but had gotten back together, the photojournalist tried to convince Jane that he has never cheated on his wife. But Jane tells Faye that she knew he was lying: "I knew, she said, that he wanted to sleep with me, had considered

148 | Knausgård and the Autofictional Novel

it thoroughly, and decided—from experience, I've no doubt, she said—that it was too much of a risk" (150).

In the narration, the connection between the story of Jane being rejected and subsequently finding herself in the work of Marsden Hartley is never made explicit. But Cusk's writing, or perhaps, Faye's elicitation, makes it possible to see Jane's story of "personal revolution" as a kind of self-deception. As she walks Jane out, Faye imagines her "in the dusk of a Paris garden, untouched in her white dress, an object thirsting if not for interpretation then for the fulfilments at least of an admiring human gaze, like a painting hanging on a wall, waiting" (151). The image suggests that Jane's infatuation with Marsden Hartley is nothing but a projection of her desire for admiration. Indeed, the answer Jane gives in response to another question about her life suggests that her desire for admiration is related to her mother, who never seemed to care for her daughter. Faye's disclosure reduces Jane's story to a fiction that she lives by and believes she has to turn into a novel. But Faye does not tell Jane this. Instead, she asks her to think about their conversation because it might help her find an "opening" (151). What that opening might be, she never tells Jane, but it is relayed in the narration and in Faye's likening of Jane to a painting as she leaves her house.

Imagining Jane's white dress against the green of the Parisian garden, Faye reverses the image of Jane in her living room where, in a lime-green pencil skirt, she sits among furniture covered with white dust sheets. Using sharp contrasts in colors (which is a feature that Marsden Hartley is known for), Faye illustrates that a commitment to reality and truth does not come at the dispense of aesthetic beauty. Rather, fiction and self-deception prevent us from seeing what already exists: we fictionalize and create stories about who we are to protect ourselves, and beauty can only be found if we abandon that fiction and seek the truth. At the same time, Faye's own story shows the difficulty of getting to that point, suggesting that finding the truth also involves a painful process of letting go. This makes Faye vulnerable in the wake of her divorce, but it also makes her hyper-attuned to the lies other people tell, as both the episode with Jane and the opening to *Outline* make clear.

After her lunch with the billionaire, Faye heads to the airport to catch her flight to Athens. Sitting aboard the flight, waiting for takeoff, she describes, with metaphorical qualities that make it one of the most striking passages in the novel, the rituals involved in every commercial flight. Evoking ecclesiastical imagery, she portrays the silence in the cabin

The Very Edge of Fiction | 149

while the passengers are listening to the safety instructions as "the silence of a congregation while the liturgy is read" (4). Continuing the metaphor, she likens the flight attendant giving the safety instruction to a priest that "leads the congregation through the details of purgatory and hell" (5). Finally, she interprets the familiar phrase about oxygen masks as a "commandment that one should take care of others only after taking care of oneself"—and, as such, emblematic of the kind of capitalistic self-interest she has just witnessed over lunch with the self-involved billionaire. Faye voices her disagreement here, however tentative: "Yet I wasn't sure it was altogether true" (5).

While using elaborate imagery to describe the rituals prior to departure might seem at odds with Faye's later-expressed aesthetics of minimizing the distance between language and the world, the result is quite the opposite: it is precisely through the ecclesiastical metaphors that Faye minimizes the distance between the two. By evoking these metaphors, she is teaching us a lesson in noticing and committing to reality. She makes us see a ritual that we go through without even noticing it and, by doing so, invites us to revisit our relationship to the world around us. It is an instance of defamiliarization, as Victor Shklovsky calls it, and that we earlier saw as a parallel to Knausgård's notion of form.[38] It is about seeing the world through a new lens that recommits us to reality and to change, or perhaps remove, the fictional veil that characterizes routines and rituals as we go through life. To that extent, Faye's use of figurative language is not an instance of the impossibility of language signifying the world but an attempt to engage that very world, in the same way she asks of her students.

Faye's attention to the lies other people tell recurs in the various discussions she has, throughout *Outline*, with a man continually and metonymically referred to as her "neighbor," because he happens to sit next to her during the flight to Athens. Despite his role as one of the most prominent characters in *Outline*, Faye never tells us his name or whether she even knows it. In Faye's narration, he is reduced to a nameless secondary character. As such, he is relegated to the place in her narrative that female characters typically have been assigned in literature written by men.

After the plane to Athens takes off, the neighbor tells Faye his life story, which includes three marriages and three divorces. But when he tells the story of his second marriage, Faye treats it as a piece of literature ripe for textual analysis, further reducing his status in the narration.

150 | Knausgård and the Autofictional Novel

Criticizing, for instance, his grasp of character development, she says that she "couldn't see the second wife half as clearly as I could see the first. In fact, I didn't entirely believe in her. She was rolled out as an all-purpose villain" (25). Admitting that he "may be somewhat biased," the neighbor nevertheless continues to criticize his second wife. Faye still does not believe him and responds to the next phase of his storytelling with a more extensive analysis, now referring to her neighbor as a "narrator":

> I remained dissatisfied by the story of his second marriage. It lacked objectivity; it relied too heavily on extremes, and the moral properties it ascribed to those extremes were often incorrect. . . . The narrative invariability showed certain people—the narrator and his children—in a good light, while the wife was brought in only when it was required of her to damn herself further. . . . I sensed the truth was being sacrificed to the narrator's desire to win. (29–30)

What Faye finds lacking in the neighbor's story is, as she notes, objectivity. Understanding that hyperbole often says more about the storyteller than the story being told, she asks for a narrative that shows the complexity of human interaction, where terms like good or bad rarely apply uniformly. (Her characterization can also work as a description of autofictional novels by male writers such as Knausgård. In his description of Linda's breakdown and hospitalization in Book 6, to take just one example, he portrays himself as the one we should feel sorry for as he has to be alone with three kids while trying to finish the novel that, as it is clear from the narrative, caused Linda's breakdown in the first place.) Conversely, what Faye wants is subdued realism that is as close to the truth as possible: her truth, that is, that in turn extends to a large female truth of women delegated to objects in the "loud" stories told by men and left only with a quiet, self-effacing realism.

The neighbor laughs and agrees with Faye's analysis, but that does not prevent him from continuing to tell her—both on the plane and, in a later chapter, on his boat—about his former wives. Where his story at first is relayed in directly quoted speech, it increasingly becomes interspersed with snippets of indirect speech, or what Dorrit Cohn calls "self-quoted monologue." These snippets of indirect speech, where the neighbor's story is relayed by Faye, are arguably more literary than those of direct speech, including more figurative language and carefully chosen metaphors. "All

The Very Edge of Fiction | 151

this did not, of course, come to pass as he had imagined it. The bump in the road hadn't only upset his marriage; it caused him to veer off on to a different road altogether, a road that was but a long, directionless detour, a road he no real business being on and that sometimes he still felt himself to be travelling even to this day" (15). The slight shift in voice in the preceding quote suggests that Faye, in using the platitude "bump in the road," borrows the neighbor's metaphor. While we are never in doubt that Faye is narrating, it is unclear whether the extension of the metaphor ("different road," "directionless detour," "a road . . . he still felt himself to be travelling") is hers or her neighbor's.[39] These snippets of indirect speech, becoming progressively longer as the neighbor keeps talking and Faye relays his story in her narration, do to his story what the religious imagery does to the description of the rituals when a plane is about to take off. They make us pause and reevaluate what we hear. They prevent us from being caught up in, and seduced by, the story the neighbor is telling. Compelling as the story might be, such figurative language reminds us it is still a story, a fabricated version of his life. And in a world dominated and constructed by male narratives, Faye suggests, there is little room for women and their stories.

Still, as Faye spends more time with the neighbor, she becomes sympathetic toward him. As Karen Valihora writes, she is "drawn in despite herself; it is as though she has caught a glimpse of herself in his story, which suggests an echo, a reflection, of her own."[40] Yet her physical descriptions make him seem increasingly predatorial, serving as a kind of concretization of what her disclosing of his stories has already hinted at, and as a counterweight to his self-portrayal as the victim of unlucky circumstances in all three of his marriages. When Faye and the neighbor first begin to talk, he is described metonymically by his "silver and grey" eyebrows that grew "unexpectedly coarsely and wildly" (6). A few pages later, Faye describes his face as a "landscape of peaks and crevices, from the centre of which rose the extraordinary hook of his nose, casting deep ravines of shadow on either side" (12). When they reunite in Athens to go sailing, his "extraordinary beak-like nose" gives him a "quizzical appearance of a seabird, crowned with his plume of silver-white hair" (59). Faye further characterizes his hands as "large and slightly claw-like, and covered with white hair" (60), while she describes his naked back, after he takes off his shirt on the boat, as "broad and fleshy" and "marked with numerous moles and scars and outcrops of course grey hair" (70). On their second trip sailing, when the neighbor attempts to give Faye

152 | Knausgård and the Autofictional Novel

an unwarranted and unwelcomed kiss, she likens him to "a prehistoric creature issuing from its cave." She writes: "The great beak of his nose loomed at the edge of my field of vision, his claw-like hands with their white fur fumbled at my shoulders; I felt myself, momentarily, being wrapped around in his greyness and dryness, as though the prehistoric creature were wrapping me in its dry bat-like wings, felt the scaly mouth miss its mark and move blindly at my cheek" (176–177). The neighbor's transformation from a bushy-haired old man to a menacing beast seems to function as a reminder to Faye, and to readers, that the neighbor's compelling life story also gives evidence of an entitled masculinity that imposes its view upon the world as a singular truth. These comparisons are not, as Merve Emre has suggested, proof that Cusk is "the cruelest novelist at work today."[41] Instead, they add an important gendered aspect to the poetics that Faye advocates in her teaching: that engaging reality and seeking truth in storytelling also means rejecting centuries of male domination.

Each installment of Cusk's trilogy consists of ten chapters, mostly occasioned by encounters with friends and strangers. But chapter 3 in *Outline* is uncharacteristically brief, a mere eight pages, and includes no interlocutor, no dialogue, and no direct speech. Instead, the chapter meticulously describes the apartment Faye lives in during her stay in Athens. The apartment belongs to Clelia, another writer, who is elsewhere. The chapter is void of life, of people, and of stories. It is a chapter about absence. Yet, in Faye's narration, the description of this absence becomes a kind of presence, even an allegory for her own selfhood.

Faye takes the reader on a tour of sorts of Clelia's apartment, beginning by the door on the city street where the apartment is located. A window at a café opposite the entryway is "entirely obscured by a photograph of more people sitting outside," creating a "convincing optical illusion" (50). Faye takes us up the stairs to the landing in front of Clelia's top-floor apartment, with a large wooden sculpture and a "cactus-like plant," and into the apartment, which, in the words of Faye, made it obvious that Clelia "regarded writing as a profession worthy of the greatest trust and respect" (52). This conclusion is based on Faye's assessment of Clelia's cave-like study, where she finds, besides a large cherry-wood desk and books, "several painted wooden models of boats, which had been mounted to the walls" (52). Faye describes how it seems as if wind blew in the boats' sails, but upon closer inspection she realizes that the effect was created by countless tiny chords, which had been fixed to the sails, "a metaphor I felt sure Clelia had intended to illustrate the relationship between illusion and reality" (52).

That Clelia perhaps just happens to like the boats—or maybe has received them as presents from someone close to her—does not seem to be an option in Faye's narration. Never does she reveal, or even hint at, why she "felt sure" that Clelia had intended the boats as a metaphor for illustrating "the relationship between illusion and reality." As with her previous conclusion—that it was obvious that Clelia considered writing a "profession worthy of the greatest trust and respect"—it is a subjective judgment, and it gives us insight into Faye's values: she finds writing a "profession worthy of the greatest trust and respect."[42] And she is interested in the "relationship between illusion and reality."

It is also herself she describes when focusing on how the apartment is set up for socializing but now is all but empty. For instance, Clelia's "formidable collection of classical recordings"—most of which were symphonies with a "marked prejudice against compositions that glorified the solo voice or instrument"—is interpreted by Faye as a blotting out of the individual: "It was, perhaps, a form of discipline, almost of asceticism, a temporary banishing of the self and its utterance" (54). She also imagines how "Clelia's friends and associates sat during the hot summer evenings" on the outside terrace with a long table and multiple chairs (56). Finally, she sees the bunk beds in one of the bedrooms as standing "for the concept of children generally," even though there are no other indications that the room is intended for children (54). These descriptions of absences suggest how alone Faye herself feels. She lingers on a three-foot-tall terracotta statue of a woman in the hallway, "where the doors to all the other rooms converged" (55). Describing how the statue stands with her face lifted and arms half raised, she continues: "Sometimes she looked as if she were about to say something, sometimes as if she were in despair" (55).

The description of Clelia's apartment reflects Faye's state of mind in the wake of her traumatizing divorce. It is a description of isolation, loneliness, and empty space, a void where community and the social world seem beyond her reach, even as others come passing through. By noticing her surroundings in the way she asks her students to do, Faye begins to provide an outline for herself—something we also see at work when she describes what she hears from the people around her.

Despite being cast as at least partly predatorial, it is the neighbor from the plane who provides one path out of loneliness. At the very end of *Outline*, Faye is back at Clelia's, talking with a writer named Anne who

154 | Knausgård and the Autofictional Novel

is about to take over both the class and the apartment, when the neighbor calls to ask if she would like to go sailing with him before she returns to England. She turns him down, as she already has talked to Anne about going to see the headless women at the Athenian Agora. With that the novel concludes with the following exchange:

> In that case, he said, I will spend the day in solicitude.
> You mean solitude, I said.
> I do beg your pardon, he said. Of course, I mean solitude. (249)

The exchange, with its curbed humor, echoes their first meeting on the plane, in which the neighbor mistakes the word "proximity" for "prolixity" and Faye corrects him (8). In that scene, it becomes evident that the mispronunciation is no mere coincidence: literally meaning a "tedious lengthiness of spoken or written matter," according to the *OED*, "prolixity" speaks to the neighbor's truth and is precisely what characterizes his continued stories about his marriages and divorces. Likewise, the mispronounced word in the novel's final exchange—solicitude—simply means to care for someone, where his slip in language reveals that he cares for Faye but her correction suggests that she does not believe him to be sincere. By turning him down, the novel suggests that Faye has moved on: she is ready, as the title of the second installment in the trilogy suggests, to transition into a new life. In the company of Anne, a woman, who has just given a more seemingly truthful account of her life than the male neighbor, Faye is also no longer in solitude.

Faye's pursuit of truth propels all three books forward, and that pursuit is also what Cusk praises in her review of Book 2 of *My Struggle*. After opening with a short description of the controversy surrounding the publication in Norway, she quotes at length Knausgård's thoughts on being fed up with fiction. The crisis he describes, she writes, is "the crisis of narrative's distance from reality," something she sees him showing "as personal."[43] Knausgård, she explains, resists turning his life into a narrative: "Instead, he shows us, by the route of life, that there is no story, and in so doing he finds, at last, authenticity. For that alone, this deserves to be called perhaps the most significant literary enterprise of our times."[44] Cusk seems to agree that "there is no story," and this, perhaps, is why she refuses to create a narrative from Faye's life. Indeed, the relentless pursuit

The Very Edge of Fiction | 155

of truth and reality, inside or in spite of the stories that others tell, is what makes Faye find authenticity.

Making that pursuit central to her own novelistic endeavor, Cusk charts a different path for contemporary autofiction. By giving her protagonist a name other than her own while foregrounding biographical similarities, Cusk invites readers to examine both Faye's and her own story more critically than Knausgård with his homology of names to get closer to the reality of his life. Cusk's version of autofiction also differs from Knausgård's in its insistence on Faye's self-effacement where she, as the novel's narrator, proposes a quiet realism, with a focus on listening and questioning. In the trilogy, this is shown as a counterweight to a male perspective that is more subjective and more totalizing. And gender is an ongoing concern in the three books: the neighbor on the plane telling about his three marriages, Jane's identification with Marsden Hartley, and Faye's staring match with a man peeing in the ocean that concludes the trilogy, to name just a few examples. But Faye's perspective is not presented solely as a contrast to a male perspective. Rather, it is presented as a truer portrayal of the world, a way for anyone to get close to reality. Consequently, the female perspective of the *Outline* trilogy is not gender specific but compatible with human experience as such and in the trilogy is suggested to be universal and objective.

Ben Lerner: Autofictionalization in the Future Tense

Like Knausgård, Cusk, and Heti, Ben Lerner seems well aware that, while readers seek out differences and errors in autobiography, they seek out similarities between author and protagonist in fiction.[45] Lerner plays with this tendency in his multifaceted novel *10:04*, using autofictionalization to create a continual oscillation between possibility and reality, between the fictional and the nonfictional. Where Knausgård's autofictionalization is directed toward the past, Lerner's version is directed toward what the novel refers to as "possible futures." Redrawing the line between fiction by showing the need to understand and question what is to come, *10:04* reveals a very different version of the contemporary autofictional novel than we have seen so far.

In *10:04*, the autobiographical aspect is never stated positively through homology, but Lerner hints at it throughout the novel, most evidently

156 | Knausgård and the Autofictional Novel

with the protagonist also being the author of "The Golden Vanity," a story originally published under Lerner's byline in the *New Yorker* and included in full in the novel.[46] Several other biographical facts line up too: both Lerner and the novel's protagonist were born in Topeka, Kansas; live in Brooklyn; and are English professors and poets whose first novel was met with critical acclaim. Indeed, as Marta Figlerowicz writes about *10:04* and *Leaving the Atocha Station*, Lerner's first novel, both books "implicitly depend on the wide online accessibility of his personal information" and create the impression that "little separates the limited fictional worlds they represent from an expansive real world."[47]

At the same time, Lerner seems to go out of his way not to positively confirm the autobiographical pact. In terms of homology, the name "Ben" appears twice in *10:04*, both times in fake emails that the protagonist has written to himself as if from famous writers.[48] But these emails are fake, and the fact that the protagonist deletes them—"*Dear Ben*, I deleted"—adds a layer of doubt to the autobiographical aspect (210, original italics). Many readers might also know that the Ben Lerner of the real world is married—his wife's name even appears in the novel when the protagonist at one point is asked by his sister where she is—whereas the protagonist of *10:04* is in a causal relationship with a young artist while being asked to father the child of his best friend, Alex.[49]

The autobiographical ambiguity and the novel's deliberate play with the autobiographical pact mean that the protagonist on one hand is Ben Lerner and on the other is not. Reaching a similar conclusion, Pieter Vermeulen writes that Lerner's narrator-character "is clearly a partly fictional entity" but "is also *identifiably* the real Ben Lerner."[50] Alison Gibbons similarly refers to the protagonist as the "autofictional counterpart of the Brooklyn-based author Ben Lerner."[51] This duality reflects how the autobiographical pact functions in the incorporated short story in the novel in which the protagonist says that he has "divided myself into two people," as the novel invokes the autobiographical pact while simultaneously undermining it (78). While the protagonist shares many of Lerner's biographical traits, Lerner seems determined to tell us that he is fiction. In the novel's acknowledgments Lerner informs the reader that he, contrary to the novel's protagonist, "never had the chance to see *The Clock* reach midnight" and that one of the novel's characters indeed is "a work of fiction" (244). This is corroborated on the title page of the novel, where it is stated in a small font that all characters, events, and more "are either products of the author's imagination or are used fictitiously" (xiii).[52]

The relationship between the protagonist and Lerner can be summed up in the last phrase of the novel's epigraph: "The same as it is now, just a little different."[53]

Lerner's *10:04* fluctuates so incessantly between the fictive and the real that there hardly seems a reason to distinguish between the two. Still, the characters in the novel try, as when the protagonist apologizes to his friend Alex a day after trying to seduce her. He says he was drunk and stupid, and she confronts him with a quote from "The Golden Vanity":

> "I don't want it to be one of the things you get to deny you wanted or deny ever happened."
>
> "What do you mean?"
>
> " 'It was the only kind of first date he could bring himself to go on, the kind you could deny after the fact had been a date at all.' "
>
> "That's fiction and we're not talking about a first date."
> (136)

The protagonist might insist in conversation that the quote is just fiction, but in the novel he has already revealed to his readers that his short story should, in essence, be read as a roman à clef, even translating the names in the story to those in the novel.[54] Now, he seems either to undermine his own explanation of the short story or his trustworthiness as an interlocutor. Even more broadly, the incongruence suggests that we can trust neither the fictional aspect of the novel nor its truth claims.

As the two of them keep arguing, Alex informs the protagonist that she would sleep with him, if he asked, as part of a "reproductive strategy." But thinking about the two of them as a couple makes them laugh out loud:

> We had no idea how it would work out. But I knew how we could pay for it: I told her I'd sent off the proposal, described my plans to expand the story.
>
> She was quiet for half a minute, then: "I don't know." I'd expected her to say it sounded brilliant, which was what she normally said whenever I ran a literary idea by her—an adjective she'd never applied to any of my nonliterary ideas.
>
> "What don't you know?"
>
> "I don't want what we're doing to just end up as notes for a novel."

158 | Knausgård and the Autofictional Novel

"Nobody is going to give me strong six figures for a poem." (137)

The scene suggests, of course, that the novel we are reading is the novel with which the protagonist offers to pay for his and Alex's future child.[55] Showcasing the complex friendship between the two, the shift from plural to singular personal pronouns indicates how the protagonist and Alex both are and are not to be seen as a couple. Describing his plans "to expand the story" to Alex but not to the reader creates what Fredric Jameson (with Ernst Bloch) has called a "utopian hole or absence" at the center of the novel: what those plans are, how they have altered as the novel progresses, and how they relate to the novel at hand.[56] Attempting to answer those questions takes us back to the opening pages of the novel and the autofictionalization that Lerner uses as a formal strategy.

On the first pages of *10:04*, the protagonist walks and talks with his agent after an "outrageously expensive celebratory meal that included baby octopuses the chef had literally massaged to death."[57] The reason for the celebratory meal is a contract with a major publishing house for a book based on a story of his "that has appeared in *The New Yorker*" (4). His agent notes that the contract comes with "a 'strong six-figure' advance," a direct quote that lays bare the capitalistic conditions of contemporary literature; the agent's excitement has to do with her own profits from the deal. Reflecting on the "indefinite proposal" he sent out for the competitive auction, the protagonist asserts the novel he is commissioned to write starts with "eating cephalopods in what would become the opening scene." And when his agent asks how he plans to expand the story from the *New Yorker*, the narration slips to a Whitmanian allusion about what "I should have said," namely that "I'll project myself into several futures simultaneously" (4). This allusion to "Crossing Brooklyn Ferry," a poem invoked throughout the novel, and here by addressing future readers, lends Lerner's novel a utopian component.

Metafictionally, the opening scene tells us that the novel we are about to read is the one Lerner sketches out here, and that it will explore possible futures, unfolding at once. A few pages later, Lerner includes two relevant images stacked atop one another. The first is a detail from Jules Bastien-Lepage's *Joan of Arc*, in which the hand of Joan of Arc starts to dissolve as she is summoned to rescue France by three translucent angels that "hover in the top left of the painting." The reprint of the painting is in the novel captioned as "the presence of the future" (9–10). The second,

The Very Edge of Fiction | 159

a still from Robert Zemeckis's iconic 1985 movie *Back to the Future*, shows Michael J. Fox's Marty, in the past, observing how his own hand dissolves as the possibility of making it "back to the future" is vanishing. It is captioned: "The absence of the future" (10).

The two overarching narrative lines of *10:04* are pulled between these poles of present and absent futures.[58] The future is most present in the protagonist's agreement to father a child with Alex, while a looming climate crisis threatens to make the future dissolve.[59] In the novel, the climate crisis is made concrete by the two tropical storms that hit New York in 2012 and frame the narrative.[60]

Exploring possible futures also prompts Lerner's version of autofictionalization. In *My Struggle*, Knausgård uses fictionalization to affect the reader's understanding of the past by situating consciousness with his former self, as we saw in chapter 2. But in *10:04*, Lerner uses autofictionalization to project the protagonist of the novel into possible and potential futures. Where Knausgård uses it to make the past present, Lerner uses it to further blur the distinction between fiction and reality.

Indeed, in a review of Book 3 of *My Struggle*, Lerner pays special attention to how Knausgård situates the narrative consciousness with his former self. Lerner investigates what is at stake in Knausgård's narration through an episode in which a young Karl Ove is sitting in the kitchen eating cornflakes. Referring to "the strange evenness of Knausgaard's attention," Lerner engages with the description's "childishness," which "involves a susceptibility to absorption and enhancement that we associate with intoxicants in adults."[61] He turns to a quotation by Baudelaire in which the French poet and essayist explores the similarities between childhood and genius and states that genius "is no more than childhood recaptured at will . . . and with the analytical mind that enables it to bring order into the sum of experience, involuntarily amassed." Lerner writes: "What's unnerving about Knausgaard is that it's hard to decide if he's just a child who stares at everything, who makes no distinctions, or if he indeed qualifies as a Baudelairean man-child, as a genius who can 'bring order into the sum of experience, involuntarily amassed.' Another way to put it: does *My Struggle* ultimately have an aesthetic form? Or is it just one thing after another?"[62]

What Lerner is attempting to distinguish, I believe, is Knausgård's use of autofictionalization in *My Struggle*. By focusing on the "childishness" of the description, he ultimately touches upon the issue of the narrative consciousness of the passage and how that consciousness is situated

160 | Knausgård and the Autofictional Novel

with the young Karl Ove as he is sitting in the kitchen reflecting upon whether cornflakes are best soft or crispy. His interest in what he refers to as "unnerving" in Knausgård's narration is unmistakably a question of the compositional principle behind the autofictionalization. But instead of trying to decipher what is at stake in the passage through a narratological lens, Lerner turns it into a question about form. This brings him to the end of *My Struggle* and Knausgård's pronouncement that he no longer is a writer (which Lerner could only have known about from interviews with Knausgård, as Book 6 had not yet been translated into English). Lerner argues that Knausgård's minute, childlike descriptions, with their "vast quantities of essential undifferentiated material," only become significant because of the promised ending. The promise of this ending, he continues, "places a tremendous pressure on the end of the book, on closure as a moment when form is achieved and retrospectively organises the work."[63] That ending where Knausgård sacrifices writing for his family is the potential of a future outside the novel. And this very promise is precisely what Lerner believes gives weight to the autofictionalization in *My Struggle*.

Lerner's interest in Knausgård's autofictionalization as a promise of a potential future, and how such a promise relates to the form of the novel, says as much about his own use of autofictionalization as it does about Knausgård's. After proclaiming that he should have told his agent at the celebratory dinner that he would "project myself into several futures simultaneously," Lerner shows how he is both himself and someone else by taking on the qualities of the "baby octopuses" they have just eaten and that "the chef had literally massaged to death" (3). After claiming that he "intuited an alien intelligence," feeling subject to images and memories "that did not, properly speaking, belong to me," he describes "a conflation of taste and touch as salt was rubbed into the suction cups" (3). A few pages later, the protagonist visits a cardiologist who happens to have a giant octopus "painted on the wall of the room," and the transformation continues; he notes that he felt "as if my limbs had multiplied" (6). In this description, Lerner makes the notion of autofictionalization physical—the word made flesh, only this time, coyly so. But as the protagonist takes on the qualities of an octopus and thus feels subject to emotions "that did not, properly speaking, belong to me," Lerner also seems to mock any readerly desire to seek identity between protagonist and author. While we might seek out Lerner's autobiographical traits in the novel, he is both himself and an octopus.

The Very Edge of Fiction | 161

When writing about the novel he should have told his agent about, he announces not just that he will project himself "into several futures simultaneously," but also that he will work his "way from irony to sincerity in the sinking city, a would-be Whitman of the vulnerable grid" (4). His autofictionalization is certainly ironic; so are the moments of direct address to the reader, which play with the autobiographical ambivalence and the question of whether the protagonist is Lerner himself. When he, for instance, writes about how Alex and he often went for walks, he turns to the reader: "You might have seen us, walking on Atlantic, tears streaming down her face . . . or perhaps you've seen me during one of my own increasingly frequent lacrimal events being comforted in kind while we moved across the Brooklyn Bridge" (8). While addressing the reader is an attempt to establish an authenticity—this truly happened and you might even have seen us walking there—it also points to the fictional status of the narration: that it, indeed, is made up. As is the case of metafictional instances in general, the paradoxical effect is that while revealing its own constructedness it simultaneously makes it seem fictional by pretending not to be. It is the permanent parabasis of irony, very different from the sincerity that characterizes Knausgård.[64]

That addressing the reader points to both the fictional and nonfictional status of his text is made explicit when Lerner asks the reader: "Have you seen people pause in revolving doors . . . ?" (43). The possible allusion to Paul de Man's revolving door that, as we saw in chapter 1, illustrates the indeterminacy between the fictional and the nonfictional, furthers the irony of the address: Lerner is not only aware of the implications of addressing his readers but also knows which theoretical text scholars would use to analyze these readerly addresses.[65]

In the last few pages of the novel, Lerner seemingly signals the shift from "irony to sincerity" as the narrative describes how the protagonist and Alex are walking the streets of a Manhattan devastated by Hurricane Sandy. "Reader, we walked on," he writes in what is both an invocation of the reader, in line with the ones earlier in the novel, and an allusion to the famous opening of the final chapter in Charlotte Bronte's *Jane Eyre*: "Reader, I married him" (234). While both direct address and the devastation of the city suggest sincerity, the allusion to Bronte and the sentimental novel suggests that we might take the shift from "irony to sincerity" with a grain of salt: on the one hand, he seems to be talking to us, simulating reality in the manner of sentimental novels; on the other,

162 | Knausgård and the Autofictional Novel

he positions himself and Alex as putting a new spin on an old trope, such that we see them as fictional characters, constructed from literary history. Indeed, after writing how the protagonist waved as he passed a TV camera, and suggesting, again to the reader, that "maybe you saw me," Lerner seems to suggest that here, at the end of the novel, the protagonist is finding the affirmation of an external reader, newly important, as a signal of the novel's "reality."

The readerly addresses culminate two pages later, when Lerner adds another metafictional comment. Among the photos of the city that he would later see from that night, there is one he decided to "use for the cover of the book—not the one I was contracted to write about fraudulence, but the one I've written in its place for you, to you, on the very edge of fiction" (237). By revealing that the book is both "for you" and "to you," the readers are integrated into the novel as both the intended audience and as receivers, as if the novel was a gift. It functions, simultaneously, as a performance of what the protagonist earlier described as the novel's trajectory—a shift from irony to sincerity—and a sign that the fictional and the nonfictional are impossible to separate.

As promised, Lerner certainly situates his novel "at the very edge of fiction," but a very different edge than Knausgård's. Where Knausgård places his novel up against that edge to engage reality, and to insist on that reality's existence, Lerner redraws the line between fiction and reality. Yet he does not suggest that there is no difference between the two, and that everything is fiction. Instead, he uses autofictionalization to direct us toward potential futures, and to show how imperative it is to engage with, understand, and question what, if anything, may come. The novel makes this tangible by suggesting two intertwined futures: one of hope, where the protagonist becomes a father, and one of death and destruction, as a result of climate change. By displaying those two futures, the novel suggests how a potential future of connection and care is threatened by capitalism's unhinged pursuit of profit where climate change has brought us to the brink of existence.[66]

All this might not have been possible had it not been for the publication of Book 1 of *My Struggle* in the US three years prior to Lerner publishing his novel. Knausgård's influence can be found not only in Lerner's use of autofictionalization but in the projecting into possible futures, with Knausgård announcing his future by declaring that he no longer is an author. But Lerner turns up the dial on Knausgård and explores what happens if these features are used even more radically than in *My Struggle*.

The Very Edge of Fiction | 163

Read this way, the novel seems to explore if, and how, autobiographical writing after Knausgård is possible.[67]

Contemporary Autofiction

Sheila Heti, Ben Lerner, and Rachel Cusk might not have been directly inspired by Knausgård, but their autofictional novels, like his, challenge and renew the genre, using some of the same techniques and arriving at some of the same conclusions. All four share a mistrust in fiction in various forms: the lies of neoliberalism the financial crisis has helped throw into relief, the self-deception in so many of the stories we tell about ourselves, the structures we unthinkingly inhabit. But they choose radically different ways to handle what can come off as a skepticism, disappointment, and fatigue with fiction.

And it is, I suggest, because of the mistrust in fiction that the four writers often have been lumped together and seen as representing what I earlier referred to as the first wave of contemporary autofiction. Their shared questioning of fiction and fictionality revitalizes both writing and our understanding of the world it records. It also lays the foundations for the many autofictional novels that were to come as the second decade of the twenty-first century came to a close: autofictional novels that often were written by authors of color, who embraced the genre to show the devastating personal consequences of centuries of intertwined capitalism, white supremacy, and sexual violence.

Over the past few decades, quite a few scholars and critics have declared the novel dead, seeing it as stuck in the tropes of reality fiction. No wonder, perhaps, that many autofiction novels have captured so much attention, as the kind of formal experimentation professional readers so often like seems to be finding mainstream appeal with autofiction. Yet what seems unique about the autofictional novels of the twenty-first century is not just their commentary on literary history, but the way they seem to help readers examine their own lives. Many reader responses to these novels speak of devotion, absorption, and a feeling of trust toward the writer as a result of what Alison Gibbons calls "metamodern affect."[68] Literary studies has often frowned upon such responses, whether by ignoring it, or rejecting it outright as naïve, but to do so misses an important aspect of these novels' appeal.[69]

Some of that engagement comes from the way these novels play with both the autobiographical and fictional pacts, which encourages readers

164 | Knausgård and the Autofictional Novel

to read them both as autobiography and novels. While the duality of these pacts reflects certain formal patterns, the very notion of the pacts discloses that autofiction should not, and cannot, be defined by formal characteristics alone and that mode of reading—the proximity between author, narrator, and protagonist—matters. To that end, the discussion of the three novels here confirms what we already saw in *My Struggle*: that we, when speaking of autofiction, also need to speak of it as a mode of reading that precisely activates two seemingly contradictory readings at one and the same time, with Heti and Cusk reminding us that gender cannot be ignored in that equation.

Afterword

After Autofiction

In the early fall of 2020, during a global pandemic, Knausgård's *Morgenstjernen* (*The Morning Star*) was published in Norway. It was far from Knausgård's first book since he concluded *My Struggle*; in spite of *My Struggle*'s closing proclamation that he would "revel, truly revel, in the thought that [he is] no longer a writer," he went on to author twelve books in Norwegian since then.[1] But *The Morning Star* was the first book since *My Struggle* that, on the cover, is designated a novel. And more than that: it was a novel concerning fictional characters in a highly fictional, even fantastic, story.[2] Set mostly in Bergen, Norway, it follows the lives of nine different people, in great detail, over the course of two days, after a huge new star has appeared in the sky. No one can explain its presence, and it might signal the apocalypse.

Since publishing *The Morning Star*, two more volumes in what Knausgård has announced will be a series of five novels have been published in Norway. The second installment, *Ulvene fra evighetens skog* (*The Wolves from the Forest of Eternity*) was published in Norway in October 2021 and the third, *Det tredje riket* (*The Third Realm*) was published in late 2022. In all three novels a formal dualism, similar to that in *My Struggle*, dominates the narrative; all three novels also revisit themes familiar to readings of Knausgård's six-volume novel: the mundane, shame, struggles with self-doubt and insecurity, and a conflict between self and world.[3] Indeed, both pull "conceptions about life," whether the advent of a new star or the longing for something beyond, into "the human sphere, where it no longer stands alone but collides with myriad impressions, thoughts, emotions, and actions," as Knausgård writes in a recent essay about why the novel matters.[4]

166 | Knausgård and the Autofictional Novel

Almost twenty years earlier, Knausgård announced another series of novels, a trilogy, made up of his first two novels and third that was never realized; instead, he suffered from a case of writer's block in which he questioned the merits of fiction. He began writing what became *My Struggle* as a cure. It seems safe to say that, with the new series, he has moved beyond the crisis of fiction that led him to write, in *My Struggle*, that "fictional writing has no value" (2.562). While that claim might seem at odds with his embrace of fiction in *The Morning Star* series, the first three books reflect his abiding desire, from his very first novel all the way through *My Struggle* and into the present, to find a way out of what he calls a "linguistically structured world." He wants to explore something more authentic, more real, and more engaging. For the many characters in the new novels, whose lives we are introduced to, the new phenomenon in the sky prompts them to confront their own lives, including the fictions they have lived by for years.

It took Knausgård a full decade—with a new status as a literary star, a new family, and a new country to call home—before he ventured back into fiction. Rachel Cusk moved a little more quickly. Her 2021 novel *Second Place* also marks a shift away from autofiction and nonfiction. Where the setting of the three novels in the *Outline* trilogy was always significant, and lent an additional level to the narration, the setting in *Second Place* is strangely blurred and unspecific, and with the location only referred to as "the marsh." The female narrator, known only as "M," invites "L," a well-known artist, to stay in a guest house she and her husband have had built on their property: their "second place." Like Jane in *Transit*, who after seeing the paintings of Marsden Hartley felt that the artist knew her, the narrator has felt an affinity toward L since she first saw his paintings years earlier and felt seen by them.

L arrives in the marsh during a global crisis—presumably the COVID pandemic—and finds a creative streak he has been missing for years. But when the narrator asks him why he does not want to paint her, but only her husband, he says that it is because he can't see her. This sets in motion a chain of events that threatens the narrator's marriage, the relationship between her and her daughter, and her sense of self. As in the *Outline* trilogy and the work that preceded it, Cusk investigates male privilege and power, and what it means to be, and attempt to create art as, a woman. But the novel can also be read as a warning about the personal and ethical consequences of pushing the quest for truth to

Afterword | 167

its extreme, and using other people in that quest, as M's desire to know why L will not paint her pushes her to do things at odds with her ethics. Such a reading seems supported by a final note in the novel, where Cusk informs us that her novel "owes a debt to *Lorenzo in Taos*, Mabel Dodge Luhan's 1932 memoir of the time D. H. Lawrence came to stay with her in Taos, New Mexico."[5]

Sheila Heti continued exploring autofiction but with increased, and more ironic, distance to her novelistic self in the 2018 novel *Motherhood*. But in 2022, she returned to the fictional with the novel *Pure Colour*. An abstract fable, the novel starts with creation and how God, dissatisfied with the "first draft of existence," created three kinds of people on his second attempt, "hoping to get it more right this time": those who view life from a distance, interested in "beauty, order, harmony, and meaning" and who are born from a bird egg; those concerned with "fairness and justice here on earth" and who are born from a fish egg; and those who "claim few people to love and protect" and who are born from a bear egg.[6] Starting her novel with creation—a literary creation made by her, that is—emphasizes the fictional nature of the novel. It shows that Heti still intends to reveal the constructedness of the few characters we meet in the novel. The small, fabricated universe of the plotless novel in which we follow Mira, born from a bird egg and an aspiring critic, dealing with the loss of her father (born from a bear egg) and her love for a woman named Annie (born from a fish egg) indicates a continued commitment to foregrounding and examining the complexities and intersection of living and creating art.

Ben Lerner, on the other hand, has pushed his experiments with autofiction forward. In *The Topeka School*, he returns to the character of Adam from his first novel. Though the novel has numerous autobiographical correspondences, and even reads more autobiographically than *10:04*, he seems less interested in investigating, and playing with, the relationship between himself as an actual person and as a novelistic character than in *10:04*. His experimentation with autofictionalization is replaced by an interest in how he and his parents use language and narrative differently.

For Knausgård, this exercise was temporary. He merged his life with his novelistic aspiration, making it impossible to separate the two, for the course of *My Struggle*; after bidding farewell to that kind of writing at the end of Book 6, he had to start anew. Few, if any, contemporary authors dedicate their whole literary career to writing autofiction; it seems safe

168 | Knausgård and the Autofictional Novel

to say that it functions, for many writers, as a kind of transitional genre.[7] Responding to crises that both seem existential, artistic, and political, they seek some perception of reality, truth, or authenticity, for both their novels and the lives those novels reflect, whether of characters, authors, or readers. They find it by embracing a literary practice that blurs fiction and nonfiction.

Whatever comes next, it seems clear that Knausgård's *My Struggle* has helped change the field, and that by thinking both with and about it, we can not only better understand his six books but also—as I have endeavored to do here—arrive at new understandings about autofiction, the novel, and indeed what literary criticism can do. The first of these is that old notions of formalism and genre studies, which treat specific formal features in isolation to identify a certain genre, do not always serve us; certainly, they cannot account for the workings of autofiction. This also means that we must accept that modes of reading matter, and can coexist. When we read, it matters if the name of a character in a novel is identical to that of the author, and it matters if the autobiographical pact that this invokes continually is positively stated throughout the work and supported by paratextual and extratextual information.

The narrative strategy of autofictionalization, through which writers are able to treat their former self as a character in the novel, might be the most important formal feature of current autofiction. Treating a former self as a novelistic character by placing the narrative consciousness with that former self creates a sense of presence and authenticity. The paradoxical effect of autofictionalization is that it is the fictive elements that make the autofictional novel feel true and real. This blurring of fiction and reality serves a sense of truth and authenticity. And it all happens within the constraints of the novel.

The previous chapters also show how the autofictional novel is neither formless nor a form happened upon by accident. Instead, writers embrace novelistic form in specific and deliberate ways, conforming to major properties of canonical theories of the novel, with the gold standard set by Lukács. Knausgård, for his part, has never not referred to *My Struggle* as a novel, even before it was published. In an onstage interview with his friend and writer-colleague Tore Renberg from 2009, Knausgård recounted the first time he revealed that he intended to "write a novel about my own life here and now, using full names and all."[8] He was, he said, giving a guest lecture to a group of aspiring writers at the writer's academy in Bergen that he himself had attended years earlier. His revelation was met

Afterword | 169

with silence: "they became somewhat quiet, and while they didn't exactly shake their heads, I sensed their skepticism" (24).[9]

Perhaps these young writers assumed that novels were fiction—possessed of autobiographical elements at times, to be sure, but fictions nonetheless. They certainly had reason to think so, given that this conception has been with us for some three centuries. But autofictional writers challenge the notion that novels are fiction, and they do so in part to rescue a genre that they and others fear has lost its importance and relevance. I believe that Knausgård, more than anyone, has helped change that.

It may be that, when future literary and cultural histories are written, *My Struggle* will come to represent the pinnacle of a certain phase of autofiction—one that arises in the wake of numerous crises in the early twenty-first century and that I earlier referred to as a first wave of autofiction. In this wave that has been associated predominantly with the four white writers discussed in the previous chapters, Knausgård represents the beginning, middle, and end with Sheila Heti, Rachel Cusk, and Ben Lerner as the three writers most often invoked in discussion of his branch of autofiction. And together, the four of them paved the way for a second wave of autofictions.

In this second wave, many of the writers are still white, though autofiction, as I mentioned in the introduction, also has been taken up by a number of authors of color. In *A Particular Kind of Black Man*, for instance, Tope Folarin explores the complexities of race and identity in a story that closely mirrors his own, "written under the influence of autofiction," as he puts it.[10] Similarly, in *Real Life*—a title that, along with an evident homage to Knausgård, invites us to read it as autofiction—Brandon Taylor, in a story that closely mimics his own, investigates loneliness, isolation, and belonging at the intersections of race, sexuality, and academia.[11] And in *Homeland Elegies*, Ayad Akhtar turns to autofiction, with homology between author, narrator, and character, to tell the story of being a Muslim American in a post-9/11 America where Ayad, the narrator and protagonist, struggles to reconcile his Muslim heritage with his American upbringing, mirrored in his troubled relationship with his father.

What these authors of color in the second wave of contemporary autofiction show is that autofiction is not merely a gimmick or a marketing strategy, as some critics have suggested, though it certainly also is that, but is more importantly a way for them to engage with the present and the intersections of their identities in the genre that historically most successfully has interpreted modern life: that of the novel.

Notes

Introduction

1. Throughout this book, I use the original Norwegian spelling of Knausgård's last name with an "å" instead of the Anglicized "aa," which otherwise is the spelling dominating in much of the English-language criticism on his work. I will, however, maintain the Anglicized spelling in quotes and titles when used. In addition, all quotations from *My Struggle* are marked in the text with reference to volume and page, where (3.127) refers to page 127 in Book 3 of the FSG edition of *My Struggle*.

2. Jonathan Lethem refers to Knausgård as "a living hero who landed on greatness by abandoning every typical literary feint." In addition, James Wood talks about *My Struggle* as an "extraordinary example of literary courage," and Jeffery Eugenides admits that he is one of those who "have fallen under Knausgaard's spell." Cf. Jonathan Lethem, "My Hero," *The Guardian*, online; James Wood and Karl Ove Knausgård, "Writing *My Struggle*," *Paris Review*, online; and Jeffrey Eugenides, "Karl Ove Knausgaard's *My Struggle*," *New York Times*.

3. For instance, Miller has declared that the "end of literature is at hand." J. Hillis Miller, *On Literature*, 1.

4. Anna Kornbluh stresses the concreteness of what such world-building entails: "realism builds houses," she answers after asking rhetorically what it builds. Cf. Anna Kornbluh, *The Order of Forms*, 33.

5. Dorrit Cohn, *The Distinction of Fiction*.

6. Alex Clark, "Drawn from Life," *The Guardian*, online; Jessica Winter, "Our Autofiction Fixation," *New York Times*, online.

7. Taylor Johnston identifies the myth of *My Struggle* as a novel without form in the criticism of James Wood, Zadie Smith, and Jonathan Lethem, but numerous other critics and scholars have embraced the notion of formlessness in Knausgård's novel. Taylor Johnston, "The Corpse as Novelistic Form," *Critique: Studies in Contemporary Fiction*, 369.

8. James Wood, "Total Recall," *New Yorker*, online.

172 | Notes to Introduction

9. The relationship, and part 1 of the novel, culminates when Vankel rapes Miriam in what he deludes himself into thinking is a consensual sexual relation. In an interview from 2000, Knausgård expressed surprise that few critics had noticed the problematic aspect of the book's Lolita motif: "Yes, it is definitely a rape [*overgrep*] that is described in the book. I have been very, very surprised that nothing has been written about this." Cf. Alf van der Hagen, *Dialoger 3*, 203.

10. Toril Moi, "Shame and Openness," 207.

11. Knausgård writes about his obsession with *Pan* in Book 4 of *My Struggle*. Recounting a New Year's Eve from his late teens, he writes about his reaction when a piece of firework landed on his feet: "I shouted that I was Hamsun's Lieutenant Glahn and had shot myself in the foot so that Hanne would realize how much I loved her, jumped around in tattered trousers and with the bandage soaked in blood, 'I'm lieutenant Glahn, I yelled'" (4.95).

12. The number thirty thousand comes from NRK's *Datoen*, a Norwegian documentary on Knausgård from 2018.

13. Øystein Rottem, "Høstens sensasjon," *Dagbladet*; Jeanette Sky, "Et monument over den modern mannen," *Morgenbladet*.

14. Henrik Kayser Pedersen's "Karl Ove Knausgård bibliografi" is an invaluable resource for anyone studying Knausgård: http://www.bibliografi.no/kok.pdf. *Ute av verden* will be retranslated into English and is scheduled for publication in 2024.

15. Frederik Wandrup, "Engler daler ned i skjul," *Dagbladet*; Jon Helt Haarder, "Monumental og vildt elektrisk," *Jyllands Posten*.

16. Hans H. Skei, "Mangfoldig, rikt, rystende," *Aftenposten*.

17. Morten Abrahamsen, "En plass for alt," *VG*.

18. "On its own terms, I wasn't anticipating the novel making any major impact, and neither were the publishers, ten thousand copies were being printed to start with, that was a lot," Knausgård writes (6.190).

19. Information on the Norwegian sales of *My Struggle* used to be available on the website of Knausgård's Norwegian publisher, Oktober, but unfortunately not anymore: http://oktober.no/nor/Presse/Pressemeldinger/Diverse-fakta-om-Karl-Ove-Knausgaards-forfatterskap. Last accessed February 13, 2018.

20. "Knausgård for dummies," *Dagbladet*.

21. The Language Council of Norway (Språkrådet) recorded in early 2010 the advent of the verb *at knause*, which in addition to the definition mentioned earlier also referred to discussions about Knausgård and *My Struggle*. See https://www.sprakradet.no/Vi-og-vart/Publikasjoner/Spraaknytt/Arkivet/Spraknytt-2010/Spraknytt-22010/Nyord/.

22. "Norges mest sexy man: Karl Ove Knausgård," it reads on the cover of *Elle*, no. 12, 2010.

23. Jan Kjærstad, "Den som ligger med nesen i grusen, er blind," *Aftenposten*.

24. In *På vakt skal man være*, I give a thorough introduction to Kjærstad's op-ed and its context. Claus Elholm Andersen, *På vakt skal man være*, 15–18.

25. Melberg's term "a literary centaur" (a term I borrowed from Melberg in an earlier article on Knausgård printed in *Critical Quarterly*) was the first of numerous terms applied to *My Struggle* by Scandinavian scholars. Arne Melberg, "Vi mangler ord," *Aftenposten*. For more on this, see Andersen, *På vakt skal man være*, 17–20.

26. The term "fictionless fiction" was introduced by Hans Hauge and "performative biographism" by Jon Helt Haarder. The term autofiction was first used in 2010 in a review in a Danish newspaper of Book 1 of *My Struggle*. For more on the many different terms applied to *My Struggle* in the early scholarship, see Andersen, *På vakt skal man være*, 17–20. In his MA thesis "Ut i det åpne," Martin Hegstad Otterbech compares the very dissimilar reception of *My Struggle* in the different Scandinavian countries through an analysis of twenty-six reviews of *My Struggle* from Norway, Denmark, and Sweden. Cf. Martin Hegstad Otterbech, "Ut i det åpne," online.

27. Despite the Danish translation, the majority of the numerous Danish scholars who have written on *My Struggle* (myself included) have read and quoted from the Norwegian original. This includes some of the first scholarship on the novel by scholars such as Poul Behrendt, Jon Helt Haarder, Stefan Kjerkegaard, and Hans Hauge.

28. In a *New York Review of Books* article from 2014, Tim Parks points out the paradox revolving around *My Struggle* in the US and the UK: that while the novel is continually talked about and praised by critics and news outlets, the sale of the three first volumes both in the US and the UK are not impressive, compared to typical international bestsellers from Scandinavia such as Peter Høeg's *Smilla's Sense of Snow* or Stieg Larsson's *The Girl with the Dragon Tattoo*. In 2014, *My Struggle* had sold only about twenty-two thousand copies in the UK and thirty-two thousand copies in the US, but those numbers changed drastically in the next couple of years and by 2016 it had sold about sixty-eight thousand copies in the UK and two hundred thousand in the US, as Günter Leypoldt reports. Cf. Tim Parks, "Raise Your Hand if You've Read Knausgaard," *New York Review of Books*, online; Günter Leypoldt, "Knausgaard in America," 62.

29. Myra Bloom, "Sources of the Self(ie)," *ESC*, 10; Siri Hustvedt, "No Competition," 85. Hustvedt relays how she in an interview asked Knausgård about his knowledge of the term autofiction—and of which he said he had none.

30. Paul West, "Sheer Fiction," *New Literary History*, 556. I thank Myra Bloom for directing my attention to West's review in the *New York Times*.

31. Serge Doubrovsky's definition of autofiction on the back cover of *Fils* is quoted widely in numerous discussions on autofiction. Here, I quote from: Sam Ferguson, *Diaries Real and Fictional in Twentieth-Century French Literature*, 29.

174 | Notes to Introduction

32. Myra Bloom, "Sources of the Self(ie)," 6.

33. Hywel Dix, *Autofiction in English*, 2–6. Doubrovsky's stylistic definition reflects according to Dix a "departure from a linear, sequential, chronological time frame and his interest in temporal experimentation"; his sociological definition an insistence that autofiction fills the gap created when more traditional forms of autobiography are rendered sociologically unavailable by the status of the writer; and his historical definition his belief that "historical conditions have changed since the days of classical autobiography such as that of Rousseau."

34. Annabel L. Kim, "Autofiction Infiltrated," *PMLA*, 560.

35. Karen Ferreira-Meyers, "Does Autofiction Belong to French or Francophone Authors and Readers Only?," 29–30.

36. Philippe Gasparini, quoted in Sam Ferguson, *Diaries Real and Fictional*, 29.

37. Gérard Genette, *Fiction and Diction*, 76–77. Alluding to Philippe Lejeune, Genette also characterizes autofiction as an "intentional contradictory pact" and singles out Dante's *Divine Comedy* as an example of it. Both Gasparini's and Genette's definitions can be traced back to Doubrovsky, not because his definition is flawed, as Arnaud Schmitt writes, but because the term is inherently vague and problematic. Schmitt writes: "since *autofiction* as a substantive lays stress on the non-referential part of the personal discourse, where Doubrovsky's textual practice [inspired by psychoanalysis] went rather in the opposite direction." Cf. Arnaud Schmitt, "Making the Case for Self-Narration against Autofiction," *a/b*, 126. The contradictory definitions of autofiction have also made their way into an English-speaking context. On the one hand, Marjorie Worthington defines autofiction as "a text in which the protagonist shares a name with the author, but the work itself is fictional." On the other, Tim Parks, writing in the *New York Review of Books*, sees autofiction as synonymous with autobiographical writing, making it a matter of whether "this or that character in a novel is identical to the writer." Cf. Marjorie Worthington, "Fiction in the 'Post-Truth' Era," *Critique*, 472; Tim Parks, "How Best to Read Autofiction," *New York Review of Books*.

38. Marjorie Worthington, *The Story of "Me,"* 19.

39. It is worth mentioning that Worthington's argument about the maleness of autofiction, at least in contemporary literature, is somewhat qualified by writers such as Sheila Heti, Rachel Cusk, Jenny Offill, Maggie Nelson, and Olivia Laing, to name just a handful of the writers who are often invoked as English-language practitioners of current autofiction. Indeed, Myra Bloom writes that the majority of "autofiction's contemporary practitioners . . . are woman" who have turned to autofiction to "diagnose and denounce the constraints faced by female creators in a patriarchal society." Myra Bloom, "Sources of the Self(ie)," 7.

40. Hywel Dix, *Autofiction in English*, 11.

41. The list of works is, to say the least, a mixed bag of works in English that spans from evidently autofictional novels by Rachel Cusk and Ben Lerner

Notes to Introduction | 175

to traditional autobiographies such as Vladimir Nabokov's *Speak, Memory* and novels such as Jonathan Franzen's *Freedom*, Paul Auster's *New York Trilogy*, and Kurt Vonnegut's *Slaughterhouse Five* that typically have been perceived as fiction, though they might have autobiographical components.

42. We see this, for instance, when Knausgård uses hyperbole to describe how he by attending a public baby gym class (that metonymically designates the Swedish welfare state) is "rendered completely harmless, without dignity, impotent," and shortly thereafter holds up the world of boxing as a badge of honor as it is a culture where "the values that the welfare society had otherwise subverted, such as masculinity, honor, violence, and pain, were upheld" (2.78, 2.126).

43. Hywel Dix extends his claim about autofiction and women writers to "the field of postcolonial writing" where "new and diverse themes have emerged, often requiring new forms for their expression." This argument is supported by a short reference to Chimamanda Ngozi Adichie, who has "called for a new literary form, capable of expressing a growing and diverse range of experiences and subjectivities within and across postcolonial cultures." Yet less than a handful of postcolonial writers have made it to his list of seventy-one works of contemporary autofiction, somewhat countering his argument about autofiction as a genre embraced by contemporary postcolonial writers.

44. Tope Folarin, "Can a Black Novelist Write Autofiction?," *New Republic*, online.

45. In a Scandinavian context, Helle Egendal argues that "multilingualism is a key autofictional strategy in transcultural autobiographical literature" and "postmigrant literature in Denmark." Helle Egendal, "Multilingual Autofiction," 141, 147.

46. In an analysis of visual autofictional art, Karen Ferreira-Meyers and Bontle Tau argue that autofiction can be seen as a step "toward establishing more cultural inclusion and social cohesion in the tradition of self-portraiture, by challenging the pre-structured and compartmentalized views on self and singular cultural identity. Karen Ferreira-Meyers and Bontle Tau, "Visual Autofiction," 181.

47. Sarah Wasserman, "Critical Darlings, Critical Dogs," *American Literary History*, 563.

48. Lee Konstantinou, "Autofiction and Autoreification," Substack, online. The short article, published on Substack, consists of Konstantinou's notes from a panel on autofiction at MLA 2021.

49. Christian Lorentzen, "Sheila Heti, Ben Lerner, Tao Lin," *Vulture*, online.

50. Hywel Dix, in an article discussing why the theory of autofiction has been less influential than other French theory, refers in his title to autofiction theory as "The Forgotten Face of French Theory." Hywel Dix, "Autofiction: The Forgotten Face of French Theory," *Word and Text*, 69.

51. In the case of *My Struggle*, as Poul Behrendt observes, the term autofiction was used in a review by the Danish critic Per Krogh Hansen in 2010,

176 | Notes to Introduction

though it was never used in the debate between both critics and scholars about Knausgård that took place that same year. Poul Behrendt, "Fra skyggerne af det vi ved," *Kritik*, 92.

52. Timothy Bewes, for instance, implies such criticism when he in the 336 pages that make up his book *Free Indirect* never mentions autofiction and the extensive scholarship on the autofiction novel, despite his attempt to understand the contemporary novel in what he calls the "postfictional age." In addition, among academics in the Twittersphere, criticism of, or rejection of, autofiction has become a recipe for guaranteed "likes" by fellow scholars. Timothy Bewes, *Free Indirect*.

53. Fredric Jameson, *Postmodernism*, xxii.

54. The symposium had a bilingual title, "Nordisk stemmer: Nordiche Identität?," and took place on November 20–21 at the Goethe University in Frankfurt. The schedule for the symposium can be found here: https://www.uni-frankfurt.de/52070877/nordiskstemmerflyer_301012.pdf.

55. Claus Elholm Andersen, "Den nordiske illusion," unpublished talk.

56. Monika Fagerholm is also one of the few female writers whose work Knausgård seems to admire in *My Struggle*. Discussing Fagerholm's *The American Girl* with a journalist in Book 2 of *My Struggle*, he says: "It's a very good novel" (2.514).

57. Here, I paraphrase Toril Moi, who luminously writes: "London exists. As does Harry Hole's Oslo." Toril Moi, "Å lese med innlevelse," *Morgenbladet*, online.

58. Annabel L. Kim, "Autofiction Infiltrated," 560.

59. Alison Gibbons, "Contemporary Autofiction and Metamodern Affect," 120. Gibbons continues: "Narrowly defined, autofictional texts identify as fiction to a greater or lesser extent, and the central character or narrator bears the name of the author" (121). From this also follows that an autobiography is not necessarily autofiction, as Kim otherwise would have us believe. Kim, "Autofiction Infiltrated," 562.

60. Myra Bloom, "Sources of the Self(ie)," 8.

61. Alexandra Kingston-Reese sees autofiction's metafiction as a sign of "the contemporary novel's built-in investment in the critical language and structures used in its own interpretation." Alexandra Kingston-Reese, *Contemporary Novels and the Aesthetic of Twenty-First Century American Life*, 121.

62. Myra Bloom, "Sources of the Self(ie)," 8.

63. Fredric Jameson, *Postmodernism*, 8–15. With references to *My Struggle* and other contemporary novels, Jonathan Sturgeon writes that "the postmodern novel is dead," as these novels "point to a new future wherein the self is considered a *living thing* composed of fictions." Cf. Jonathan Sturgeon, "The Death of the Postmodern Novel and the Rise of Autofiction," *Flavorwire*.

64. Using the term "neorealism," Lee Konstantinou suggests that writers such as Knausgård, Heti, and Lerner "paradoxically renounce fictionality in the name of something called reality, often retaining postmodernist genres such as

Notes to Introduction | 177

metafiction, but rejecting postmodernist critiques of representation." Lee Konstantinou, "Neorealist Fiction," 111.

65. Jonathan Sturgeon, "The Death of the Postmodern Novel and the Rise of Autofiction."

66. Alison Gibbons, "Contemporary Autofiction and Metamodern Affect," 120. Both Marjorie Worthington and Stefan Kjerkegaard also describe an earlier iteration of autofiction that seems more aligned with postmodernism—Worthington, as mentioned, through a historical approach to autofiction, spanning from the late 1960s till today; Kjerkegaard through a case study of Phillip Roth's so-called "Roth Books." Marjorie Worthington, *The Story of "Me"*; Stefan Kjerkegaard, "Getting People Right. Getting Fiction Right," *JTN*.

67. Johannes Voelz, "The American Novel and the Transformation of Privacy," 329.

68. Sheila Heti, "An Interview with Dave Hickey," *Believer*, online.

69. David Shields, *Reality Hunger*, 71, 115. Cf. Marta Figlerowicz, "The Novel of Infinite Storage," 206–207.

70. According to Shields, these chunks of reality appear "seemingly unprocessed, unfiltered, uncensored, and unprofessional," and a central component is an emotional urgency and intensity as well as "a blurring (to the point of invisibility) of any distinction between fiction and nonfiction" (5).

71. See, for instance, Ane Farsethås, *Herfra til virkeligheten*, 30, and Hans Hauge, *Fiktionsfri fiktion*, 20. Figlerowicz, however, gives a more nuanced account of the parallel between Knausgård and Shields.

72. Günter Leypoldt, "Knausgaard in America," *Critical Quarterly*, 56.

73. Kyle Buckley, " 'The Novel Is Like a Room'—an Interview with Karl Ove Knausgaard," *Hazlitt*.

74. The controversy has been subject to numerous critical investigations, often concerning the fictional aspect of autobiography. See, for instance, Micaela Maftei, *The Fiction of Autobiography*, 36–39; Arnaud Schmitt, *The Phenomenology of Autobiography*, 36.

75. The quote comes from an unpublished manuscript by Alice Marshall, which most commentators of Shields have missed. Shields list his sources in the back of his back but nothing in the text suggests that it is a quote.

76. The very composition of *Reality Hunger*—which consists of a little more than six hundred short epigrams loosely organized in thematic chapters, about half of which are quotes by writers, thinkers, and artists—is a deliberate blurring of the line between copy and original, between fiction and nonfiction. It is a practical illustration of what Knausgård, writing about being fed up with fiction, writes: that the distance to reality has become the same whether something is true or not. It also suggests that Shields, contrary to Knausgård, believes that the answer to any reality hunger is an abandonment of these boundaries altogether.

178 | Notes to Introduction

77. The idea that all narrative accounts essentially are fiction is what Marie-Laure Ryan has labeled "panfictionality." Cf. Marie-Laure Ryan, *Avatars of Story*, 46.

78. Toril Moi, "Description in *My Struggle (Min kamp)*," unpublished MLA paper.

79. Fully in line with Knausgård, who writes about how he had grown tired of fiction and novels, Shields also writes: "I doubt very much that I'm the only person who's finding it more and more difficult to want to read and write novels" (81). Several critiques have also mentioned Kenneth Goldsmith's thoughts on the novel in the age of the world wide web as relevant for understanding *My Struggle*. But Goldsmith's call for a conceptual, almost formless, literature (as, for instance, in the preface to his and Craig Dworkin's *Against Expression*) seems inadequate to explain how Knausgård consciously works with the form of the novel. Cf. Kenneth Goldsmith and Craig Dworkin, *Against Expression*, xix.

80. Ralph Keyes, *The Post-Truth Era*, 13.

81. Most Scandinavian newspapers even had stories about how subprime had been voted "Word of the Year" in the US.

82. That year the accumulated debt by US households reached a staggering $13 trillion dollars—more than thirty times what they held just a few decades earlier. See Dan Sinykin, *American Literature and the Long Downturn*, 7.

83. Here, quoted from the *Guardian*'s online version: https://www.theguardian.com/business/2008/oct/24/economics-creditcrunch-federal-reserve-greenspan.

84. That the crisis only momentarily led to self-reflection on Wall Street that soon was forgotten should not have come as a surprise to anyone. For more on the culture of investment banks and Wall Street, and the ideology of bankers, see Karen Ho's excellent ethnographical study, *Liquidated*.

85. Fredric Jameson, "The Aesthetics of Singularity," *New Left Review*, 118.

86. Fredric Jameson, "Itemised," *London Review of Books*.

87. Lee Konstantinou, "Autofiction and Autoreification," online.

88. In the book *Cool Characters*, Lee Konstantinou coins the term "postirony" to describe "what comes after postmodernism," and which he applies to a group of late twentieth-century and early twenty-first-century writers, some associated with autofiction, that "wish to preserve postmodernism's critical insight (in various domains) while overcoming its disturbing dimensions." Yet in his reading of autofiction in the aforementioned talk, he seems to situate autofiction firmly in postmodernism. Lee Konstantinou, *Cool Characters*, 37.

89. Anna Kornbluh (on the podcast *The American Vandal* with Merve Emre and Matt Seybolt), "Bootstrapping across America."

90. Mitch R. Murray, "All Auto All the Time," online.

91. In her introduction to a special issue of *ESC: English Studies in Canada* on autofiction, Myra Bloom notes that "many of the writers who submitted to this special issue are emerging scholars." Myra Bloom, "Sources of the Self(ie)," 2.

92. Sarah Wasserman, "Critical Darlings, Critical Dogs," 563.

Notes to Introduction | 179

93. Toril Moi, "Descripting *My Struggle*," *The Point*, online.

94. Arne De Boever, *Finance Fictions*, 15.

95. Paul Crosthwaite, *The Market Logics of Contemporary Fiction*, 3.

96. Timotheus Vermeulen and Robin van den Akker, "Notes on metamodernism," 4 & 2.

97. Timotheus Vermeulen and Robin van den Akker, "Periodising the 2000s, or the Emergence of Metamodernism," 4.

98. Alison Gibbons, Timotheus Vermeulen, and Robin van den Akker, "Reality Beckons," 54.

99. Timotheus Vermeulen and Robin van den Akker, "Utopia, Sort of," *Studia Neophilologica*, 56.

100. Ferrante's "anonymity continues to inspire unease in readers, critics, and academics, and it has become a popular obsession to attempt to track her down," Inge van de Venn notes. Inge van de Venn, "Guys and Dolls," *Scandinavian Studies*, 299.

101. See also Eric Hayot, who coins the term "aesthetic worlds" to describe "the sum total of the activity of the diegetic work of art." Cf. Eric Hayot, *On Literary Worlds*, 14.

102. In the essay "Die Singularität der immerwährenden Gegenwart," I read contemporary autofiction in the light of the financial crisis and use Marx's notion of "mute compulsion" to help explain why Knausgård started writing a 3,600-page autobiographical novel. Claus Elholm Andersen, "Die Singularität der immerwährenden Gegenwart," 83–98.

103. Cleanth Brooks, *The Well-Wrought Urn*, 203. Provocatively, Caroline Levine suggests that "far from being too much of a formalist, Brooks is actually *not formalist enough*." Caroline Levine, *Forms*, 31.

104. Timothy Aubry and Florence Dore, "Introduction," *Post45*, online.

105. Marjorie Levinson, "What Is New Formalism?," *PMLA*, 559.

106. Joseph North, *Literary Criticism*, xi.

107. Two of the scholars I have in mind, Caroline Levine and Anna Kornbluh, seem to distance themselves from the auspices of new formalism, with Kornbluh specifically referring to her view of form as "political formalism." Anna Kornbluh, *The Order of Forms*, 4.

108. Caroline Levine, *Forms*, 3 (original italics).

109. Sarah Chihaya, "The Sight of Life," *Post45*, online. As part of *Post45*'s slow burn on *My Struggle* in 2016, Chihaya noted the importance of form in *My Struggle* and characterized Knausgård as "a manipulator of forms." Sarah Chihaya, "*My Struggle*, Vol. 2," *Post45*, online.

110. Anna Kornbluh, *The Order of Forms*, 10.

111. Form, as Cara L. Lewis writes, "describes many possible actions and relations that can obtain at the same time, or within the same social or cultural sphere." Cara L. Lewis, *Dynamic Form*, 10.

180 | Notes to Chapter 1

112. Joshua Rothman, "Knausgaard's Selflessness," *New Yorker*; Martin Hägglund, *This Life*, 91.

113. My reading of this particular instance follows and augments Poul Behrendt's. Poul Behrendt, "Autonarration som skandinavisk novum," *Spring*, 304–305.

114. Henrik Skov Nielsen, James Phelan, and Richard Walsh, "Ten Theses about Fictionality," 62.

115. Including Gallagher among these formalist scholars might surprise those who associate her work with new historicism. But in the article "The Rise of Fictionality," she reverts, as I show in chapter 5, to formal techniques for distinguishing fictive first-person narrations.

116. As mentioned, I build on newer rhetorical approaches to fictionality in my definition of the term, specifically the work of Henrik Skov Nielsen, James Phelan, and Richard Walsh. See Henrik Skov Nielsen, James Phelan, and Richard Walsh, "Ten Theses about Fictionality," *Narrative*; Richard Walsh, *The Rhetoric of Fictionality*.

117. In the most elaborate study of shame in *My Struggle* to date, Kaye Mitchell, in her 2020 book *Writing Shame*, addresses shame in *My Struggle* in the context of masculinity. Kaye Mitchell, *Writing Shame*.

118. My reading of shame as a formalistic conflict between ethics and aesthetics is inspired by Timothy Bewes's admirable study *The Event of Postcolonial Shame*.

119. Using Kierkegaard's *The Concept of Anxiety* as a point of departure, my reading of this existential aspect also draws on Kierkegaard's discussion of the novel in the review *From the Papers of One Still Living*. See also Yi-Ping Ong, *The Art of Being*.

120. Numerous other writers, such as Jenny Offill, Maggie Nelson, Teju Cole, Chris Kraus, Olivia Laing, Ocean Vuong, to name just a few, have also been named in connection with Knausgård. But the three previously mentioned—Heti, Lerner, and Cusk—are most frequently included in these mentions. In addition, all three of them have expressed their admiration for *My Struggle* in criticism and interviews and have reviewed *My Struggle* in various journals and publications.

Chapter 1: A Commitment to Reality

1. His description of death soon takes on metaphorical qualities as Knausgård describes the bacteria that moves through "the Havers Channels, the Crypts of Lieberkühn, the Isle of Langerhans" of the dead body as an "invasion." Indeed, it concludes with an allegory of workers at a production plant.

2. The actual opening line of the novel—"For the heart, life is simple: it beats for as long as it can"—alludes to Knausgård's second novel *A Time for Everything* in which he writes: "As far as the heart is concerned, everyone is the

Notes to Chapter 1 | 181

same. All it wants to do, all it knows how to do, all it can do, is beat. All it wants, all it can do, all it does is beating." The somber description of death that opens *My Struggle* is also reminiscent of the tone in this novel, where Knausgård, among other things, writes about how Noah of the Old Testament was fascinated with death and that which did not easily confine to the categories of either the living or the dead. Cf. Karl Ove Knausgård, *A Time for Everything*, 468.

3. In *Bagdad Indigo*, a book published by Knausgård's own publishing house, Geir Angell Øygarden, who plays an important part in *My Struggle*, describes Baghdad during the Iraq War in 2003 as such a city: "The bodies lie across the bridge. Some without head, others without stomach . . . all covered by insects." Cf. Geir Angell Øygarden, *Bagdad Indigo*, 857, and my analysis of the similarities between *My Struggle* and Øygarden's book: Claus Elholm Andersen, "Forfatteren og sociologien," 2014.

4. In an interview with James Wood, Knausgård reiterates what he writes in Book 6: "When we were publishing that first book, my editor asked me to remove those pages because they are so different from the rest, and he was right—he is right—it would have been better, but I needed one place in the book where the writing was good. I spent weeks and weeks on that passage, and I think it's modernist, high-quality prose." Cf. James Wood and Karl Ove Knausgaard, "Writing *My Struggle*. An Exchange."

5. Karl Ove Knausgård, "Om framtiden," 103.

6. Walter Benjamin, "The Storyteller," 84.

7. Peter Brooks, *Reading for the Plot*, 95.

8. James Wood, "Total Recall."

9. Though this latter term originated in the first part of the twentieth century, it is often associated with the development in literary studies in the past four decades and the idea that language is our only means of knowing and engaging the world. That the world is linguistically structured, and that there is nothing beyond language, is therefore a reproach often thrown at poststructuralism and deconstruction by its critics. Ian Buchanan offers a brief but concise description of the phrase "the linguistic turn" in *A Dictionary of Critical Theory*, 295.

10. These thoughts on a "linguistically structured world" are also part of the essay about the future, published a year earlier. Cf. Knausgård, "Om framtiden," 109.

11. Alexandra Kingston-Reese, *Contemporary Novels and the Aesthetic of Twenty-First Century American Life*, 12. Gísli Magnússon argues that it is a demonstration of "the accidental character of the privileged moment," writing deftly about this particular instance. Cf. Gísli Magnússon, "The Aesthetics of Epiphany in Karl Ove Knausgård's *Min kamp*," 360.

12. From the episode on the commuter train, Knausgård turns to arts. What he felt that day on the commuter train, he says, is similar to the feeling that only certain paintings evoke in him. These paintings—painted by canonical figurative artists such as Rembrandt, Caravaggio, Turner, and Vermeer—were all

182 | Notes to Chapter 1

painted before the 1900s and "within the artistic paradigm that always retained some reference to visible reality" (1.223). This historical understanding finds its precursor in *A Time for Everything* in which the narrator, Henrik Vankel, sketches a similar history. Yet, in his book on Anselm Kiefer, Knausgård describes a similar experience when seeing one of Kiefer's painting in his studio outside Paris: "Something in me opened itself, when I looked at it." Cf. Karl Ove Knausgård, *A Time for Everything*, 341, and *Skoven og floden*, 37.

13. Dean Krouk, "'Gres, isstykker'—Knausgård som leser av Paul Celan i *Min kamp*," 190.

14. Ferdinand de Saussure, "Nature of the Linguistic Sign," 10.

15. In his anthology, David Lodge uses an excerpt from Roy Harris's 1983 translation of Saussure, where signifier and signified is translated as signal and significance. See also Toril Moi's extensive and engaging discussion of Saussure in Toril Moi, *Revolution of the Ordinary*, chapter 5.

16. Toril Moi, *Revolution of the Ordinary*, 15–16.

17. Terence Hawkes, *Structuralism and Semiotics*, i.

18. Discussing Jacques Derrida's reading of Saussure, Jonathan Culler writes how the French philosopher showed that the "difference between signifier and signified cannot be one of substance and that what we may at one point identify as a signified is also a signifier." That the signified turns out to be a signifier suggests the linguistic sign can only refer to other linguistic signs. Derrida's conclusion is, Culler asserts, "that there are no final means that arrest the movement of signification." As Culler presents it, Derrida reduces the relationship between signifier and signified to what Saussure explicitly tells us it is not, namely a "link between a thing and a name." Jonathan Culler, *On Deconstruction*, 188.

19. In *Inadvertent*, Knausgård repeats the metaphor about opening the world, almost verbatim: "Yes, I write because I want to open the world." Cf. Karl Ove Knausgård, *Inadvertent*, 46.

20. Numerous critics and scholars have misinterpreted Knausgård's description of how he tried to "combat fiction with fiction" as a testament to his intention with *My Struggle*—and not, as is evident from the context, a statement about his first two novels. See, for instance, Arnaud Schmitt and Stefan Kjerkegaard, "Karl Ove Knausgaard's *My Struggle*," *a/b*, 568.

21. As for writers who revel in the outside world, I believe he could be thinking about Jan Kjærstad, "the greatest Norwegian postmodernist writer," as he calls him in Book 4, and to whom he returns repeatedly in his narration. In Book 4, Knausgård writes about how as a young aspiring writer he admired Jan Kjærstad and wanted to write like him: "Writing in a postmodern style like Kjærstad was way beyond my reach, I couldn't do it" (4.392). But slowly he realizes that everything he admires in Kjærstad is stylistics and mechanics, which he soon learns to imitate. The point seems to be that postmodernism is nothing but surface, and it is thus rejected by Knausgård, the older narrator, as he looks back upon his younger self.

Notes to Chapter 1 | 183

22. Arguably, it also extends to Knausgård's 2020 novel *Morgenstjernen* (*The Morning Star*), as he touches upon this longing as it investigates the supernatural.

23. Released in 2018—almost a decade after the first volume of *My Struggle* hit Norwegian bookstores—most of *Inadvertent* has been published previously in one form or another: the story of how he came to write *My Struggle*, his thoughts on Joyce and Hamsun, and the comparison between *Game of Thrones* and Lars von Trier's *Antichrist*. But what is truly original in the little book is, in fact, his discussion of Ursula K. Le Guin's *A Wizard of Earthsea* (1968). When Knausgård in April 2019 received the Swedish Academy's Nordic Prize, a prize often referred to as the little Nobel Prize, he verbatim mentioned how *A Wizard of Earthsea* influenced him again. His acceptance speech, "Språket, bildene og litteraturen," was later published in the Norwegian newspaper *Klassekampen*.

24. Karl Ove Knausgård, *Inadvertent*, 24. On her Twitter account, Ursula K. Le Guin, who died in 2018, wrote the following in response to Knausgård's acknowledgment of her writing: "Thank you, Karl Ove Knausgaard's mother, for bringing the book home to your son."

25. In the book *The Abyss or Life Is Simple*, the collective of authors addresses the questions of religion in *My Struggle*. In their introduction, they write: "Central to Knausgaard's mission in the six books of *My Struggle* is the challenge of saturated fragments and of arranging them so that they open, even within these finite limits, into glimpses of, gestures towards, the infinite." Courtney Bender et al., *The Abyss or Life Is Simple*, 4.

26. See, for instance, 2.454, when he, during the christening of his oldest daughter Vanja, realizes that the sacred is what he wants to archive with his writing.

27. The phrase originates in Paul de Man's seminal "The Rhetoric of Temporality" in which he famously concludes the first part of the essay, on allegory, with the following: "The meaning constituted by the allegorical sign can then consist only in the *repetition* (in the Kierkegaardian sense of the term) of a previous sign with which it can never coincide." See also my critical reading of de Man's "Autobiography as De-Facement" later in this chapter. Cf. Paul de Man, "The Rhetoric of Temporality," 207.

28. With decades of poststructuralism and deconstruction dominating both literary fiction and literary studies, it would, perhaps, be more accurate to characterize the continual insistence on this ideology as reactionary. But instead, it is typically the attempts to criticize poststructuralism that are deemed reactionary. For more on this discussion, see Rita Felski, *The Limits of Critique*, chapter 1.

29. See also Ane Farsethås's short but excellent reading of this novel, which I'm indebted to here. Ane Farsethås, *Herfra til virkeligheten*, 274–279.

30. Writing that "it began to dawn on me that to understand *My Struggle*, I would have to unlearn a generation's worth of literary theory," Toril Moi stands out among the exceptions. She warns us that if we ignore the challenge *My Struggle* poses to the poetics of poststructuralism and continue with business as usual, it will only lead to the conclusion "that *My Struggle* is a complete failure." Cf. Toril

184 | Notes to Chapter 1

Moi, "Describing *My Struggle*." Moi also discusses how *My Struggle* challenges the way we read in the essay "Å lese med innlevelse." Further, Poul Behrendt, in the article "Autonarration som skandinavisk novum," discusses this as early as 2011, while Jon Helt Haarder spends several chapters in his *Performativ Biografisme* from 2014 showing how *My Struggle* and other recent autobiographical novels challenge what he refers to as a new critical mode of reading.

31. William Deresiewicz, "Why Has *My Struggle* Been Anointed a Literary Masterpiece?," *Nation*, online.

32. Timothy Bewes, "What Does It Mean to Write Fiction? What Does Fiction Refer To?," *Amerikastudien*, 535.

33. This is in the expanded part of the article where he also discusses the papers of his fellow panelists and offers a harsh criticism of Gerald Prince's paper, misrepresenting the much-debated notion of fictionality, as proposed by Nielsen, Phelan, and Walsh, which Prince took up in his paper.

34. Bewes's insistence of the difference between direct and indirect discourse also seems to have the unfortunate side effect that it does away with any distinction between first- and third-person narrator, and fiction and nonfiction as genre designations.

35. Anna Kornbluh, "Freeing Impersonality," 37.

36. James Wood, *How Fiction Works*, 11.

37. Recently, numerous scholars have proposed that free indirect discourse does extend to first-person narrations. But the literary examples cited in such discussions are all cases of something clearly not narrated by the first-person narrator. See, for instance, Henrik Skov Nielsen, "The Impersonal Voice in First-Person Narrative." Contrarily, Anna Kornbluh makes a strong case for rejecting any notions of FID in first-person narrators—and invokes Bewes in that discussion, too. See Anna Kornbluh, "Freeing Impersonality."

38. When Bewes further generalizes that "every programmatic claim or moment of description in *My Struggle*" is in free indirect discourse, it is quickly disproved by the programmatic passages that we have seen so far and that often come in more essayistic passages. These do certainly not adhere to an alienation of the speaking subject, as he would otherwise like us to believe.

39. In his 2022 book *Free Indirect*, Bewes defines free indirect as a "mode of thought" in the contemporary novel. In an earlier article, he attempts to "liberate" free indirect discourse from the notion of "discourse," asking if a "concept of 'free indirect' "—free indirect discourse without discourse—can provide "the basis of an authentically political thought." But in his reading of *My Struggle* in the present article, Bewes seems to take this a step further and tries to liberate free indirect discourse from "free," too. Cf. Timothy Bewes, *Free Indirect*, 5, and "Free Indirect," *Political Concepts*, online.

40. In *Free Indirect*, Bewes seems to have moved beyond such formalist understandings of fiction, writing what he calls the principle of fiction is "not

Notes to Chapter 1 | 185

a form but a principle that exists in tension with the genre category." Timothy Bewes, *Free Indirect*, 10.

41. Taylor Johnston, "The Corpse as Novelistic Form," 373. Focusing on Knausgård's description of objects, Johnston claims that his indexing of these objects both "frustrate sense-making schemes" and "resist assimilation to narrative" (372). Because of that, a structure of sorts emerges in *My Struggle*: "a nihilistically paratactic one that never really coheres into meaning" (373).

42. Dan Sinykin, "*My Struggle*, Vol. 1," *Post45*, online.

43. David Attridge, *Reading and Responsibility*, 96.

44. In a review of an anthology on *My Struggle* edited by me, Toril Moi points to the irony that de Man is the critic whose name most frequently appears in the index. Cf. Toril Moi, "Knausgårds udfordring," 111. But it is not only in my anthology that "Autobiography is De-facement" has been invoked in relation to Knausgård: see Hans Hauge, "Forfatteren står frem som den, han er," *Politiken*, 7–8, and *Fiktionsfri fiktion*.

45. A simple Google search confirms the use of this nickname, often used as "Paul 'the man' de Man." I first heard the nickname from fellow students as an exchange student at the Department of Comparative Literature at the University of Bergen in 1996, the same department where Knausgård was enrolled at the time and that he writes about extensively in Book 5.

46. Talking about how he and his fellow students worshipped those professors who advanced the theories of deconstruction, Knausgård writes about two of his old professors, Per Buvik and Arild Linneberg: "Both of them had immense power over us. . . . They had such high status it was as if the gods had descended from Mount Olympus to sit among us in the canteen. Which, of course, they never did. That Buvik had asked me a question twice during a lecture was a sign of favor from the Sun God in my eyes" (5.304).

47. Linda Anderson, *Autobiography*, 12. Just as de Man's essay signaled the end of autobiography, it also paradoxically caused it to return. The discovery of his wartime journalism in 1987 led critics to read him in a new light. Suddenly, de Man's critical text was read autobiographically, where some critics, in the words of Linda Anderson, "tried to interpret de Man's work as complicated, lingering acts of expiation through which he was producing the analytical tool that would have enabled him to cut through the subjective mystification he had succumbed to in his youth," while others "saw de Man's undermining of authorial responsibility and voiding of autobiographical selfhood as driven by personal necessity: his own need to repress his past" (15). The point being that his rejection of autobiography in light of his past is what justified biographical readings of his own works: referentiality suddenly had become important again.

48. Hans Hauge, "Forfatteren står frem som den, han er," 7–8. Hans Hauge has also written extensively about Knausgård in his 2012 book, *Fiktionsfri fiktion*.

186 | Notes to Chapter 1

49. Paul de Man, "Autobiography as De-facement," 67. In chapter 2, I return to Philippe Lejeune and his attempt to define autobiography in depth.

50. Bruss, for instance, addresses the notion of simple definitions head on in her *Autobiographical Acts* from 1976, writing: "Faulty or naïve assumptions about the nature of a genre impair the criticism of autobiographical writing." Cf. Elizabeth W. Bruss, *Autobiographical Acts*, 1.

51. In his important study of genre, David Fischelov identifies four metaphors that permeate genre theory: biology, family, social institutions, and speech act. Of these, the closest to what Paul de Man seems to subscribe to in his essay on autobiography is that of biology. Cf. David Fischelov, *Metaphors of Genre*.

52. Toril Moi, *Revolution of the Ordinary*, 93.

53. Martin McQuillan argues that de Man does not believe "that real events are determined by the author's desire to write a book." Yet, that seems to be exactly what de Man claims in this widely cited quote. Cf. Martin McQuillan, *Paul de Man*, 75.

54. In *Revolution of the Ordinary*, Toril Moi identifies a similar longing for ideal concepts in her reading of Derrida. Toril Moi, *Revolution of the Ordinary*, 72.

55. "In the end there is only writing," as Linda Anderson summarizes de Man's argument. Cf. Anderson, *Autobiography*, 13.

56. It also is the case for some of the rejections of autofiction more broadly that I reference in the introduction by scholars such as Lee Konstantinou, Sarah Wasserman, and Mitch Murray.

57. Writing about *My Struggle*, Poul Behrendt astutely states that "*the work itself cannot be separated from its creation*." Poul Behrendt, *Fra skyggerne af det vi ved*, 62 (original italics).

58. Knausgård, *Inadvertent*, 37. In Book 6, he also recounts how he, around the time he started writing *My Struggle*, was reading Witold Gombrowicz's diaries and in those found both a voice and reflections on life and literature that immediately resonated with him. He also writes that his working title for the book was *Argentina*: the country in which Gombrowicz lived in exile and wrote his diaries.

59. Another example of such diaristic stamps of authenticity occurs a few pages later, when Knausgård writes: "It is now a few minutes past eight o'clock in the morning. It is the fourth of March 2008" (1.28). And Book 2 opens, as if it was an actual diary, with the recording of date and year in the upper-right corner: "July 29, 2009" (2.3).

60. Martin Hägglund, *This Life*, 112.

61. Philippe Lejeune, *On Diary*, 181.

62. Philippe Lejeune, *On Diary*, 202. The notion of "antifiction" is presented jokingly as a reference to Doubrovsky and autofiction: "These days, the minute you invent a word, you have to take out a patent," Lejeune writes.

63. Dorrit Cohn, *The Distinction of Fiction*. 107.

Notes to Chapter 1 | 187

64. Arnaud Schmitt and Stefan Kjerkegaard, "Karl Ove Knausgaard's *My Struggle*," 569.

65. Rita Felski, *Hooked*, 93.

66. I explore the question of readerly identification in more depth in chapter 4.

67. Knausgård, *Ute av verden*, 10. See also Ane Farsethås, *Herfra til virkeligheten*, 265ff.

68. As Rita Felski writes, a central concept of modernism is that "selfhood becomes self-reflexive [and] literature comes to assume a crucial role in exploring what it means to be a person." Rita Felski, *Uses of Literature*, 25.

69. See, for instance, Evan Hughes, "Karl Ove Knausgaard Became a Literary Sensation by Exposing His Every Secret," *New Republic*; Tore Renberg, "I røykeavdelingen på havets bunn"; and Jesse Barren, "Completely without Dignity."

70. Alexandra Kingston-Reese, *Contemporary Novels*, 117. Kingston-Reese asserts this in relation to Chris Kraus's *I Love Dick* and Sheila Heti's *How Should a Person Be?*

71. Toril Moi reminds us that the Knausgård we meet in Book 6 "is simply not the same writer as in Book One." From an impoverished writer, longing for recognition, he has become an overnight literary sensation and celebrity. See also my discussion of this in chapter 3. Cf. Toril Moi, "Knausgaard's Ruthless Freedom," *Public Books*, online.

72. As discussed in the introduction, while I believe that Shields's diagnosis of a reality hunger—how we "yearn for the 'real' " and how we "want to pose something nonfictional against all the fabrication"—is similar to that of Knausgård's, his remedy is the opposite, as he, fully in line with Paul de Man, suggests that all autobiographical writing is fiction—and that we need to embrace that fiction. Cf. David Shields, *Reality Hunger*, 82.

73. Paul de Man, "Autobiography as De-facement," 72. In chapter 2, I argue for the possibility of a figure of duality in reading *My Struggle* as part of a larger theoretical discussion of fiction and autobiography.

74. Tore Renberg, "I røykeavdelingen på havets bunn," 24.

75. Karl Ove Knausgård, "Sjelens Amerika," 96.

76. Victor Shklovsky, "Art as Technique," 720.

77. Karl Ove Knausgård, *Inadvertent*, 31.

78. M. H. Abrams, *A Glossary of Literary Terms*, 72.

79. Paul de Man, "Semiology and Rhetoric," 4.

80. Caroline Levine, *Forms*, 7

81. Jeremy Biles, "Incidentals (When the Slugs Come) (In the Cut)," 155.

82. In talking about form-making in this context, I also follow Caroline Levine.

83. I vehemently disagree with Martin Hägglund, who, without any further evidence, claims that Knausgård in the last sentence of Book 1 expresses "a

188 | Notes to Chapter 2

strict materialist view of death," as his reading of the last sentence of Book 1 of *My Struggle* ignores the fact that the dead body is not merely an object among others, but an integral part of life. Hägglund uses his reading of the materialist view of death as a basis for his further reading of Knausgård as part of a secular tradition. This reading, however, also ignores Knausgård's continual invocation of what he calls the religious and how he writes about the sacred as a literary ideal. Cf. Martin Hägglund, "Knausgaard's Secular Confession," *boundary 2*, and *This Life*.

84. Knausgård's sense of death is not, to borrow Paul de Man's phrase from "Autobiography as De-Facement," merely "a displaced name for a linguistic predicament." In de Man's gridlock, death is that which cannot be faced or named, but Knausgård does both. J. Hillis Miller interprets de Man's conclusion this way: "'Displaced name,' that is, a substitute trope for what has no proper name. The word *death* indicates a blind spot within knowledge. This blind spot de Man calls 'a defacement of the mind.' . . . The word *defacement* names both a disfiguring of the mind, as vandals disfigure a statue, and a disabling of the trope of prosopopoeia that projects a human face and a human personality into the mind. Death is an area in the mind that cannot be humanized. This defaced area is a product of the inherence of language in consciousness and of consciousness's dependence on language. This place cannot ever be faced and named directly." Cf. J. Hillis Miller, *Ariadne's Thread*, 250.

85. The TV program was originally broadcast on October 6, 2009—about a month after the publication of Book 1. Here, *My Struggle* was presented as one of several new novels that fall. But, as Espen Børdahl writes, the interview with Knausgård was relatively short in the original broadcast, but later, when *My Struggle* repeatedly had made headlines in Norway, was shown in an extended version with the title "Quiet Before the Storm" ("Stille før stormen"). See *Bokprogrammet: Store norske* and *Bokprogrammet: Stille før stormen*. Cf. Espen Børdahl, " 'Livet er en gamp, sa kjerringa, hun kunne ikke si k.' "

86. Caroline Levine, *Forms*, 40.

87. See Cara L. Lewis, *Dynamic Form*, 16.

Chapter 2: Reforming the Form

1. David Bugge interprets this mark as a Cain's mark in a reading of *My Struggle* in light of the story of Cain and Abel—a story Knausgård also retells in his second novel, *A Time for Everything* from 2004. Cf. David Bugge, "Mennesket," 27–54.

2. I follow Poul Behrendt's register of the chronological events in Book 2 of *My Struggle*, and, later, of *My Struggle* as such. See Poul Behrendt, *Fra skyggerne af det vi ved*, 123, 441.

Notes to Chapter 2 | 189

3. His descriptions of each episode are less than one page long and lack the short, intense sentences that Knausgård typically resorts to when his writing intensifies. Perhaps jealousy, the feeling that motivates Knausgård's younger self to cut his own face, is melodramatic enough on its own that he needs no additional amplification, though use of repetition in between a slight dramatization or buildup. In the article "Narratives of a Life," I show how, elsewhere in *My Struggle*, Knausgård dramatizes with numerous narrative strategies. Claus Elholm Andersen, "Narratives of a Life," *Critical Quarterly*.

4. See the Gospel of John 1:14.

5. Jeremy Biles, "Incidentals (When the Slugs Come) (In the Cut)," 156.

6. Nora Hämäläinen, *Är Trump postmodern?* 123.

7. Caroline Levine, *Forms*, 25.

8. Judith Butler, *Gender Trouble*, 17. To Butler, the physical performativity of gender is more important in the construction of gender categories than any essential notion that arises from the mind.

9. Jonathan Arc, "What Kind of History Does a Theory of the Novel Require?," *Novel: A Forum on Fiction*, 191.

10. Georg Lukács, *The Theory of the Novel*, 29.

11. Lukács writes that "a purely interior reality which is full of content and more or less complete in itself enters into competition with the reality of the outside world." Lukács, *The Theory of the Novel*, 112.

12. Peter Brooks, *Reading for the Plot*, 52.

13. Lee Konstantinou, *Cool Characters*, 8. In an American context, numerous commentators identified 9/11 as what led to the death of irony, though Konstantinou rejects such historization as too simplified and shows how postirony can be traced further back in time.

14. Karl Ove Knausgård, "Litteraturen og det onde," 310.

15. The critic Knausgård refers to is the Swedish professor, critic, and feminist Ebba Witt-Brattström, who was also my *Doktormutter*, or dissertation advisor, when I wrote my dissertation on *My Struggle*. While applying a feminist lens to *My Struggle* helps identify a troubling ideology in the novel, I find it problematic when readings of the novel are directly extended and translated to Knausgård's life and marriage.

16. Though the formalism of Lukács's theory has "often remained latent in the reception of the work," as Anna Kornbluh notes, his language on the conflict between interior and exterior suggests that he does think of it in terms of literary form. Cf. Anna Kornbluh, "We Have Never Been Critical," *Novel: A Forum on Fiction*, 403.

17. Lukács, *The Theory of the Novel*, 89. According to Lukács, the novel "is essentially biographical," by which he is thinking of the fictional biography of the novel's protagonist (77). The novel, whether it's Cervantes's *Don Quixote*

190 | Notes to Chapter 2

or Pontoppidan's *Lucky Per*, which Lukács refers to by its German title *Hans im Glück*, tells that story of the problematic individual.

18. Writing about the monumentality of *My Struggle*, and in a comparison with Bolano's *2666*, Inge van de Ven notes: "Starting as a quest to restore meaning to lost time, Knausgård's search leads to the creation of a monument so comprehensive that it finally exceeds the self-centered and exhibitionist perspective that we would expect from a six-volume autobiography." Inge van de Ven, "Size Matters," 114.

19. In her reading of *The Theory of the Novel*, Anna Kornbluh argues that Lukács's tropes of architecture and construction point to a "yet unactualized formalist theory of literary realism: realism is architecture, a projective composition of integral space." Anna Kornbluh, *The Order of Forms*, 48.

20. Guido Mazzoni, *Theory of the Novel*, 3, 38.

21. See, for instance, Guido Mazzoni, *Theory of the Novel*, 149, 220, 319, and 335.

22. Mazzoni here singles out authors such as Philip Roth, J. M. Coetzee, Michel Houellebecq, and, somewhat ironically in a history of the novel, Raymond Carver and Alice Munro, both of whom write short stories.

23. "Knausgaard's novel is something like an empirical confirmation of Mazzoni's thesis about the tendency of the novel towards absolutely private particularity, absent any transcendent justification." Cf. Ben Parker, "What Is a Theory of the Novel Good For?," *boundary2*.

24. It is worth adding that Watt also historicizes the novel, which he considers a product of the industrial revolution in the eighteenth century.

25. "The narrative method whereby the novel embodies this circumstantial view of life may be called its formal realism." Cf. Ian Watt, *The Rise of the Novel*, 32.

26. Ian Watt, *The Rise of the Novel*, 32.

27. Ian Watt, *The Rise of the Novel*, 13.

28. Taylor Johnston, "The Corpse as Novelistic Form," 369. Alexandra Kingston-Reese also implies a notion a formlessness when suggesting, as previously quoted, that the "novel form is often happened upon by accident in the self-reflexive texts of the early twenty-first century." Cf. Kingston-Reese, *Contemporary Novels*, 117.

29. Case in point: In the US, magazines and newspapers reported widely on *My Struggle* before the translation of Book 1 appeared in English in June 2012. In my native Denmark, several articles had appeared in *Politiken*, the country's newspaper of record, before a translation of Book 1 was released. That included an article on "The Norwegian Wonder Boy" who published six autobiographical novels within a year and an essay about the debate in the wake of the publication in Norway. In Norway, the blurb of the first edition of Book 1 stressed the autobiographical aspect of the novel, saying that the book was about "the author Karl Ove Knausgård's struggle to master life and himself, and his own ambitions

Notes to Chapter 2 | 191

in terms of writing." Cf. Larry Rohter, "He Says a Lot, for a Norwegian," *New York Times*; Carsten Andersen, "Norsk wonder boy er våd anmelderdrøm," *Politiken*; and Janus Kramhøft, "Balladen om Karl Ove," *Politiken.*

30. Arnaud Schmitt and Stefan Kjerkegaard, "Karl Ove Knausgaard's *My Struggle*," 561.

31. Such a potential stumbling onto *My Struggle* without any knowledge actually characterizes my own first reading in 2009/2010, where I, after only skimming a review in a Danish newspaper declaring it a masterpiece, checked out Book 1 from the university library and started reading.

32. J. Hillis Miller, *Reading for Our Time*, 40.

33. Roland Barthes declared the author dead in 1966, based on a claim that "writing is the destruction of every voice, of every point of origin." Arnaud Schmitt might be right when downplaying the actual significance of Barthes's proclamation, saying that he finds it hard to believe that anyone "was so naïve as to believe in the death of the author" and claiming that most literary scholars were aware that "this trend was simply the result of a theoretical rebalancing measure." Yet, the notion of the death of the author certainly became a trope in literary studies in the decades following Barthes, to which my own education is a testament. But while the author *within* the literary work was dead, she was very much alive outside of it and perhaps, as Sean Burke suggests, as a result of it, with the author being "identified with the entirety of the work, while being nowhere visible within the work." Cf. Roland Barthes, "The Death of the Author," 142; Sean Burke, *Authorship from Plato to the Postmodern*, xxii; and Arnaud Schmitt, *The Phenomenology of Autobiography*, 5.

34. Philippe Lejeune, *On Autobiography*, 4, original italics. Published in 1989, *On Autobiography* is compiled from several of Lejeune's French-language books, most importantly *Le Pacte autobiographique* from 1975.

35. In a later book, Lejeune turns his attention to the diary. Cf. Philippe Lejeune, *On Diary*, 2009.

36. Lejeune "reduces the issue of fiction vs. non-fiction to a simple matter of pragmatics," Helga Schwalm writes in *The Living Handbook of Narratology*. See Helga Schwalm, "Autobiography."

37. The sensory impressions of that spring night when he was eight is another example of what Fredric Jameson, in relation to *My Struggle*, calls itemization. In the preceding quote, Knausgård lists every detail as it through itemization becomes possible to distill that which he otherwise cannot approach in his narration.

38. Dorrit Cohn, *Transparent Minds*, 162.

39. Marta Figlerowicz rightly observes that this skepticism is invited by *My Struggle*, and part of the novel's project. Figlerowicz, "The Novel of Infinite Storage," *Poetics Today*, 211.

40. In chapter 4, I give a more extensive analysis of Uncle Gunnar's accusations and their implications.

192 | Notes to Chapter 2

41. Fredric Jameson suggests that Uncle Gunnar constitutes "that 'ideal reader' of whom great critics have talked so much." Jameson, "Itemised," *London Review of Books*.

42. Sheila Heti recounts her meeting with Knausgård, and asking him if this detail was made up, in a review of Book 2 of *My Struggle*, says how, after his admission, she "was unable to pick up his books for another year." Cf. Sheila Heti, "So Frank," *London Review of Books*.

43. Dorrit Cohn, *The Distinction of Fiction*, 33.

44. In a Scandinavian context, Poul Behrendt introduced the concept of a double pact—*dobbeltkontrakten*—in a book with that title from 2006. In Behrendt's version, the first pact—what he calls the reality contract—is a work's claim to be autobiographical. Using Peter Høeg's *Borderliners* as his prime example, he argues that the second pact—the fictional pact—came into existence when Høeg admitted that his novel was not autobiographical *after* publication, leading Behrendt to conclude that the second pact replaces the first, very much in line with Lejeune. Behrendt's concept has been widely debated in Scandinavia and has been an influential pedagogical reading tool in readings of contemporary texts in high schools and colleges. But in his most recent book, Behrendt reevaluates his notion of a double pact and distinguishes between two contracts in regard to events and one in terms of narrations. And in the latter, similar to what I propose earlier, he finds room for *My Struggle*: "This is the double pact as pronouncement/narrative fiction [*udsigelsesfiktion*] in Karl Ove Knausgård's *My Struggle*. Not measured any more by a confusing of events but of the nature of voices." But in Behrendt's version, one of the pacts will always dominate—an argument that *My Struggle* seems to disprove. Cf. Poul Behrendt, *Dobbeltkontrakten*, 17–18, and *Midnatssolen på Dramaten*, 32.

45. Referring to "evidence in psychology and neuroscience," Alison Gibbons writes: "When reading an autofiction, readers will encounter a character that either explicitly or implicitly represents the author, prompting them to create a text-world—first at a micro-level but this is extrapolated (both in the diagram and in the reading experience) to a macro-level—which includes that enactor of the author. Depending on the choice of name for this author-enactor and on a reader's assessment of the accuracy of the depiction (of the author, of events in text-worlds or the storyworld at large), this text-world will be assigned either a referential or fictional status and thus read in relation to corresponding factual or fictional pacts. At some point in reading the autofiction, scenarios or identity attributes of the enactor will contradict a readers' initial ontological assignation, and in such a way that they cannot neatly revise the interpretation by replacing fictionality with referentiality or vice versa. As such, readers will be required to create a new, distinct text-world, contrasting in its ontological status. The felt effect of this tension can be described as 'ontological dissonance,' the experience of nonfitting ontological relations. Because both text-worlds apply to the reading

and interpretation of the autofictional narrative, neither can be dismissed: Readers must maintain these parallel mental representations, thus giving rise to the simultaneous doubling of incompatible yet co-referential narrative structures." Arnaud Schmitt, on the other hand, in a discussion of Philippe Gasparini's notion of simultaneity in reading, rejects any such notion, claiming that "simultaneity, appealing as it may seem, simply cannot be pulled off because it does not rest on any cognitive reality." Though I agree with Gibbons in this particular debate, I am not qualified to enter into a discussion of reading cognition. But in one of the more classical studies on this that I am familiar with, Richard Gerring seems to confirm Gibbons's arguments about autofiction and reading, writing that a sense of simultaneity happens in reading itself with "the duality of inhabiting the real and narrative worlds as real and narrative character." Cf. Alison Gibbons, "A Cognitive Model of Reading Autofiction," *English Studies*, 481; Arnaud Schmitt, "Making the Case for Self-Narration against Autofiction," *a/b*, 128; and Richard J. Gerring, *Experiencing Narrative Worlds*, 22.

46. As mentioned earlier, Arnaud Schmitt reminds us that "the truth value of a single event, or of a single fact might be a complicated, multisided, holistic, much-debated issue." Schmitt, *The Phenomenology of Autobiography*, 36.

47. In *The Art of Memoir*, Mary Karr also insists on complexity when it comes to a conception of truth, as the "line between *memory* and *fact* is blurry, between *interpretation* and *fact*." Mary Karr, *The Art of Memoir*, 86–87.

48. Roland Barthes, "The Reality Effect," 146. I am not the first to apply the concept of the reality effect to *My Struggle*. Trond Haugen did so in an essay from as early as 2010. Also, Poul Behrendt and Toril Moi have discussed the concept in relation to *My Struggle*, though more critically. See Trond Haugen, "Sirkulasjonen av virkelighet," *Prosa*; Behrendt, "Autonarration som skandinavisk novum," 298–302; and Moi, "Description in *My Struggle* (*Min kamp*)."

49. The exact number of copies in the Norwegian purchasing program changes from year to year. The purchasing program is administered by the Arts Council Norway. More information—mostly in Norwegian—can be found at: https://www.kulturradet.no/innkjopsordningene. A short introduction to the council's work in English can be found at: https://www.kulturradet.no/english/vis/-/arts-council-norway-main.

50. In Book 1 of the English paperback version, a short blurb on the back cover informs readers that *My Struggle* is an "autobiographical novel." In the German version of Book 1, the word *roman* is printed just beneath the title of the book, which in German has been translated into *Sterben* and it reappears on the very first page. In the French version, the translated title *La mort d'un père* is followed by the pronouncement that this is a "Roman traduit du Norvégien" (Novel translated from Norwegian).

51. Serge Doubrovsky's definition of autofiction on the back cover of *Fils* is quoted widely in numerous discussions on autofiction. Here, I quote from:

194 | Notes to Chapter 2

Sam Ferguson, *Diaries Real and Fictional in Twentieth-Century French Literature*, 29.

52. The letter from Doubrovsky to Lejeune is dated October 17, 1977, and quoted in Philippe Lejeune, *Moi aussi*, 63.

53. As Sean Kelly accurately writes about autofiction concerning Vigdis Horth's *Will and Testament*: "The definition of the genre was never very clear, not even at the start. With time, it has become intensely unclear, especially because it can feel, these days, as though every new book is in imminent danger of being stuck with the label because of the newfound ease with which we can trace the similarities between a novelist's life and their work." Cf. Sean Kelly, "Smile, Mingle, Inherit," *Sydney Review of Books*.

54. In my analysis of this particular scene, I'm indebted to Poul Behrendt's analysis of this very scene, "Autonarration som skandinavisk novum," 304–305.

55. I agree with Liane Carlson that Knausgård's description of where his father stands can be linked to a grave as he is standing in a "hollow" that is a few meters deep. She writes: "He is powerful. He is primal. He is standing in a grave." Liane Carlson, "Aesthetics of an Abused Child," 58.

56. For a definition of synthetic character narration, see James Phelan, *Reading People, Reading Plots*, 2.

57. It eventually turns out that it had nothing to do with his father being all-knowing but simply a result of him being able to hear Karl Ove running through the open window.

58. This kind of narration also mirrors what Genette calls paralipsis, where the narrator keeps information from the reader. Genette first identifies paralipsis in Proust, while later discussing it in relation to Stendhal and Agatha Christie. Without venturing into a discussion of the narratological differences between Knausgård and Proust, I will add that it should not be a surprise that Genette also identifies this kind of narration in *La Recherche*, as the complex and multifaceted narration in Proust's novels encompasses numerous narrative modes, which Genette's study in *Narrative Discourse* is testament to. Where the mode is one of many in *La Recherche*, it dominates in *My Struggle*, where Knausgård uses this kind of narration throughout the six volumes. Cf. Gérard Genette, *Narrative Discourse*, 196.

59. Marcel Proust, *Swann's Way*. Inge van de Ven talks about Knausgård's "anaphoric, singular form" in contrast to Proust's selective and syntagmatic narration. Cf. Inge van de Ven, "Den monumentale Knausgård," 67.

60. In Book 6 of *My Struggle*, it is made explicit that Linda, whose mother is a Swedish actress, certainly knows what Chekov's gun is. Railing against Karl Ove's friend Geir Angel, who has given Karl Ove a knife for his birthday, she is convinced that the reason he gave it to Karl Ove was so he would kill her: "A pistol mentioned in the first act is fired in the fifth" (6.1059).

61. Siri Hustvedt, for instance, reads *My Struggle* in the context of automatic writing and stream of consciousness. Relaying an interview with Knausgård, she

Notes to Chapter 2 | 195

writes: "Knausgaard might be called the contemporary king of automatic writing. *My Struggle* is an uncontrolled text. That is the nature of the project. I asked him about automatic writing in the interview, but he knew nothing about its history in either psychiatry or Surrealism." Siri Hustvedt, "No Competition," 85.

62. Hans Ulrich Gumbrecht, *Production of Presence*, xv; Poul Behrendt, *Fra skyggerne af det vi ved*, 103; and Peter Sjølyst-Jackson, "Confession, Shame and Ethics in Coetzee and Knausgård," 280.

63. Marta Figlerowicz, "The Novel of Infinite Storage," *Poetics Today*, 211.

64. Indeed, in Book 6, he writes that it was his intention to match "the reflections as closely as possible to the age of the first-person narrator," where his ten-year-old self "reflected on sweets, the twenty-nine-year-old on pop-music, the thirty-five-year-old on parenting" (6.69).

65. Joshua Rothman, "Knausgaard's Selflessness," *New Yorker*; and Hägglund, *This Life*, 91.

66. Martin Hägglund, *This Life*, 91; and Peter Sjølyst-Jackson, "Confession, Shame and Ethics," 288.

67. Poul Behrendt and Mads Bunch, *Selvfortalt*, 17; and Anna Rühl, " 'Lite og stygt, men alt som var,' " 148.

68. Paul John Eakin, *How Our Lives Become Stories*, 22–23.

69. Schmitt, "Making the Case for Self-Narration against Autofiction," 130. Schmitt originally coined the term "autonarration" and translated it himself into "self-narration." As autonarration, the term has been applied to Knausgård by Schmitt, writing with Stefan Kjerkegaard, and arguing that self-narration is "Knausgaard's best estimate of how to represent a real life in a novel." As autofiction, the term has been applied by Poul Behrendt, who sees it as an attempt "not to fictionalize but to maintain the actual and the particular. . . . Not as a representation of reality but as a production of reality." Later, Behrendt also relates it to a history of autobiographical novels in Scandinavia in recent years, where autonarration is the latest and most advanced stage. Cf. Schmitt and Kjerkegaard, "Karl Ove Knausgaard's *My Struggle*," a/b, 555; and Behrendt, *Fra skyggerne af det vi ved*, 94–95.

70. Schmitt, "Making the Case for Self-Narration against Autofiction," 133.

71. Cf. Dorrit Cohn, *Transparent Minds*, 166. Building on Cohn (among others), Henrik Skov Nielsen has referred to this kind of narration as "free-indirect speech in first-person narrative," thus contesting the common notion in narratology that free indirect speech is only possible in third-person narration. Cf. Henrik Skov Nielsen, "The Impersonal Voice in First-Person Narrative," *Narrative*, 136.

72. See Genette, *Narrative Discourse*, 52.

73. Cohn believes that fiction and nonfiction are ontologically dissimilar and that it is possible to distinguish between the two through formal features in the texts themselves, with fiction offering clues to its own fictionality. Cf. Dorrit Cohn, *The Distinction of Fiction*, vii. Marie-Laure Ryan uses Roland Barthes and Hayden White as examples of scholars representing the notion of panfictionality,

196 | Notes to Chapter 2

with a critical analysis of both of their arguments. Marie-Laure Ryan, *Avatars of Story*, 46–52.

74. Catherine Gallagher, "The Rise of Fictionality," 336–363. Though Gallagher's article has been quoted widely, it has also been the subject of serious criticism both from a narratological point of view (Monika Fludernik, "The Fiction of the Rise of Fictionality," *Poetics Today*, 67–92; and Simona Zetterberg Gjerlevsen, "A Novel History of Fictionality," *Narrative*, 174–189) and a historical one (by Julie Orlemanski in "Who Has Fiction?," *New Literary History*, 145–170). I discuss Gallagher's article in the context of *My Struggle* in chapter 4.

75. Henrik Skov Nielsen, James Phelan, and Richard Walsh, "Ten Theses about Fictionality," 71.

76. Richard Walsh, *The Rhetoric of Fictionality*, 30.

77. Cf. Rolf Reitan's thorough introduction to Richard Walsh's complex universe. Rolf Reitan, "The Rhetoric of Fictionality," *Spring*, 35.

78. In the textbook *Fiktionalitet*, written by a host of Danish scholars (including Henrik Skov Nielsen and Stefan Kjerkegaard), Knausgård is briefly discussed in relation to Walsh's thoughts on fictionality. Though it provides an overview of different discourses of fictionality—in politics, social media, and genre-bending movies and TV shows—the concept of fictionality remains vague. Concerning Knausgård, the authors write: "Our suggestion is to call *My Struggle* fictionalized non-fiction, because empirical real and autobiographical factors are exposed for techniques of fictionalization." Cf. Louise Brix Jacobsen et al., *Fiktionalitet*, 28.

79. In chapter 4, I discuss this alignment of novel and fiction further in relation to Catherine Gallagher's "The Rise of Fictionality."

80. With references to *My Struggle* and other autofictional novels, Jonathan Sturgeon, as mentioned in the introduction, writes that "the postmodern novel is dead," as these works "point to a new future wherein the self is considered a *living thing* composed of fictions." Cf. Jonathan Sturgeon, "The Death of the Postmodern Novel and the Rise of Autofiction," *Flavorwire*.

81. Fredric Jameson, *Postmodernism, or, The Cultural Logic of Late Capitalism*, 8–15.

82. Fredric Jameson, "Itemised," *London Review of Books*.

83. Frederic Jameson is not the first to observe how itemization is a defining feature of *My Struggle*. Marta Figlerowicz notes how *My Struggle* is "organized as a parataxic of repetitions, lists, and synonyms," adding that Knausgård seems to test the limits of how "lists are fundamentally non-narrative; forms of representation." James Wood also notes how Knausgård, when talking about his favorite bands, lists all of them, instead of a few. Cf. Marta Figlerowicz, "The Novel of Infinite Storage," *Poetics Today*, 208; and James Wood, "Total Recall," *New Yorker*.

84. In Book 1, Knausgård's eight-year-old self refers to it as "the new supermarket," thus validating the memory of it being built in Book 6 (1.22). For mentions of B-MAX, see also Book 3: 15, 164, 264, and 351.

Notes to Chapter 3 | 197

85. While Jameson demands that the estrangement, or defamiliarization as Shklovsky calls it, must be poetic or nightmarish, Shklovsky, in "Art as Technique," expresses no such demand. Instead, he writes the following about the concept: "The purpose of art is to impart the sensation of things as they are perceived and not as they are known. The technique of art is to make objects 'unfamiliar,' to make forms difficult, to increase the difficulty and length of perception because the process of perception is an aesthetic end in itself and must be prolonged." Cf. Victor Shklovsky, "Art as Technique," 720.

86. Presumably referring to the passages when Knausgård discusses his poetic and novelistic ambitions, Jameson writes that he finds "himself growing impatient" when reading the essayistic passages in *My Struggle*, missing that these should not be seen as a reflection of Knausgård's thoughts at the time of writing but, as Martin Hägglund convincingly has suggested, as the thoughts of Knausgård's former self at the time of the narration—and thus another instance of autofictionalization. Hägglund writes: "The theoretical reflections exist on the same plane as the practical actions; they reflect how someone thinks and feels at a particular time rather than expressing the perspective of someone who is outside the narrative and in control of its meaning." Cf. Martin Hägglund, *This Life*, 100.

87. Michael Riffaterre famously opens *Fictional Truth* by stating that what his term designates is generic fiction: "The only reason that the phrase 'fictional truth' is not an oxymoron, as 'fictitious truth' would be, is that fiction is a genre whereas lies are not." Michael Riffaterre, *Fictional Truth*, 1.

88. As Arnaud Schmitt and Stefan Kjerkegaard remind us: "To read *My Struggle* as fiction is to strip it of its originality." Schmitt and Kjerkegaard, "Karl Ove Knausgaard's *My Struggle*," *a/b*, 568.

Chapter 3: A Son of Shame

1. Jesse Barron, "Completely without Dignity," *Paris Review*, online.

2. Jesse Barron, "Completely without Dignity," *Paris Review*, online.

3. In the same interview, Knausgård also says that he would burn all the copies of *My Struggle* if he could. Cf. Jesse Barron, "Completely without Dignity," *Paris Review*, online.

4. In his interpretation, Poul Behrendt, without textual support in Knausgård's novel, claims that the father laughs because he is ashamed that he has turned on the late TV news because his son has told him about the face he saw. Behrendt also claims that the father "gets up and turns off the TV the second the story [about the fishing boat] is over," though Knausgård writes nothing to support such a claim. Cf. Poul Behrendt, *Fra skyggerne af det vi ved*, 129.

5. Surprisingly, the letter is not part of her wonderful epistolary collection of essays to Knausgård. Kim Adrian, "Karl Ove Knausgaard's Feats of Shame and Openness," *Lithub*, online. See also her epistolary *Dear Knausgaard*.

198 | Notes to Chapter 3

6. Peter Sjølyst-Jackson calls this first scene of shame the "urtext for the whole autobiographical project." See "Confession, Shame and Ethics in Coetzee and Knausgård," 288.

7. Accordingly, it can be seen as Karl Ove reverting to an Oedipal conflict that he, at the age of eight, ideally should have moved beyond. I discuss this aspect in my article "Som far, så søn," 174.

8. Knausgård both "names and describes shame" in this particular scene, as Sjølyst-Jackson notes. Peter Sjølyst-Jackson, "Confession, Shame and Ethics in Coetzee and Knausgård," 288.

9. Dorrit Cohn, *Transparent Minds*, 145.

10. According to the American Psychological Association's *Dictionary of Psychology*, shame is a "highly unpleasant self-conscious emotion" that is characterized by "withdrawal from social intercourse—for example, by hiding or distracting the attention of another from one's shameful action." Cf. *Dictionary of Psychology*, online source.

11. Giorgio Agamben, *Remnants of Auschwitz*, 115. In his discussion of shame, Agamben famously centers his reading on a passage by Robert Antelme. For a discussion on this, see Nicolai Krejberg Knudsen, "Shame, Belonging, and Biopolitics," *Human Studies*, 439–442.

12. Agamben, *Remnants of Auschwitz*, 107.

13. Sandemose formulated the Law of Jante in his 1933 novel *En flyktning krysser sitt spor* (*A Fugitive Crosses His Tracks*). Commenting on the Law of Jante in Book 6 of *My Struggle*, Knausgård writes: "Only a writer could have penned the Law of Jante. The fact that the Law of Jante found so much widespread resonance is ironic, since what Sandemose's rules express is the very tyranny of the majority" (6.237).

14. This, I believe, is also what Toril Moi has in mind when asserting that contemporary writers do not deny "the subject may well be a construction" but simultaneously want to express "what it feels like to exist as a particular subject in a particular time and place." Cf. Toril Moi, "Real Characters," *The Point*, online.

15. Numerous other critics have written about the centrality of shame in *My Struggle*, and their different understandings help reveal the complexity of Knausgård's treatment of the feeling. In *Writing Shame*, Kaye Mitchell suggests that *My Struggle* shows "the dilemma of writing masculine shame," where Knausgård's attempt "to engage with a particular species of masculine shame cannot but be presented and received as an heroic 'struggle' for authenticity, where authenticity too often means 'authentic masculinity.'" Arguing that no one "has written better about shame than Knausgård" and that his first novel, *Out of the World* (*Ute av verden*) is "one long investigation of the phenomenology of shame," Toril Moi asserts that Knausgård in *My Struggle* must come "into the open" by "revealing his inner life" if he wants to "escape the alienating division of shame." Echoing Moi, Barry Sheils and Julie Walsh write that Knausgård attempts to "escape his

Notes to Chapter 3 | 199

shame by writing about it," while Peter Sjølyst-Jackson, in his notable investigation of shame's relation to ethics, concludes that "shame in Knausgård is a debilitating obstacle to both self-understanding and understanding others." Cf. Kaye Mitchell, *Writing Shame*, 236; Toril Moi, "Shame and Openness," *Salmagundi* (Moi's article first appeared in Norwegian in the weekly *Morgenbladet*); Barry Sheils and Julie Walsh, introduction to *Shame and Modern Writing*, 11; and Peter Sjølyst-Jackson, "Confession, Shame and Ethics in Coetzee and Knausgård," 290.

16. Silvan Tomkins, *Affect, Imagery, Consciousness*, vol. 2, 351.

17. Timothy Bewes, *The Event of Postcolonial Shame*, 22.

18. Building on Tomkins in *Touching Feeling*, Sedgwick focuses on shame as visible, performative, and theatrical, and she discounts internal shame felt by a subject. Though agreeing that one "*is something* in experiencing shame," she also stresses that it does not follow that shame is "the place where identity is most securely attached to essences, but rather the place where the question of identity arises most originally and most relationally." Eve Kosofsky Sedgwick, *Touching Feeling*, 36.

19. D. A. Miller, *The Novel and the Police*, 162, original italics.

20. In the English translation, the word "brendte" from the Norwegian original is translated as both "burned" and "seared."

21. Tomkins, *Affect, Imagery, Consciousness*, vol. 2, 360.

22. The title of the 1997 exhibition in Barcelona was *Flying over Water = Volar damunt l'aigua*, and the image is also printed on the cover of the catalogue. Cf. Peter Greenaway, *Flying over Water = Volar damunt l'aigua*.

23. See Johanna Lee, "I See Faces," 106.

24. Mark Currie used the term in a paper on *My Struggle* at the symposium The Cult in Context: Historical and Comparative Perspectives on Karl Ove Knausgaard at the Goethe-Universität Frankfurt in June 2017. In *10:04*, Ben Lerner describes the term at length. Cf. Mark Currie, "Pareidolia and Struggle," unpublished conference paper; and Ben Lerner, *10:04*, 69.

25. See Poul Behrendt, "Autonarration som skandinavisk novum," *Spring*, 306; Ane Farsethås, *Herfra til virkeligheten*, 303; Olivia Noble Gunn, "Growing Up," *Scandinavian Studies*; and my own article "Som far, så søn," 167.

26. In the aforementioned interview with the *Paris Review*, Knausgård also refers to himself as "a classic Proustian." Cf. Jesse Barron, "Completely without Dignity;," online source.

27. Ane Farsethås, *Herfra til virkeligheten*, 303, original italics.

28. Knausgaard, *A Time for Everything*, 485.

29. In the Norwegian original, Knausgård writes: "Jeg er så glad for Linda, og jeg er så glad for barna våre," which is a clear but understated declaration of love. Yet the English translation has a different connotation with Knausgård stating: "I am so happy about Linda and I am so happy about our children" (6.1152).

30. Poul Behrendt, *Fra skyggerne af det vi ved*, 57 and 190.

200 | Notes to Chapter 3

31. Nils Gunder Hansen, Review of *Fra Skyggerne af det vi ved*, *Kristeligt Dagblad*, online. In my review of Behrendt's book, I expand and problematize his reading of Knausgård further. Cf. Claus Elholm Andersen, Review, *Scandinavian Studies*.

32. Poul Behrendt, *Fra skyggerne af det vi ved*, 113.

33. Even after adding a section on when he met Linda in Book 2, which by his own admission gave it "the light the novel needed," Book 2 became subject to criticism in Knausgård's adopted home country of Sweden. The critic Ebba Witt-Brattström faulted Knausgård for his portrayal of women in general and Linda in particular. Calling the criticism "stupid and unworthy," Knausgård attempted to counter it by invoking the ethical side of his novel: "I have described my life, and a critic says that my life is not good enough." He continued: "Witt-Brattström's criticism of *My Struggle* is about the protagonist (me) suppressing his wife (Linda), and that it is wrong. It is consequently a moralistic and ideological reading of a book, but it is unclear to me what it wants to achieve since it is me personally that it accuses." Cf. Ebba Witt-Brattström, "En kamp för det första kønet," *Dagens Nyheter*; and Knausgård, "Literaturen og det onde," 309.

34. Timothy Bewes, *The Event of Postcolonial Shame*, 44. Bewes rightly notes that the word "shame" does not appear once in Lukács's text. In a review of *The Event of Postcolonial Shame*, Hamish Dalley notes that Bewes's book "lays claim to a much broader theoretical territory than its apparent postcolonial focus would suggest" and that in making shame an effect of formal incommensurability "Bewes' theory is really applicable to literature in general, regardless of its place of origin or thematic concerns." Hamish Dalley, Review of *The Event of Postcolonial Shame*, 385.

35. Bewes further extends his notion of aesthetics and ethics to the discrepancies between form and content, idea and reality, vehicle and tenor, and subject and object. Timothy Bewes, *The Event of Postcolonial Shame*, 13, 46.

36. "The shame of being a man—is there any better reason for to write?" Gilles Deleuze asks in a quote Bewes returns to throughout his study. Where Bewes reads Deleuze's question as a question about being and writing—and very much as a confirmation of his view of shame—Kaye Mitchell sees the question in relation to gender and the shame of male writing, even naming her chapter on Knausgård "The Shame of Being a Man." Timothy Bewes, *The Event of Postcolonial Shame*, 28; and Kaye Mitchell, *Writing Shame*, 199.

37. Jon Helt Haarder, "Hvordan er en forfatter (ikke)?," 256–257.

38. Arne Melberg writes, "If Proust's project has concisely been summarized in three words—'Marcel becomes a writer'—Knausgård's answer is: 'Karl Ove stops being a writer.'" Cf. Ben Lerner, "Each Cornflake," *London Review of Books*, online; and Arne Melberg, Essä/roman," 278.

39. Knausgård seeing his father naked for the first time can also be seen as belated experience of the primal scene in a Freudian sense.

Notes to Chapter 3 | 201

40. In his second novel, *A Time for Everything*, Knausgård recounts a similar episode where the father tries to step out of his shell as he buys a boat and takes the family sailing, though embarrassing himself and Henrik (the protagonist) because he does not know how to sail.

41. Silke-Maria Weineck, *The Tragedy of Fatherhood*, 9–10.

42. Though *My Struggle* consists of six books, it also consists of nine numbered parts, with Books 1, 2, and 6 each consisting of two parts. It seems likely that the two parts in Book 1 are a remnant of the original idea to publish *My Struggle* in twelve installments, whereas the two parts in both Books 5 and 6 indicate an unexpected change of the narration.

43. This can also be seen in the context of honor and honor culture, as discussed in a great article by Per Thomas Andersen in relation to *My Struggle*. Per Thomas Andersen, "Karl Ove Knausgaard and the Transformation of Honor Culture in Late Modern Welfare States," *Journal of World Literature*, 555–568.

44. Siri Hustvedt is undoubtedly correct when claiming that *My Struggle* is "a highly feminine text" in that it is "attentive to the nuances of feeling that accompany ordinary domestic life." Siri Hustvedt, "No Competition," 89.

45. Knausgård's mother often worked late and even spent two full years away from the family home to go to school, as we hear in Books 1 and 3. Poul Behrendt, *Fra skyggerne af det vi ved*, 71.

46. Poul Behrendt, *Fra skyggerne af det vi ved*, 129; and Martin Hägglund, *This Life*, 112.

47. This tendency originated in the Modern Breakthrough of the 1870s and was central to a number of writers in the 1970s, many of whom Knausgård has read, and has reemerged in the twenty-first century.

48. Søren Kierkegaard, *The Concept of Anxiety*, 145.

49. Italics in the original. The word "reserved" in Alistair Hannay's translation is "indesluttet" in the Danish original, which means confined and contained, and points toward being introverted more than reserved.

50. "Helt grundlæggende skildrer *Min kamp* et menneske i dyb eksistentiel krise." Cf. Hans Nørkjær Franch, "Knausgårds absolutte blik og dobbeltrettede længsel," *Dansk Kirketidende*, 22.

51. Martin Hägglund, *This Life*, 112.

52. Though the father certainly fastens his gaze on Karl Ove as an all-knowing and all-seeing deity in the earlier volumes of *My Struggle*, Knausgård portrays that gaze as a gaze that only judges and condemns, but that does not see.

53. In the English translation, the phrase is translated differently in Books 5 and 6. In Book 5, the phrase is translated as "vital to have a focus," whereas in Book 6 it is translated as "fasten one's gaze." As the latter seems closer to the Norwegian original—"Det gjelder å feste blikket"—I extend that translation to both instances.

202 | Notes to Chapter 4

54. The phrase reappears in Knausgård's 2020 novel *Morgenstjernen* (*The Morning Star*), where Kathrine, a pastor, and one of the novel's numerous characters, sees it as a guiding principle for her life. Knausgård, *Morgenstjernen*, 59.

55. Martin Hägglund, *This Life*, 112.

56. Toril Moi, "Knausgaard's Ruthless Freedom," *Public Books*, online.

57. Sebastian Köhler, " 'Det gjelder å feste blikket,' " *Norsk litterær årbok*, 224. Köhler's article, in which he reads *My Struggle* in the light of René Girard's notion of triangular desire, is a revised version of an essay for a seminar on *My Struggle* that I cotaught with Hadle Oftedal Andersen at the University of Helsinki in 2013.

58. Writing in 1905, Georg Brandes asserted that Kierkegaard's attachment to Andersen was "something nearly unreadable now." Georg Brandes, quoted in Kim Andersen, " 'Genius' and the Problem of 'Livs-Anskuelse,' " 147.

59. Søren Kierkegaard, *From the Papers of One Still Living, Published against His Will*, 76.

60. More than a dogma or philosophy in a novel, a life-view, as Yi-Ping Ong asserts in a brilliant reading of *From the Papers of One Still Living*, is "the condition of the totalization demanded by the novel as a work of art," where it is "only by virtue of a life-view that a novel may succeed at representing anything at all." Yi-Ping Ong, *The Art of Being*, 60.

61. Yi-Ping Ong, *The Art of Being*, 64.

Chapter 4: Fiction and Trust

1. In Book 6, Knausgård recalls the interview via phone with the journalist Finn Bjørn Tønder: "It is the most unpleasant voice I have heard in the forty-nine years I have been alive and it was the most unpleasant conversation I have ever had" (6.923).

2. Finn Bjørn Tønder, "Familien føler sig uthengt in ny Knausgård-roman," *Bergens Tidende*.

3. Finn Bjørn Tønder, "Familien føler sig uthengt in ny Knausgård-roman," *Bergens Tidende*.

4. Two weeks later, on Saturday, October 3, 2009, the conflict escalated, when the family published an open letter in the newspaper *Klassekampen* and in which they insisted that *My Struggle* was not a novel: "It is confessional literature and non-fiction we are talking about. Judas literature. It is a book full of insinuations, untruths, erroneous personal characterizations and exposures that most clearly is a violation of Norwegian law concerning this area." They further claimed that the novel was a "dangerous mixture of reality, fantasy, and lies," impossible for ordinary readers and critics alike to separate, making it hard for those concerned, "dead or alive, to defend themselves." Cf. 14 berørte familiemedlemmer, "Klassekampen, Schiøtz og Knausgård," *Klassekampen*, 37.

Notes to Chapter 4 | 203

5. See, for instance, Janus Kramhøft, "Balladen om Karl Ove," *Politiken*; and Evan Hughes, "Karl Ove Knausgaard Became a Literary Sensation by Exposing His Every Secret," *New Republic*.

6. Bjørge Knausgård identified himself as "Uncle Gunnar" in an op-ed in the daily *VG*. At the time of publication, he was also a high school teacher and not, as we otherwise hear in *My Struggle*, an accountant. Bjørge Knausgård, "*Min kamp 6*," *VG*. See also Poul Behrendt, "Fra skyggerne af det vi ved," *Kritik*, 81.

7. In the dissertation, Vold og visjoner i sjette bind av Karl Ove Knausgårds *Min Kamp* (Violence and Visions in Book Six of Karl Ove Knausgård's *My Struggle*), Kjersti Irene Aarstein, in an intricate and controversial reading of Book 6, argues that Knausgård in Book 6 raises the suspicion that his "father Kai Åge did not die of natural courses but was killed" by no other than his own brother, Gunnar, in a parallel with Shakespeare's *Hamlet*, which Knausgård also discusses on Book 6. The accusation—that Uncle Gunnar should have killed his own brother—is, Aarstein claims, the reason he cleaned the house before Karl Ove and his brother arrived. Because of this particular reading, Aarstein's dissertation was heavily debated and criticized in the Norwegian media. Kjersti Irene Aarstein, Vold og visjoner i sjette bind av Karl Ove Knausgårds "Min Kamp," dissertation, University of Bergen, 2018, 102.

8. Sianne Ngai, *Ugly Feelings*, 28.

9. Distinguishing between "voice" and "tone," and in regard to Ngai's treatment of the latter, Lilian Munk Rösing turns to film: voice, she suggests, is equivalent to a voice-over in a film, while tone can be seen as the score. Cf. Lilian Munk Rösing, "Strindbergs vrede stemme," *K&K*, 123–124.

10. While some scholars argue for a difference between feeling and affect, Ngai uses them synonymously. For a concise account of Ngai's notion of tone, I refer to Jennifer Greiman's review in *Leviathan*, 72–74.

11. Though Ngai sees tone as a negative affect, Charles Altieri (in his otherwise positive review of the book) takes issue with this, reminding us that tone "is by its nature not an ugly feeling at all." Charles Altieri, Review of *Ugly Feelings* by Sianne Ngai, *Contemporary Literature*, 146.

12. Andrea Schou Christensen also uses Ngai's notion of tone in an analysis of *My Struggle* but distances herself from Ngai in arguing that tone is "an emotionally affective phenomenon that the text is influenced by and moves toward." Andrea Schou Christensen, "Det autentiske er en klang," 7.

13. I have previously written on Geir Angell's ideological influence on Knausgård—and vice versa. Cf. Claus Elholm Andersen, "Forfatteren og sociologen," *Edda*, 104–119.

14. In claiming that no one picked up *My Struggle* without prior knowledge, I (as I also write in chapter 2) follow Arnaud Schmitt and Stefan Kjerkegaard, "Karl Ove Knausgaard's *My Struggle*," 561.

15. That he is not interested in the attention, and did not anticipate it, is furthered, when he writes: "I wasn't anticipating the novel making any major

204 | Notes to Chapter 4

impact, and neither were the publishers, ten thousand copies were being printed to start with" (6.190).

16. Fredric Jameson, "Itemised," *London Review of Books*, online.

17. Knausgård eventually gives up the idea of calling Engdahl as his witness, as he finds placing him opposite Uncle Gunnar problematic: on the one hand, Engdahl is a "literary aristocrat" who has "something essentially elitist and superior about him," and on the other, Uncle Gunnar, who contrary to Engdahl is "coming across as the man in the street, the everyman." Knausgård speculates that people would think that it could happen to them too, that someone in their family also could expose them in the name of literature, fearing this would make him seem like "the basest of human beings, a kind of literary vampire, brutal, and without consideration, self-seeking and egoistic," which is why he—just as he is interrupted in the laundry room thinking about the trial—comes to the following conclusion: "Perhaps an aristocrat wouldn't be the right person to argue in favor of such a practice?" (6.195).

18. J. Hillis Miller, *Others*, 206.

19. Recall the definition of fictionality defined by Nielsen, Phelan, and Walsh, as "the intentional use of invented stories and scenarios" used as "a vehicle for negotiating, weighing options, and informing beliefs and opinions." Henrik Skov Nielsen, James Phelan, and Richard Walsh, "Ten Theses about Fictionality," 62.

20. Fredric Jameson, "Cosmic Neutrality," *London Review of Books*, online.

21. Catherine Gallagher, "The Rise of Fictionality," 341.

22. Julie Orlemanski refers to Gallagher's article as both "commanding and widely-cited." Julie Orlemanski, "Who Has Fiction?," 145.

23. What exactly Gallagher refers to with the term "fantasy" is "tellingly undefined," as Julie Orlemanski points out. Cf. Orlemanski, "Who Has Fiction?," 146.

24. One reason for this might be that Gallagher speculates about our "psychic investment in, or even identification with, the characters" we encounter in novels—speculation mainly based on how she believes we perceive literary characters but without any apparent evidence. She equates character with the genre of realism, as if identification only happens with the illusion of realism. In *Hooked*, Rita Felski offers a more dynamic view of fictional characters, arguing that the draw of a character "has far less to do with realism than with qualities of vividness and distinctiveness." Rita Felski, *Hooked*, 80.

25. Chapter 7 of *The Distinction of Fiction* is, for instance, titled "Signposts of Fictionality." Dorrit Cohn, *The Distinction of Fiction*, 109.

26. That these supposedly distinctive features are easily identifiable in third-person narration is also the reason why these epic narratives often have been given priority in narratology, most famously by Käte Hamburger, who does not even include first-person narrations in her section on epic narrative in *The Logic of Literature*.

Notes to Chapter 4 | 205

27. I also read Gallagher's notion of an allegory of reading as an (unintentional?) allusion to Paul de Man's influential *Allegories of Reading* from 1979, where de Man in his preface defines this as "a process of reading in which rhetoric is a disruptive intertwining of trope and persuasion"—a definition that seems to be at odds with Gallagher's historical-pragmatic approach. Cf. Paul de Man, *Allegories of Reading*, ix.

28. These instances are vastly different from the literary techniques Gallagher points to in her discussion of third-person narrations. Instead of seeing them as formal techniques, she sees surfacing in the narration thematically.

29. Anna Rühl, "'Lite og stygt, men alt som var,'" 148. Another example can be found in Book 3, where Knausgård explicitly addresses why he hardly has any memories of his mother from his childhood, and, as previously mentioned, in Book 6, where he, prior to talking with Hannah from high school, reiterates how he had made up most of the dialogue from conversations.

30. Mikhail M. Bakhtin, "Epic and the Novel," *Theory of the Novel*, 322, 324.

31. Amazon.com, September 24, 2016, and January 13, 2016. A third reviewer, an Australian by the name of David Bradford, emphasizes that his life "has been nothing like this man's [Knausgård's] life," how he not only is older and lives in a different part of the world but also neither is heterosexual nor has children. Yet he stresses how Knausgård's "thoughts resonate with me" and how he kept his daily reading "to a limited number of pages to spin out the enjoyment" (Amazon.com, July 22, 2013). The sentiment expressed in the review—that Knausgård's writing resonated with the reviewer despite obvious differences—is one that I have found when teaching *My Struggle* at various institutions.

32. Zadie Smith, "Man vs. Corpse," *New York Review of Books*, online; and Toril Moi, "Describing *My Struggle*," *The Point*, online.

33. It was on his now-defunct blog "Den store litteratyr," that Kjerkegaard referred to Stig Larsson as "Knausgård's Godfather." In an interview from as early as 2000, Knausgård uses the exact same metaphor of a "clenched fist" to describe how he felt reading Larsson initially: "When I read *Natta de mina*, I was completely knocked out. It hit me as a clenched fist in the stomach." Cf. Alf van der Hagen, *Dialoger 3*, 222.

34. Stig Larsson, "Så drabbades jag av Knausgård," *Dagens Nyheter*, online.

35. In *The Verbal Icon*, William K. Wimsatt and Monroe Beardsley name aesthetic absorption the "affective fallacy" and warn that it "begins by trying to derive the standard of criticism from the psychological effect of the poems and ends in impressionism and relativism." To them, the goal of any critical engagement with a text is an objective criticism. To that end, when readers report how "a poem or story induces in them vivid images, intense feelings, or heightened consciousness," these accounts can neither be refuted completely nor are they "possible for the objective critic to take into account" (35). Instead, the critic

206 | Notes to Chapter 4

should leave his feelings at the door, because he (and, of course, they assume the critic is a he) is "not a contributor to statistically countable reports about the poem, but a teacher or explicator of meanings" (38).

36. Rita Felski, *Hooked*, 80.

37. William Deresiewicz, "Why Has *My Struggle* Been Anointed a Literary Masterpiece?," *The Nation*; Taylor Johnston, "The Corpse as Novelistic Form," 368.

38. Poul Behrendt, "Face off," 116–117.

39. Günter Radden and Zoltán Kövecses, "Towards a Theory of Metonymy," 335–359. See also Lakoff and Johnson's short chapter on metonymy in George Lakoff and Mark Johnson, *Metaphors We Live By*, 35–40.

40. Claus Elholm Andersen, "Narratives of a Life," *Critical Quarterly*, 24–38.

41. Reading a passage from Book 5, where Knausgård reads Blanchot, Stefan Kjerkegaard and Dan Ringgaard also identify two modes of reading in *My Struggle*, one, which they refer to as "more traditional literary criticism," and the other, which they see as an example of what Felski has labeled "postcritical." Stefan Kjerkegaard and Dan Ringgaard, "Hvordan forfattere læser," 71.

42. Knausgård mentions very few female writers in *My Struggle*. One exception is the Finnish author Monika Fagerholm, whom he mentions in Book 2 during an interview, after both of them have been nominated for the Nordic Council's Literary Prize. Asked by the journalist who he thinks will win, Knausgård points to Fagerholm: "It's a very good novel," he says (2.515). Reading mainly male writers becomes a way for him to "construct his ideal-ego, the intellectual, male bohemian," Camilla Schwartz argues, where the bookcase in *My Struggle* is the place "where Knausgård attempts to measure and evaluate his own potency." Camilla Schwartz, "Forfatteren som læser," 169, 170.

43. In her dissertation on the intersection of criticism and authorship in Knausgård's writings, Ida Hummel Vøllo discusses a radio segment Knausgård did when he worked at the student radio station at the University of Bergen. Making a list of what he calls "The Ten Most Overrated Authors," he is quick to dismiss Dostoyevsky as nothing but pulp fiction. In her reading, Vøllo opens "to a satirical reading of this segment," where the segment potentially "could be a humoristic nod to his fellow members of Studentradioen." Ida Hummel Vøllo, *The Functions of Autoreception*, 105.

44. Rita Felski, *Uses of Literature*, 75.

45. Rita Felski, *Uses of Literature*, 67.

46. Dora Zhang, *Strange Likeness*, 39.

47. Georg Lukács, "Narrate or Describe?," 110–111.

48. Georg Lukács, "Narrate or Describe?," 118–119.

49. Dora Zhang, *Strange Likeness*, 37.

50. Georg Lukács, "Narrate or Describe?," 128.

51. In the aforementioned essay, "Cosmic Neutrality," Jameson provides a condensed history of the end of the novel from the eighteenth century to the

Notes to Chapter 4 | 207

earlier twentieth with Henrik Pontoppidan's *Lykke-Per* (*Lucky Per*)—a novel that Lukács also discusses in *The Theory of the Novel*. In the article "A Stranger in His Own House," I challenge Jameson's reading of Pontoppidan as well as giving an overview of Lukács's. Cf. Claus Elholm Andersen, "A Stranger in His Own House," *Scandinavian Studies*, 522–538.

52. Sharon Marcus, Heather Love, and Stephen Best, "Building a Better Description," 5.

53. Toril Moi, "Description in *My Struggle* (*Min kamp*)," unpublished MLA paper.

54. Toril Moi, "Description in *My Struggle* (*Min kamp*)," unpublished MLA paper.

55. See, for instance, Toril Moi, "Describing *My Struggle*," *The Point*, online, and "Description in *My Struggle* (*Min kamp*)," unpublished MLA paper.

56. Karl Ove Knausgård, "Dit ut der fortellingen ikke når," in *Sjelens Amerika*, 384. In an interview with James Wood, Knausgård reiterates this story: "When we were publishing that first book, my editor asked me to remove those pages because they are so different from the rest, and he was right—he is right—it would have been better, but I needed one place in the book where the writing was good. I spent weeks and weeks on that passage, and I think it's modernist, high-quality prose." Cf. James Wood and Karl Ove Knausgaard, "Writing *My Struggle*," *Paris Review*, online.

57. In September 1970, the fishing boat *Jøviktind* mysteriously disappeared off the coast of northern Norway with its crew of seven. What exactly happened has never been solved. Knausgård could also be thinking about the disappearance of the fishing boat *Tulipan* in 1977. While this resonates with his age at the time, there are numerous circumstances that differ from the description in *My Struggle*: It did not disappear in northern Norway but by the west coast. In addition, the crew only consisted of five, not seven. The mystery of *Jøviktind*'s disappearance is described by Liv-Karin Edvardsen, "Jøviktind-forliset ble aldri gransket," *Kyst og fjord*, online. A list of Norwegian shipwrecks from 1945 to 2002, can be found here: https://www.nordlys.no/nyheter/forliste-fartoy-1945-2002/s/1-79-567529.

58. Georg Lukács, "Narrate or Describe?," 112.

59. Moi hints at a similar conclusion, writing that "Zola writes in the third person, Knausgård in the first. Zola writes as an external spectator, Knausgård writes as a person fully immersed in the actions described, however insignificant they may appear." Toril Moi, "Description in *My Struggle* (*Min kamp*)," unpublished MLA paper.

60. Gérard Genette, *Narrative Discourse*, 100.

61. Gérard Genette, *Narrative Discourse*, 106.

62. Dora Zhang, *Strange Likeness*, 47.

63. While Dora Zhang undoubtedly is right when arguing scale and form are important when we determine whether something is a narrative or a descrip-

208 | Notes to Chapter 5

tion, Knausgård makes it impossible for any such distinction, scale or form aside.

64. Arnaud Schmidt and Stefan Kjerkegaard, "Karl Ove Knausgaard's *My Struggle*," a/b, 570.

Chapter 5: The Very Edge of Fiction

1. Rachel Cusk, *Kudos*, 151.

2. Katy Waldman, " 'Kudos,' the Final Volume of Rachel Cusk's 'Faye' Trilogy, Completes an Ambitious Act of Refusal," *New Yorker*, online.

3. Cusk might, of course, also be seeking to avoid a potential lawsuit, though the entire trilogy bears that out, with Faye's name only appearing once in each book.

4. Megan O'Grady, "Rachel Cusk on Her Quietly Radical New Novel, *Outline*," *Vogue*, online.

5. Megan O'Grady, "Rachel Cusk on Her Quietly Radical New Novel, *Outline*," *Vogue*, online.

6. Since this initial meeting, Heti has, among other things, interviewed Knausgård onstage—an interview that is available on YouTube.

7. Cf. Sheila Heti, "So Frank," *London Review of Books*, online.

8. Heti's interpretation is very much in line with my reading of Knausgård's rejection of fiction in chapter 1.

9. In an interview with Dave Hickey, Heti—four years before Book 1 of *My Struggle* came out in English—expressed how she, similar to Knausgård, was fed up with fiction, which might account for why she is drawn to this aspect of *My Struggle*: "Increasingly I'm less interested in writing about fictional people, because it seems so tiresome to make up a fake person and put them through the paces of a fake story. I just—I can't do it." Cf. Sheila Heti, "An Interview with Dave Hickey," *Believer*, online.

10. Jennifer Cooke, *Contemporary Feminist Life-Writing*, 65.

11. Sheila Heti, *How Should a Person Be?*, 3.

12. Dena Fehrenbackher writes about what she calls the "punchline aesthetics" in both Heti and Cusk and in which a "pointed juxtaposition of cheap tricks and aesthetic aspirations plays out." She writes: "Punchlines about personal failure have the capacity to challenge the social scripts dictating that failure—but they do not necessarily avoid reinforcing those scripts, nor do they in themselves provide a full escape from the strictures those scripts entail or the assumptions that undergird them." Dena Fehrenbackher, "Punchline Aesthetics, *Post45*," online.

13. Sheila Heti, "So Frank," *London Review of Books*, online.

14. Myra Bloom, "Messy Confessions," 180. Bloom offers an extended discussion of sex in Heti's novel.

Notes to Chapter 5 | 209

15. Myra Bloom, "Messy Confessions," 180–181. Bloom offers an extended discussion of sex in Heti's novel.

16. The paratextual information is also confirmed by a simple Google search where the *Wikipedia* entry on Margaux Williamson mentions that her "former partner is Misha Glouberman" who has "collaborated with Williamson's friend and oft-co-creator Sheila Heti." See https://en.wikipedia.org/wiki/Margaux_Williamson.

17. This designation is curiously enough missing on the grayish American paperback edition published by Picador.

18. Relating the commissioned play-turned-into-a-novel in *How Should a Person Be?* to Barthes's notion of "Wanting-to-Writing" novel, Rachel Sagner Buurma and Laura Heffernan writes that it involves a "renegotiation of the terms of novelistic realism in order to reconfigure their imagined relations to literature's commissioning and canonizing institutions. Rachel Sagner Buurma and Laura Heffernan, "Notation after 'The Reality Effect,'" *Representations*, 89.

19. Beth Blum reads *How Should a Person Be?* as one of several contemporary novels that depict how "self-help has become a transmedia industry that implicates us all—aesthetes and entrepreneurs, critics and lay readers—in its expanding cultural matrix." In addition to Heti's novel, Blum analyzes Mohsin Hamid's *How to Get Filthy Rich in Rising Asia* and Tash Aw's *Five Star Billionaire*. Cf. Beth Blum, "The Self-Help Hermeneutic," 1104.

20. Heti writes the scene like a play, starting with italicized stage directions: "Margaux, Sholem, Misha, Jon, and Sheila gather in Jon and Sholem's living room. . . . Everyone sits on the couch or on chairs except for Sholem, who stands before everyone" (287). The form reminds readers of the play Sheila has been trying to write, suggesting that she has found an alternate way of fulfilling her promise.

21. Saying that she intended to have "a rainbow coming out of a hole with a sunrise" and that she mainly used yellow and black, Margaux explains that while it was abstract at first, it "became a vagina" (293).

22. By seeing the novel as "framed at either end by the challenge of the Ugly Painting Competition," Jennifer Cooke identifies the artistic paradox that Sheila faces in the competition: "This is the audacious risk at the heart of *How Should a Person Be?*: to abandon imperatives to beauty, and make ugly art from the ugly self." Jennifer Cooke, *Contemporary Feminist Life-Writing*, 78–79.

23. Here I diverge from other scholars who have asserted that Heti's novel, like Knausgård's, is so committed to transparent realism that it lacks form. Zara Dinnen, for instance, argues that the "novel is undone by the e-mails and the scripts because they are not within the constraints of the fiction." Instead, these "attest to Sheila Heti's social life, mediation as becoming-with, and Sheila Heti's work as author." Rachel Sykes agrees, seeing Heti's use of "emails, transcripts, and the minutes, even boring, details of her 'real' social life," as disclosures that "often seem to have no point; they do little to advance the story or enable." Zara

210 | Notes to Chapter 5

Dinnen, *The Digital Banal*, 86, 90; Rachel Sykes, "'Who Gets to Speak and Why,'" 162; and James Wood, "True Lives," *New Yorker*, online.

24. "As the transcripts slowly come to form a novel, Sheila's friend Margaux ceases to be just a character in the novel and becomes a collaborator in its writing," Buurma and Heffernan suggest. Cf. Rachel Sagner Buurma and Laura Heffernan, "Notation after 'The Reality Effect,'" *Representations*, 92.

25. Jennifer Cooke, *Contemporary Feminist Life-Writing*, 74.

26. Lee Konstantinou writes: "And *How Should a Person Be?* presents itself as the very play . . . that Sheila struggled to complete, a play whose content is imaged to be the unvarnished audio recordings, emails, and other affective records of body-to-body contact (friendship, sex, and so on). That is, Heti's novel constructs a fantasy that the novel might become a self-justifying or self-vouchsafing *document*, a document that gives us not the reality effect but rather reality." Lee Konstantinou, "Neorealist Fiction," 119

27. Alexandra Kingston-Reese, *Contemporary Novels*, 113, 117.

28. James Wood, "True Lives," *New Yorker*, online.

29. Paul Crosthwaite reads the titular question as a question of how the artwork should be and answers by relating it to capitalism and the market: "first, the artwork should be *desired*—not really an artwork at all, that is, but a pure commodity given over to the satisfaction of consumer demand; or second, that it should be *admired*, an object of veneration by virtue of its originality and aesthetic importance. The third answer is more distinctive: that the artwork should be *used* or at least *usable*." Paul Crosthwaite, *The Market Logics of Contemporary Fiction*, 248.

30. Heidi Julavits. "Choose Your Own Rachel Cusk," *The Cut*, online.

31. In an unpublished conference paper, Ricarda Menn writes: "However, the narrator shares some conspicuous details with author Rachel Cusk: both are female, middle-aged novelists, divorced mothers. Whereas Cusk is mother to two daughters, Faye has two sons. Moreover, certain events can be linked to public appearances of Cusk—most notably a visit to a literary festival in *Kudos*, whose description directly points to LitCologne, which Cusk attended in 2016. Yet, the narrative leaves the name of the city unmentioned." Cf. Ricarda Menn, "Reading Serial Autofictions—Knausgård and Cusk," unpublished conference paper.

32. By setting *Outline* in Athens, Cusk also, as Karen Valihora rightly observes, invokes the city's mythical connotations. She writes: "Cusk's engagement with the project and form of the novel begins with a return to its beginnings. If the trilogy's interconnected, dream-like stories, as well as its repetitions, transitions, and echoes, recall Ovid's series of myths in the *Metamorphoses*, its trajectory suggests the fixed arc of Homeric epic." Karen Valihora, "She Got Up and Went Away," 22.

33. Pieter Vermeulen also points to this instance but sees the banker's question as a "belated emergence . . . to full subjecthood." Pieter Vermeulen, "Against Premature Articulation," 90.

Notes to Chapter 5 | 211

34. Fredric Jameson is one who refers to the economy that led up to the financial crisis in 2008 as fictional.

35. Indeed, in addition to Cusk, the figure of the billionaire is "everywhere in contemporary culture and has taken a pride of place in popular literature, too," Mark McGurl notes in *Everything and Less*. He also points out how the "billionaire stands as the last redoubt of heroic individual agency in a world otherwise given over to abstract systems and bureaucracies." Cf. Mark McGurl, *Everything and Less*, 8, 26.

36. What Faye asks her students to do also seems parallel to what Knausgård attempts to do in the first two volumes of his *Seasonal Quartet* with their short phenomenological descriptions of the world that surrounds him, as he introduces that world to his newly born daughter.

37. Interestingly, the story of Jane shares numerous similarities with Cusk's novel *Second Place*, published in 2021, after the *Outline* Trilogy.

38. Victor Shklovsky, "Art as Technique," 720.

39. With that, I believe Pieter Vermeulen is wrong when suggesting that the novel is characterized by free indirect discourse. Except in a very few, special cases, which Nielsen has labeled "impersonal voice in first-person narrative," I reject the notion that free indirect discourse can be applied to a first-person narrator. When Heti, as I showed earlier, turns to something closer to free indirect discourse, it is also a departure from the first-person narration that otherwise characterizes her novel. Cf. Pieter Vermeulen, "Against Premature Articulation," 89; and Henrik Skov Nielsen, "The Impersonal Voice in First-Person Narrative," 136.

40. Karen Valihora, "She Got Up and Went Away," 23.

41. Merve Emre, "Of Note," *Harper's Magazine*, online.

42. As Josie Mitchell notes on Cusk, "The manner in which you describe others reveals a lot about yourself: your values, desires, epistemology." Josie Mitchell, "To Endure the Void," *Los Angeles Review of Books*, online.

43. Rachel Cusk, "A Man in Love by Karl Ove Knausgaard—Review," *The Guardian*, online.

44. Rachel Cusk, "A Man in Love by Karl Ove Knausgaard—Review," *The Guardian*, online.

45. In "The Autobiographical Pact," Philippe Lejeune reminds us that if the autobiographical pact is not stated positively (as in fiction), the reader will attempt to establish resemblances, despite the author." Philippe Lejeune, *On Autobiography*, 14.

46. Ben Lerner, "The Golden Vanity," *New Yorker*, online. To complicate matters, parts of "The Golden Vanity" have, as Juliet Lapidos points out, been published in an essay by Lerner in *Harper's*. Juliet Lapidos, "When Are Metafictional Games a Mask for Laziness," *New Republic*, online; and Ben Lerner, "Damage Control," *Harper's Magazine*, online.

47. Marta Figlerowicz, "The Novel of Infinite Storage," *Poetics Today*, 206.

212 | Notes to Chapter 5

48. This is also evident in "The Golden Vanity," in which the protagonist, only referred to as "the author," hears his name called out at a coffee shop: "Someone said his name because his coffee was ready" (61). The announcement leads to an interest in the author's proper name, which we are never told.

49. In "The Golden Vanity," the name of Lerner's wife Ari (Ariana Mangual) appears when he takes Hannah on a weekend with his parents, brother, and sister-in-law. The author late at night sits by the beach and his brother asks: "Where is Ari?" to which the author answers: "She isn't in this story" (77).

50. Pieter Vermeulen, "How Should a Person Be (Transpersonal)?," 666.

51. Alison Gibbons, "Metamodernism, the Anthropocene, and the Resurgence of Historicity," *Critique*, online.

52. This standard, legal disclaimer can also be found in Cusk's *Outline*, but it is noticeably missing in the FSG edition of *My Struggle*.

53. In the acknowledgments, Lerner informs us that he first encountered the text of his epigraph in Giorgio Agamben's *The Coming Community* and that it is "typically attributed to Walter Benjamin." To be sure, the epigraph does appear word for word in Agamben's *The Coming Community*, where it is also attributed to Benjamin, though Agamben does not relay that the quote is from one of Benjamin's so-called "think-images." Prior to quoting Benjamin, Agamben explains that the aphorism is based on a "well-known parable about the Kingdom of the Messiah" that Benjamin one evening told Ernst Bloch, who transcribed it in *Traces* (*Spuren*) from 1930. In Bloch's version, the story is about how it "is sufficient to displace this cup or this bush or this stone just a little, and thus everything." Cf. Giorgio Agamben's *The Coming Community*, 52.

54. In the pages of *10:04* leading up to the short story, Ben, who has an "asymptomatic and potentially aneurysmal dilation" in his "aortic root" (4), recalls how he initially started writing "The Golden Vanity" and provides a key of sorts for its characters: "The story would involve a series of transpositions: I would shift my medical problems to another part of the body . . . I would change names: Alex would become Liza, which she'd told me once had been her mother's second choice; Alena would become Hannah; Sharon I'd change to Mary; Jon to Josh; . . . the protagonist—a version of myself; I'd call him 'the author' " (55).

55. In *Finance Fictions*, Arne De Boever argues that *10:04* can be read as a contemporary novelist's response to the transcendental question that animates this book: the conditions of possibility for a financial realism today." Arne De Boever, *Finance Fictions*, 153.

56. Fredric Jameson, "Cosmic Neutrality," *London Review of Books*, online.

57. Ben Lerner, *10:04*, 3.

58. As Ralph Clare writes: "As such, the past, as both individual memory and collective history, is imbued with a virtual affective presence that at times permeates the

Notes to Chapter 5 | 213

novel's present in true Bergsonian fashion." Ralph Clare, "Freedom and Formlessness," *Open Library of Humanities*, online.

59. Asking how "Lerner's narrator makes good on his promise to project himself into different futures," Leonid Bilmes also turns to the novel's formal aspect and how "within this autofictional account of both real and imagined memories, the past is brought back to life through the narrator's play with tense and his reflections on the act of self-narration itself." Leonid Bilmes, " 'An Actual Present Alive with Multiple Futures,' " *Textual Practice*, 1082.

60. See, for instance, Andreas Malm's *The Progress of This Storm*.

61. Ben Lerner, "Each Cornflake," *London Review of Books*, online.

62. Ben Lerner, "Each Cornflake," *London Review of Books*, online.

63. Ben Lerner, "Each Cornflake," *London Review of Books*, online.

64. Friedrich Schlegel famously defined irony as permanent parabasis—a definition Paul de Man expands in his reading of both Schlegel and Kierkegaard in "The Concept of Irony," where he defines irony as "the permanent parabasis of the allegory of the tropes." Paul de Man, "The Concept of Irony," 179.

65. Lerner's wanting to seem in control of his narrative is also apparent when he shortly thereafter describes his ability to intuit Alex's grief after her friend Candice had died, and the protagonist would see her "halfway to the kitchen to put on the water for her tea before she remembered that Candice was dead" (43). And, as if he realizes that he has committed a narratological sin by narrating Alex's thoughts, he adds in parenthesis: "I don't know how I knew she briefly didn't know, or how I could tell when the fact returned to her consciousness" (43).

66. Fredric Jameson, "The Aesthetics of Singularity," *New Left Review*, 118. Paul Crosthwaite argues that *10:04* can be read as "exhibiting what a novel that simultaneously cannot and must conform to the neoliberal logic of the market might look like." Cf. Paul Crosthwaite, *The Market Logics of Contemporary Fiction*, 194.

67. Alison Gibbons considers *10:04* a "decisively metamodernist text," where metamodernism is seen as "a designation for the structure of feeling—emerging and coagulating throughout the first decade of the twenty-first century." Lerner falls under the auspice of metamodernism, she argues, because "its significance rests on the way it exemplifies the figuration of time in response to life in the Anthropocene as well as in the cultural context of metamodernism more broadly." Alison Gibbons, "Metamodernism, the Anthropocene, and the Resurgence of Historicity," *Critique*, online.

68. Speaking of an affective turn in contemporary autofiction, Gibbons defines metamodern affect as situational and experiential: "it is ironic yet sincere, skeptical yet heartfelt, solipsistic yet desiring of connection." Alison Gibbons, "Contemporary Autofiction and Metamodern Affect," 120.

214 | Notes to Afterword

69. As discussed in the previous chapter, both Rita Felski and Toril Moi have recently made the case such engagement is not at odds with a scholarly approach but should instead be integrated into our readings of the texts in question.

Afterword: After Autofiction

1. This includes two collections of essays, books on Edvard Munch and on Anselm Kiefer, and the so-called *Seasons Quartet*—four books, dedicated to his youngest daughter—that some critics have seen as a continuation of *My Struggle*.

2. The novel, as Brandon Taylor notes in the *New Yorker*, marks a "return to the more purely fictional mode of his previous novels." Brandon Taylor, "Karl Ove Knausgaard's Haunting New Novel," *New Yorker*, online.

3. In *The Third Realm* (2022), we meet a celebrity artist, an architect, who doubts his own ability to create anything new, precisely like Knausgård in *My Struggle* wondering if he can write another novel: "I couldn't do it. Nothing had changed. It was the thought that I couldn't that had made it so. And it was I that had let it grow. The problem was the doubt, not what it was doubting," the architect, Helge, is thinking, as he is about to being a new project. And ironically that new project is a center for Axel Sandemose—one of Knausgård's literary heroes and famous for penning the infamous Law of Jante: "Sandemose," Helge reflects in a phrase that could easily have been attributed to the Knausgård of *My Struggle*, "that was the Law of Jante and epitome of Scandinavian culture. But it was also the shadows of the past and the human condition." Karl Ove Knausgård, *Det tredje riket*, 116.

4. Karl Ove Knausgård, "Why the Novel Matters," *New Statesman*, online.

5. Rachel Cusk, *Second Place*, 183.

6. Sheila Heti, *Pure Colour*, 4–5.

7. One noticeable exception to this might be Annie Ernaux, who was hailed as one of the early autofictional writers in the 1980s and still, as her popularity outside France has grown in the wake her winning the 2022 Nobel Prize in Literature, continues to write autofiction.

8. Tore Renberg, "I røykeavdelingen på havets bunn," *Samtiden*, 24.

9. Also, in an interview with the Norwegian public TV broadcast *NRK*, recorded prior to the publication of Book 1 of *My Struggle*, Knausgård emphasized that what he had written is a novel, when he—as I noted in chapter 1—admits that he made up the second visit to the chapel to see the body of his deceased father because he needed it "in terms of the novel's composition." With this admission *prior* to the publication of Book 1, Knausgård confirms that writing a novel was an all-important factor in his writing process.

10. Tope Folarin, "Can a Black Novelist Write Autofiction?," *New Republic*, online.

Notes to Afterword | 215

11. One of the characters in the novel is called Yngve—the name of Knausgård's brother in *My Struggle*—suggesting that Taylor's iteration of autofiction would not have been possible without him. In a short exchange with me on Twitter, Brandon Taylor confirmed that using Yngve as a name in the novel is indeed an homage to Knausgård.

Bibliography

14 berørte familiemedlemmer. "Klassekampen, Schiøtz og Knausgård." *Klassekampen*, October 3, 2009.

Aarstein, Kjersti Irene. "Vold og visjoner i sjette bind av Karl Ove Knausgårds *Min Kamp*." Unpublished dissertation, University of Bergen, 2018.

Abrahamsen, Morten. "En plass for alt." *VG*, November 6, 2009.

Abrams, M. H. *A Glossary of Literary Terms*, 6th ed. New York: Harcourt Brace, 1993.

Adrian, Kim. *Dear Knausgaard*. New York: Fiction Advocate, 2020.

Adrian, Kim. "Karl Ove Knausgaard's Feats of Shame and Openess." *Lithub*, September 2019. https://lithub.com/karl-ove-knausgaards-feats-of-shame-and-openness/.

Agamben, Giorgio. *The Coming Community*. Minneapolis: University of Minnesota Press, 1993.

Agamben, Giorgio. *Remnants of Auschwitz: The Witness and the Archive*. New York: Zone Books, 1999.

Allamand, Carole. "The Autobiographical Pact, Forty-Five Years Later." *European Journal of Life Writing* 7 (2018): 51–55.

Altieri, Charles. Review of *Ugly Feelings* by Sianne Ngai. *Contemporary Literature* 47, no. 1 (Spring 2006): 141–147.

American Psychological Association. *Dictionary of Psychology*. https://dictionary.apa.org/shame.

Andersen, Carsten. "Norsk wonder boy er våd anmelderdrøm." *Politiken*, January 14, 2010. https://politiken.dk/kultur/boger/boganmeldelser/skonlitteratur_boger/art5013159/Norsk-wonder-boy-er-en-v%C3%A5d-anmelderdr%C3%B8m.

Andersen, Claus Elholm. "Den nordiske illusion: Findes der en nordisk litteraturhistorie?" Unpublished talk held at the symposium Nordiske stemmer: Nordische Identität, Goethe University Frankfurt, November 2012.

Andersen, Claus Elholm. "Die Singularität der immerwährenden Gegenwart: Autofiktion nach der Finanzkrise und der Fall Karl Ove Knausgårds." *WestEnd: Neue Zeitschrift für Sozialforschung*, edited by Honneth Axel, Sidonia Blättler, and Johannes Voelz, no. 1 (2022): 83–98.

218 | Bibliography

Andersen, Claus Elholm. "Forfatteren og sociologien—om Karl Ove Knausgård og Geir Angell Øygarden." *Edda* 101, no. 2 (2014): 104–119.

Andersen, Claus Elholm. "Narratives of a Life: Karl Ove Knausgård's *My Struggle* as a Literary Centaur. *Critical Quarterly* 60, no. 2 (2018): 24–38.

Andersen, Claus Elholm. "*På vakt skal man være*": Om litterariteten i Karl Ove Knausgård's "Min kamp." Nordica Helsingiensia, no. 39. Helsinki: University of Helsinki, 2015.

Andersen, Claus Elholm. Review of *Fra skyggerne af de vi ved*, by Poul Behrendt. *Scandinavian Studies* 92, no. 2 (2020): 256–261.

Andersen, Claus Elholm, ed. *Så tæt på livet som muligt: Perspektiver på Karl Ove Knausgårds "Min kamp."* Hellerup: Forlaget Spring, 2017.

Andersen, Claus Elholm. "Som far, så søn: Om fædre, sønner og litterær indflydelse i Karl Oe Knausgårds *Min Kamp*." *Norsk litterær årbok* (2013): 160–184.

Andersen, Claus Elholm. "A Stranger in His Own House: Nothingness and Alienation in Henrik Pontoppidan's *Lucky Per*." *Scandinavian Studies* 92, no. 4 (2020): 521–537.

Andersen, Kim. "'Genius' and the Problem of 'Livs-Anskuelse': Kierkegaard Reading Andersen." In *H.C. Andersen: Old Problems and New Readings*, edited by Steven P. Sondrup, 145–160. Odense, DK/Provo, UT: University Press of Southern Denmark/Brigham Young University Press, 2003.

Andersen, Per Thomas. "Karl Ove Knausgaard and the Transformation of Honor Culture in Late Modern Welfare States." *Journal of World Literature* 1, no. 4 (2016): 555–568.

Anderson, Linda. *Autobiography*. Abingdon, UK: Routledge, 2001.

Arc, Jonathan. "What Kind of History Does a Theory of the Novel Require?" *Novel: A Forum on Fiction* 42, no. 2 (2009): 190–195.

Attridge, David. *Reading and Responsibility: Deconstruction's Traces*. Edinburgh: Edinburgh University Press, 2010.

Aubry, Timothy, and Florence Dore. "Introduction: Formalism Unbound." *Post45*, no. 5, part 1. https://post45.org/2020/12/aubry-dore-introduction/#footnote_1_13233.

Bakhtin, Mikhail M. "Epic and the Novel." In *Theory of the Novel: A Critical Approach*, edited by Michael McKeon. Baltimore, MD: Johns Hopkins University Press, 2000.

Bakhtin, Mikhail M. *The Dialogical Imagination: Four Essays*. Austin: University of Texas Press, 1981.

Barren, Jesse. "Completely without Dignity: An Interview with Karl Ove Knausgaard." *Paris Review*, December 26, 2013. http://www.theparisreview.org/blog/2013/12/26/completely-without-dignity-an-interview-with-karl-ove-knausgaard/.

Barthes, Roland. "The Death of the Author." In *Image—Music—Text*, 142–148. New York: Hill & Wang, 1977.

Bibliography | 219

Barthes, Roland. "The Reality Effect." In *The Rustle of Language*, edited by François Wahl, 141–148. Berkeley: University of California Press, 1989.

Behrendt, Poul. "Autonarration som skandinavisk novum." *Spring*, nos. 31–32 (2011): 294–335.

Behrendt, Poul. *Dobbeltkontrakten: En æstetisk nydannelse.* Copenhagen: Gyldendal, 2006.

Behrendt, Poul. "Face Off: Skam som plotskaber i af *Min kamp.*" In *Så tæt på livet som muligt: Perspektiver på Karl Ove Knausgårds "Min kamp,"* edited by Claus Elholm Andersen, 113–147. Hellerup: Forlaget Spring, 2017.

Behrendt, Poul. *Fra skyggerne af det vi ved: Kunst som virkelighedsproduktion.* Copenhagen: Rosinate, 2019.

Behrendt, Poul. "Fra skyggerne af det vi ved: Ved selvfremstillingens grænse." *Kritik*, no. 213 (2015): 69–94.

Behrendt, Poul. *Midnatssolen på Dramaten: Dobbeltkontraten 2020 hos Karl Ove Knausgård.* Hellerup: Forlaget Spring, 2021.

Behrendt, Poul, and Mads Bunch. *Selvfortalt: Autofiktioner på tværs.* Copenhagen: Dansklærerforeningens Forlag, 2015.

Bender, Courtney, Jeremy Biles, Liane Carlson, Joshua Dubler et al. *The Abyss or Life Is Simple: Reading Knausgaard Writing Religion.* Chicago: University of Chicago Press, 2022.

Benjamin, Walter. "The Storyteller." In *Theory of the Novel: A Critical Approach*, edited by Michael McKeon. Baltimore, MD: Johns Hopkins University Press, 2000.

Best, Stephen, and Sharon Marcus. "Surface Reading: An Introduction." *Representations* 108, no. 1 (Fall 2009): 1–21.

Bewes, Timothy. *The Event of Postcolonial Shame.* Princeton: Princeton University Press, 2011.

Bewes Timothy. "Free Indirect." Political Concepts. https://www.politicalconcepts.org/free-indirect-timothy-bewes/.

Bewes, Timothy. *Free Indirect: The Novel in a Postfictional Age.* New York: Columbia University Press, 2022.

Bewes, Timothy. "Reading with the Grain: A New World in Literary Criticism." *differences* 21, no. 3 (2010): 1–33.

Bewes, Timothy. "Recent Experiments in American Fiction." *Novel: A Forum on Fiction* 50, no. 3 (2017): 351–359.

Bewes, Timothy. "What Does It Mean to Write Fiction? What Does Fiction Refer To?" *Amerikastudien / American Studies* 64, no. 4 (2019): 533–548.

Biles, Jeremy. "Incidentals (When the Slugs Come) (In the Cut)." In *The Abyss or Life Is Simple: Reading Knausgaard Writing Religion*, by Courtney Bender, Jeremy Biles, Liane Carlson, Joshua Dubler et al., 127–168. Chicago: University of Chicago Press, 2022.

220 | Bibliography

Bilmes, Leonid. "'An Actual Present Alive with Multiple Futures': Narrative, Memory and Time in Ben Lerner's *10:04*." *Textual Practice* 34, no. 7 (2020): 1081–1120.

Bloom, Myra. "Messy Confessions: Sheila Heti's *How Should a Person Be?*" In *Avant Canada: Poets, Prophets, Revolutionaries*. Waterloo, ON: Wilfred Laurier University Press, 2019.

Bloom, Myra. "Sources of the Self(ie): An Introduction to the Study of Autofiction in English." *ESC: English Studies in Canada* 45, no. 1 (2019): 1–18.

Blum, Beth. "The Self-Help Hermeneutic: Its Global History and Literary Future." *Publication of the Modern Language Association* 133, no. 5 (2018): 1099–1117.

Bokprogrammet: Stille før stormen: Et møte med Karl Ove Knausgård. NRK, January 12, 2010. https://tv.nrk.no/serie/bokprogrammet/2010/MKTF01000910.

Bokprogrammet: Store norske. NRK, October 6, 2009. https://tv.nrk.no/serie/bokprogrammet/2009/OATF02001609.

Børdahl, Espen. "'Livet er en gamp, sa kjerringa, hun kunne ikke si k': Om tittelens betydning og funksjon i Karl Ove Knausgårds *Min kamp*." In *Så tæt på livet som muligt: Perspektiver på Karl Ove Knausgårds "Min kamp,"* edited by Claus Elholm Andersen, 38–56. Hellerup: Forlaget Spring, 2017.

Brooks, Cleanth. *The Well-Wrought Urn: Studies in the Structure of Poetry*. New York: Harcourt, 1947.

Brooks, Peter. *Reading for the Plot: Design and Intention in Narrative*. Cambridge, MA: Harvard University Press, 1984.

Bruss, Elizabeth W. *Autobiographical Acts: The Changing Situation of a Literary Genre*. Baltimore, MD: Johns Hopkins University Press, 1976.

Buchanan, Ian. *A Dictionary of Critical Theory*. 2nd ed. Oxford: Oxford University Press, 2018.

Buckley, Kyle. "'The Novel Is Like a Room'—an Interview with Karl Ove Knausgaard." *Hazlitt*, November 4, 2014. https://hazlitt.net/feature/novel-room-interview-karl-ove-knausgaard.

Bugge, David. "Mennesket: Kain—Hitler—Knausgård." In *Knausgård i syv sind*, edited by David Bugge, Søren R. Fauth, and Ole Morsing, 27–54. Copenhagen: Eksistens, 2016.

Burke, Sean. *Authorship from Plato to the Postmodern*. Edinburgh: Edinburgh University Press, 1995.

Butler, Judith. *Gender Trouble*. New York: Routledge, 2008. Originally published 1990.

Buurma, Rachel Sagner, and Laura Heffernan. "Notation after 'The Reality Effect': Remaking Reference with Roland Barthes and Sheila Heti." *Representations* 125, no. 1 (2014): 80–102.

Carlson, Liane. "Aesthetics of an Abused Child." In *The Abyss or Life Is Simple: Reading Knausgaard Writing Religion*, by Courtney Bender, Jeremy Biles, Liane Carlson, Joshua Dubler et al., 57–76. Chicago: University of Chicago Press, 2022.

Bibliography | 221

Cercas, Javier. *The Blind Spot: An Essay on the Novel*. London: MacLehose Press, 2018.

Chihaya, Sarah. "*My Struggle*, Vol. 2." *Post45: Slow Burn*, 2016. https://post45.org/2016/07/my-struggle-vol-2-sarah-chihaya-july-5-guest-post/.

Chihaya, Sarah. "The Sight of Life." *Post45*, no. 5: "Formalism Unbound, Part 1." https://post45.org/2020/12/chihaya-the-sight-of-life/.

Christensen, Andrea Schou. " 'Det autentiske er en klang'—dødens eksitentielle og æstetiske tonalitet i Karl Ove Knausgårds *Min kamp*." *Aktualitet* 10 (2016): 1–32.

Clare, Ralph. "Freedom and Formlessness: Ben Lerner's *10:04* and the Affective Historical Present." *Open Library of Humanities* 2, no. 4. https://olh.openlibhums.org/articles/10.16995/olh.336/.

Clark, Alex. "Drawn from Life: Why Have Novelists Stopped Making Things Up?" *The Guardian*, June 23, 2018. https://www.theguardian.com/books/2018/jun/23/drawn-from-life-why-have-novelists-stopped-making-things-up.

Cohn, Dorrit. *The Distinction of Fiction*. Baltimore, MD: Johns Hopkins University Press, 1999.

Cohn, Dorrit. *Transparent Minds: Narrative Modes for Presenting Consciousness in Fiction*. Princeton, NJ: Princeton University Press, 1978.

Cooke, Jennifer. *Contemporary Feminist Life-Writing: The New Audacity*. Cambridge: Cambridge University Press, 2020.

Crosthwaite, Paul. *The Market Logics of Contemporary Fiction*. Cambridge: Cambridge University Press, 2019.

Culler, Jonathan. "The Closeness of Close Reading." *ADE Bulletin*, no. 149 (2010): 20–25.

Culler, Jonathan. *On Deconstruction: Theory of Criticism after Structuralism*. Ithaca, NY: Cornell University Press, 1982.

Currie, Mark. "Pareidolia and Struggle." Unpublished conference paper at the symposium The Cult in Context: Historical and Comparative Perspectives on Karl Ove Knausgaard, Goethe-Universität Frankfurt, 2017.

Cusk, Rachel. *Coventry*. New York: Farrar, Straus and Giroux, 2019.

Cusk, Rachel. *Kudos*. New York: Farrar, Straus and Giroux, 2018.

Cusk, Rachel. "A Man in Love by Karl Ove Knausgaard—Review." *The Guardian*, April 12, 2013. https://www.theguardian.com/books/2013/apr/12/man-in-love-knausgaard-review.

Cusk, Rachel. *Outline*. New York: Picador, 2016.

Cusk, Rachel. *Second Place*. New York: Farrar, Straus and Giroux, 2021.

Cusk, Rachel. *Transit*. New York: Picador, 2016.

Dalley, Hamish. Review of *The Event of Postcolonial Shame*, by Timothy Bewes. *MFS: Modern Fiction Studies* 58, no. 2 (Summer 2012): 386–388.

Dauenhauer, Bernard. "Paul Ricoeur." *Stanford Encyclopedia of Philosophy*. https://plato.stanford.edu/entries/ricoeur/.

222 | Bibliography

De Boever, Arne. *Finance Fictions: Realism and Psychosis in a Time of Economic Crisis*. New York: Fordham University Press, 2018.

de Man, Paul. "Autobiography as De-facement." In *The Rhetoric of Romanticism*, 67–82. New York: Columbia University Press, 1984.

de Man, Paul. "The Concept of Irony." In *Aesthetic Ideology*, 163–184. Minneapolis: University of Minnesota Press, 1996.

de Man, Paul. "Excuses (*Confessions*)." In *Allegories of Reading*, 278–302. New Haven, CT: Yale University Press, 1979.

de Man, Paul. "The Rhetoric of Temporality." In *Blindness and Insight*, 2nd ed., 187–228. Methuen, UK: Routledge, 1983.

de Man, Paul. "Semiology and Rhetoric." In *Allegories of Reading*, 3–19. New Haven, CT: Yale University Press, 1979.

Deresiewicz, William. "Why Has *My Struggle* Been Anointed a Literary Masterpiece?" *The Nation*, May 13, 2014. https://www.thenation.com/article/why-has-my-struggle-been-anointed-literary-masterpiece/.

Derrida, Jacques. *Acts of Literature*. Edited by Derek Attridge. New York: Routledge, 1992.

Dinnen, Zara. *The Digital Banal: New Media and American Literature and Culture*. New York: Columbia University Press, 2018.

Dix, Hywel. "Autofiction: The Forgotten Face of French Theory." *Word and Text* 8 (2017): 69–85.

Dix, Hywel, ed. *Autofiction in English*. Palgrave Studies in Life Writing. London: Palgrave Macmillan, 2018.

Eakin, Paul John. *How Our Lives Become Stories: Making Selves*. Ithaca, NY: Cornell University Press, 1999.

Eakin, Paul John. *Touching the World: Reference in Autobiography*. Princeton, NJ: Princeton University Press, 1992.

Edmiston, William F. "Focalization and the First-Person Narrator: A Revision of the Theory." *Poetics Today* 10, no. 4 (1989): 729–744.

Edvardsen, Liv-Karin. "Jøviktind-forliset ble aldri gransket." *Kyst og fjord*, July 31, 2020. https://www.kystogfjord.no/nyheter/forsiden/Joeviktind-forliset-ble-aldri-gransket.

Effe, Alexandra, and Hannie Lawlor. *The Autofictional: Approaches, Affordances, Form*. Palgrave Studies in Life Writing. London: Palgrave Macmillan, 2022.

Egeland, Marianne. "Forfatteren, frirommet og virkelighetslitteraturen." In *Så tæt på livet som muligt: Perspektiver på Karl Ove Knausgårds "Min kamp,"* edited by Claus Elholm Andersen, 222–243. Hellerup: Forlaget Spring, 2017.

Egeland, Marianne. "Recognition and Authenticity in Life Writing." *International Journal of the Book* 13, no. 4 (2015): 11–22.

Egendal, Helle. "Multilingual Autofiction: Mobilizing Language(s)?" In *The Autofictional: Approaches, Affordances, Form*, edited by Alexandra Effe and Hannie Lawlor, 141–159. Palgrave Studies in Life Writing. London: Palgrave Macmillan, 2022.

Emre, Merve. "Of Note: Rachel Cusk's Unforgiving Eye." *Harper's Magazine*, June 2018. https://harpers.org/archive/2018/06/of-note/.

Eugenides, Jeffrey. "Karl Ove Knausgaard's *My Struggle*: Book 4." *New York Times*, April 23, 2015.

Farsethås, Ane. *Herfra til virkeligheten: Lesninger i 00-tallets litteratur*. Oslo: Cappelen Damm, 2012.

Fehrenbackher, Dena. "Punchline Aesthetics: Recuperated Failure in the Novels of Ben Lerner and Sheila Heti." *Post45*, 2021. https://post45.org/2021/07/punchline-aesthetics/.

Felski, Rita. *Hooked: Art and Attachment*. Chicago: University of Chicago Press, 2020.

Felski, Rita. "Identifying with Characters." In *Character: Three Inquiries in Literary Studies*, edited by Amanda Anderson, Rita Relski, and Toril Moi, 77–126. Chicago: University of Chicago Press, 2019.

Felski, Rita. *The Limits of Critique*. Chicago: University of Chicago Press, 2015.

Felski, Rita. *Uses of Literature*. Malden, MA: Blackwell, 2008.

Ferguson, Sam. *Diaries Real and Fictional in Twentieth-Century French Literature*. Oxford: Oxford University Press, 2018.

Ferreira-Meyers, Karen. "Does Autofiction Belong to French or Francophone Authors and Readers Only? In *Autofiction in English*, edited by Hywel Dix, 27–48. Palgrave Studies in Life Writing. London: Palgrave Macmillan, 2018.

Ferreira-Meyers, Karen, and Bontle Tau. "Visual Autofiction: A Strategy for Cultural Inclusion." In *The Autofictional: Approaches, Affordances, Form*, edited by Alexandra Effe and Hannie Lawlor, 161–182. Palgrave Studies in Life Writing. London: Palgrave Macmillan, 2022.

Figlerowicz, Marta. "The Novel of Infinite Storage." *Poetics Today* 39, no. 1 (2018): 201–219.

Fischelov, David. *Metaphors of Genre: The Role of Analogies in Genre Theory*. University Park: Pennsylvania State University Press, 1993.

Fludernik, Monika. "The Fiction of the Rise of Fictionality." *Poetics Today* 39, no. 1 (2018): 67–92.

Folarin, Tope. "Can a Black Novelist Write Autofiction?" *New Republic*, October 27, 2020. https://newrepublic.com/article/159951/can-black-novelist-write-autofiction.

Garff, Joakim. *SAK: Søren Aabye Kierkegaard: En biografi*. Copenhagen: Gads Forlag, 2000.

Gallagher, Catherine. "The Rise of Fictionality." In *The Novel*, vol. 1, edited by Franco Moretti, 336–363. Princeton, NJ: Princeton University Press, 2006.

Genette, Gérard. *Fiction and Diction*. Ithaca, NY: Cornell University Press, 1993.

Genette, Gérard. *Narrative Discourse: An Essay in Method*. Ithaca, NY: Cornell University Press, 1980.

Gerring, Richard J. *Experiencing Narrative Worlds*. New Haven, CT: Yale University Press, 1993.

224 | Bibliography

Gibbons, Alison. "A Cognitive Model of Reading Autofiction." *English Studies* 103, no. 3 (2022): 471–493.

Gibbons, Alison. "Contemporary Autofiction and Metamodern Affect." In *Metamodernism: Historicity, Affect, and Depth after Postmodernism*, edited by Robin van den Akker, Alison Gibbons, and Timotheus Vermeulen, 117–130. Lanham, MD: Rowman & Littlefield, 2017.

Gibbons Alison. "Metamodernism, the Anthropocene, and the Resurgence of Historicity: Ben Lerner's *10:04* and 'The Utopian Glimmer of Fiction.'" *Critique: Studies in Contemporary Fiction* (2020). https://doi.org/10.1080/00111619.2020.1784828.

Gibbons, Alison, Timotheus Vermeulen, and Robin van den Akker. "Reality Beckons: Metamodernist Depthiness beyond Panfictionality." In *Fact and Fiction in Contemporary Narratives*, edited by Jan Alber and Alice Bell, 52–69. London: Routledge, 2021.

Gjerlevsen, Simona Zetterberg. "A Novel History of Fictionality." *Narrative* 24, no. 2 (2016): 174–189.

Greenaway, Peter. *Flying over Water = Volar damunt l'aigua.* Mount Olive, NC: Merrill, 1997.

Greiman, Jennifer. Review of *Ugly Feelings* by Sianne Ngai. *Leviathan* 3, no. 3 (2012): 70–75.

Goldsmith, Kenneth, and Craig Dworkin, eds. *Against Expression: An Anthology of Conceptual Writing.* Evanston, IL: Northwestern University Press, 2011.

Gumbrecht, Hans Ulrich. *Production of Presence: What Meaning Cannot Convey.* Stanford, CA: Stanford University Press, 2004.

Gunn, Olivia Noble. "Growing Up: Knausgård on Proust, Boyishness, and (Straight) Time." *Scandinavian Studies* 92, no. 3 (2020): 325–347.

Haarder, Jon Helt. "Hvordan er en forfatter (ikke)? Syv en halv note om det som Knausgård ikke længere vil være i slutningen af *Min kamp.* In *Så tæt på livet som muligt: Perspektiver på Karl Ove Knausgårds "Min kamp,"* edited by Claus Elholm Andersen, 244–266. Hellerup: Forlaget Spring, 2017.

Haarder, Jon Helt. "Monumental and vildt elektrisk." *Jyllands Posten*, June 28, 2007.

Haarder, Jon Helt. *Performativ Biografisme.* Copenhagen: Gyldendal, 2014.

Hagen, Alf van der. *Dialoger 3.* Oslo: Tiden Norsk Forlag, 2000.

Hägglund, Martin. "Knausgaard's Secular Confession." *boundary 2*, August 23, 2017. https://www.boundary2.org/2017/08/martin-hagglund-knausgaards-secular-confession-1a/.

Hägglund, Martin. *This Life: Secular Faith and Spiritual Freedom.* New York: Pantheon Books, 2019.

Haglund, David. "Her Ideal Self." *New York Times*, July 5, 2012. https://www.nytimes.com/2012/07/08/books/review/how-should-a-person-be-by-sheila-heti.htlm.

Hämäläinen, Nora. *Är Trump postmodern? En essä om sanning och populism.* Helsinki: Förlaget, 2019.

Bibliography | 225

Hamburger, Käte. *The Logic of Literature*. Indianapolis: Indiana University Press, 1973.

Hansen, Nils Gunder. Review of *Fra skyggerne af det vi ved* by Poul Behrendt. *Kristeligt Dagblad*, April 5, 2019. https://www.kristeligt-dagblad.dk/kultur/altid-en-ekstra-lille-kroelle-paa-halen.

Hauge, Hans. *Fiktionsfri fiktion: Om den nyvirkelige litteratur*. Copenhagen: Multivers, 2012.

Hauge, Hans. "Forfatteren står frem som den, han er." *Politiken*, February 28, 2013.

Haugen, Trond. "Sirkulasjonen av virkelighet: Fakta, fiksjon, selvbiografi og roman i Karl Ove Knausgårds *Min kamp*." *Prosa*, no. 5, Oslo, 2010. http://2001-10.prosa.no/artikkel.asp?ID=687.

Hawks, Terence. *Structuralism and Semiotics*, 2nd ed. London: Routledge, 2003.

Hayot, Eric. *On Literary Worlds*. Oxford: Oxford University Press, 2012.

Henderson, Desirée. *How to Read a Diary: Critical Contexts and Interpretive Strategies for 21st Century Readers*. London: Routledge, 2019.

Heti, Sheila. *How Should a Person Be?* New York: Picador, 2013. Originally published 2010.

Heti, Sheila. "An Interview with Dave Hickey." *Believer*, November 1, 2007. https://believermag.com/an-interview-with-dave-hickey/.

Heti, Sheila. *Motherhood*. New York: Henry Holt, 2018.

Heti, Sheila. *Pure Colour*. New York: Farrar, Straus and Giroux, 2022.

Heti, Sheila. "So Frank." *London Review of Books* 36, no. 1 (January 2014). https://www.lrb.co.uk/v36/n01/sheila-heti/so-frank.

Hirsch, Marianne. *Family Frames*. Cambridge, MA: Harvard University Press, 1997.

Ho, Karen. *Liquidated: An Ethnography of Wall Street*. Durham, NC: Duke University Press, 2009.

Hughes, Evan. "Karl Ove Knausgaard Became a Literary Sensation by Exposing His Every Secret." *New Republic*, April 8, 2014. https://newrepublic.com/article/117245/karl-ove-knausgaard-interview-literary-star-struggles-regret.

Hustvedt, Siri. "No Competition." In *A Woman Looking at Men Looking at Women*, 79–95. New York: Simon & Schuster, 2016.

Ivry, Henry. "Writing in the 'Second Person Plural': Ben Lerner, Ambient Esthetics, and Problems of Scale." *Critique: Studies in Contemporary Fiction* (2020). https://doi.org/10.1080/00111619.2020.1787321.

Jacobsen, Louise Brix, Stefan Kjerkegaard, Rikke Andersen Kraglund, Henrik Skov Nielsen, Camilla Møhring Reestorff, and Carsten Stage. *Fiktionalitet*. Frederiksberg: Samfundslitteratur, 2013.

Jameson, Fredric. "The Aesthetics of Singularity." *New Left Review*, no. 92 (March/April 2015).

Jameson, Fredric. "Cosmic Neutrality." *London Review of Books* 33, no. 20 (2011). https:// www.lrb.co.uk/v33/n20/fredric-jameson/cosmic-neutrality.

226 | Bibliography

Jameson, Fredric. "Itemised." *London Review of Books* 40, no. 21 (November 2018). https://www.lrb.co.uk/the-paper/v40/n21/fredric-jameson/itemised.

Jameson, Fredric. *Postmodernism, or, The Cultural Logic of Late Capitalism.* Durham, NC: Duke University Press, 1991.

Johansson, Anders. *Självskrivna män.* Gothenburg: Glänta, 2015.

Johnston, Taylor. "The Corpse as Novelistic Form: Knausgaard's Deconstruction of Proustian Memory." *Critique: Studies in Contemporary Fiction* 59, no. 3 (2017): 368–382.

Julavits, Heidi. "Choose Your Own Rachel Cusk." *The Cut*, March 6, 2017. https://www.thecut.com/2017/03/rachel-cusk-novelist-transit.html.

Karr, Mary. *The Art of Memoir.* New York: Harper, 2015.

Kellaway, Kate. "Rachel Cusk: 'Aftermath Was Creative Death. I Was Headed into Silence.' " Interview with Rachel Cusk. *The Observer*, August 24, 2014. https://www.theguardian.com/books/2014/aug/24/rachel-cusk-interview-aftermath-outline.

Kelly, Sean. "Smile, Mingle, Inherit." *Sydney Review of Books*, February 17, 2020. https://sydneyreviewofbooks.com/review/vigdis-hjorth-will-testament.

Keyes, Ralph. *The Post-Truth Era: Dishonesty and Deception in Contemporary Life.* New York: St. Martin's Press, 2004.

Kierkegaard, Søren. *The Concept of Anxiety.* Edited and translated by Alistair Hannay. New York: Liveright, 2014.

Kierkegaard, Søren. *From the Papers of One Still Living, Published against His Will: Early Polemical Writings.* Edited and translated by Julie Watkins. Princeton, NJ: Princeton University Press, 1990.

Kim, Annabel L. "Autofiction Infiltrated: Anne Garréta's *Pas un jour.*" *Publication of the Modern Language Association* 133, no. 3 (2018): 559–574.

Kingston-Reese, Alexandra. *Contemporary Novels and the Aesthetic of Twenty-First Century American Life.* Iowa City: University of Iowa Press, 2019.

Kjærstad, Jan. "Den som ligger med nesen i grusen, er blind." *Aftenposten*, January 7, 2010.

Kjerkegaard, Stefan. "Getting People Right, Getting Fiction Right: Self-Fashioning, Fictionality, and Ethics in the Roth Books." *JTN: Journal of Narrative Theory* 46, no. 1 (Winter 2016): 121–148.

Kjerkegaard, Stefan, and Dan Ringgaard. "Hvordan forfattere læser: Et bidrag til postkritikken med læsninger i Karl Ove Knausgårds *Min Kamp* og Christina Hesselholdts *Selskabet.*" In *En ny kritik*, edited by Louise Mønster, Jens Lohfert Jørgensen, and Michael Kallesøe Schmidt, 65–81. Hellerup: Forlaget Spring, 2019.

Knausgård, Bjørge. "*Min kamp 6*: Hilsen fra 'onkel Gunnar." *VG*, November 17, 2011. https://www.vg.no/nyheter/meninger/i/vaeqL/min-kamp-6-hilsen-fra-onkel-gunnar.

"Knausgård for dummies." *Dagbladet*, January 23, 2010.

Bibliography | 227

Knausgård, Karl Ove. *Det tredje riket*. Trondheim: Forlaget Oktober, 2022.

Knausgård, Karl Ove. *En tid for alt*. Trondheim: Forlaget Oktober, 2012. Originally published 2004.

Knausgaard, Karl Ove. *Inadvertent*. New Haven, CT: Yale University Press, 2018.

Knausgård, Karl Ove. "Litteraturen og det onde." In *Sjelens Amerika*, 303–336. Trondheim: Forlaget Oktober, 2013.

Knausgård, Kar Ove. "Livet vender tilbage." Oslo: Tiden Norsk Forlag, 2001. http://web.archive.org/web/20040327150836/http://www.tiden.no/alt/vis.asp?txt=0008.

Knausgård, Karl Ove. *Min Kamp*. Books 1–6. Trondheim: Forlaget Oktober, 2009–2011

Knausgård, Karl Ove. *Morgenstjernen*. Trondheim: Forlaget Oktober, 2020.

Knausgaard, Karl Ove. *My Struggle*. Books 1–6. New York: Farrar, Strauss and Giroux, 2011–2019.

Knausgård, Karl Ove. "Om framtiden." *Samtiden*, no. 3 (2008): 102–115.

Knausgård, Karl Ove. *Skoven og floden: Om Anselm Kiefer og hans kunst*. Copenhagen: Lindhart og Ringhof, 2021.

Knausgård, Karl Ove. "Språket, bildene og litteratuen." *Klassekampen*, April 27, 2019.

Knausgård, Karl Ove. *Sjelens Amerika*. Trondheim: Forlaget Oktober, 2013.

Knausgaard, Karl Ove. *A Time for Everything*. Brooklyn, NY: Archipelago, 2009.

Knausgård, Karl Ove. *Ulvene fra evighetens skog*. Trondheim: Forlaget Oktober, 2021.

Knausgård, Karl Ove. *Ute av verden*. Oslo: Tiden Norsk Forlag, 2010. Originally published 1998.

Knausgård, Karl Ove. "Why the Novel Matters." *New Statesman*, October 26, 2022. https://www.newstatesman.com/culture/books/2022/10/why-novel-matters-imperialism-absolute-karl-ove-knausgaard.

Knudsen, Nicolai Krejberg. "Shame, Belonging, and Biopolitics: Agamben among the Phenomenologists." *Human Studies*, no. 41 (2018): 437–455.

Köhler, Sebastian. " 'Det gjelder å feste blikket': Kampen mot nihilismen i Karl Ove Knausgårds *Min kamp*." *Norsk litterær årbok* (2014): 212–226.

Konstantinou, Lee. *Cool Characters: Irony and American Fiction*. Cambridge, MA: Harvard University Press, 2016.

Konstantinou, Lee. "Four Faces of Postirony." In *Metamodernism: Historicity, Affect, and Depth after Postmodernism*, edited by Robin Van den Akker, Alison Gibbons, and Timotheus Vermeulen, 87–102. Lanham, MD: Rowman & Littlefield, 2017.

Konstantinou, Lee. "Neorealist Fiction." In *American Literature in Transition 2000–2010*, edited by Rachel Greenwald Smith, 109–124. Cambridge: Cambridge University Press, 2017.

Konstantinou, Lee. "Autofiction and Autoreification." Substack, 2021. https://leekonstantinou.substack.com/p/autofiction-and-autoreification.

228 | Bibliography

Kornbluh, Anna. "Bootstrapping across American: Autofiction, Autotheory, and Autoeverything." Episode of the podcast *The American Vandal* with Matt Seybolt and Merve Emre, The Center for Mark Twain Studies, February 14, 2022.

Kornbluh, Anna. "Fifty Billion Shades of Gray." *Los Angeles Review of Books*, August 24, 2018. https://lareviewofbooks.org/article/fifty-billion-shades-gray/.

Kornbluh, Anna. "Freeing Impersonality: The Objective Subject in Psychoanalysis and *Sense and Sensibility*." In *Knots: Post-Lacanian Psychoanalysis, Literature and Film*, edited by Jean Michel-Rabaté, 35–54. New York: Routledge, 2019.

Kornbluh, Anna. *The Order of Forms: Realism, Formalism, and Social Space*. Chicago: University of Chicago Press, 2019.

Kornbluh, Anna. "We Have Never Been Critical: Toward the Novel as Critique." *Novel: A Forum on Fiction* 50, no. 3 (2017): 397–408.

Kramhøft, Janus. "Balladen om Karl Ove." *Politiken*, January 28, 2010. https://politiken.dk/debat/kroniker/ECE888480/balladen-om-karl-ove/.

Krouk, Dean. "'Gres, isstykker': Knausgård som leser av Paul Celan i *Min kamp*." In *Så tæt på livet som muligt: Perspektiver på Karl Ove Knausgårds "Min kamp,"* edited by Claus Elholm Andersen, 184–200. Hellerup: Forlaget Spring, 2017.

Lakoff, George, and Mark Johnson. *Metaphors We Live By*. Chicago: University of Chicago Press, 2003.

Lapidos, Juliet. "When Are Metafictional Games a Mask for Laziness: The Complex Style of Ben Lerner." *New Republic*, August 25, 2014. https://newrepublic.com/article/119005/ben-lerners-1004-review-repetition-and-autobiography-fiction.

Larsson, Stig. "Så drabbades jag av Knausgård." *Dagens Nyheter*, November 24, 2010. https://www.dn.se/kultur-noje/bocker/sa-drabbades-jag-av-knausgard/.

Lee, Johanna. "I See Faces: Popular Pareidolia and the Proliferation of Meaning." In *Material and Popular Culture: The Popular Life of Things*, edited by Anna Malinowska and Karolina Lebek, 105–118. New York: Routledge, 2017.

Le Guin, Ursula K. *A Wizard of Earthsea*. New York: Houghton Mifflin Harcourt, 2012. Originally published 1968.

Lejeune, Philippe. *Moi aussi*. Paris: Éditions du Seuil, 1984.

Lejeune, Philippe. *On Autobiography*. Minneapolis: University of Minnesota Press, 1989.

Lejeune, Philippe. *On Diary*. Honolulu: University of Hawai'i Press, 2009.

Lerner, Ben. *10:04*. New York: Picador, 2014.

Lerner, Ben. "Damage Control." *Harper's Magazine*, October 2012. https://harpers.org/archive/2013/12/damage-control/.

Lerner, Ben. "Each Cornflake." *London Review of Books* 36, no. 10 (May 2014). https://www.lrb.co.uk/the-paper/v36/n10/ben-lerner/each-cornflake.

Lerner, Ben. "The Golden Vanity." *New Yorker*, June 10, 2012. https://www.newyorker.com/magazine/2012/06/18/the-golden-vanity.

Lerner, Ben. *The Topeka School*. New York: Farrar, Straus and Giroux, 2019.

Bibliography | 229

Lethem, Jonathan. "My Hero: Karl Ove Knausgaard. *The Guardian*, January 31, 2014. https://www.theguardian.com/books/2014/jan/31/my-hero-karl-ove-knausgaard-jonathan-lethem.

Levine, Caroline. *Forms: Whole, Rhythm, Hierarchy, Network*. Princeton, NJ: Princeton University Press, 2015.

Levison, Marjorie. "What Is New Formalism?" *Publication of the Modern Language Association* 222, no. 2 (2007): 558–569.

Lewis, Cara L. *Dynamic Form: How Intermediality Made Modernism*. Ithaca, NY: Cornell University Press, 2020.

Leypoldt, Günter. "Knausgaard in America: Literary Prestige and Charismatic Trust." *Critical Quarterly* 59, no. 3 (2017): 55–69.

Lockwood, Patricia. "Why Do I Have to Know What McDonald's Is?" *London Review of Books* 9, no. 9 (2018). https://www.lrb.co.uk/the-paper/v40/n09/patricia-lockwood/why-do-i-have-to-know-what-mcdonald-s-is.

Lorentzen, Christian. "Sheila Heti, Ben Lerner, Tao Lin: How 'Auto' Is 'Autofiction'?" *Vulture*, May 2018. https://www.vulture.com/2018/05/how-auto-is-autofiction.html.

Lukács, Georg. "Narrate or Describe?" In *Writer and Critic: And Other Essays*, 110–148. London: Merlin Press, 1970.

Lukács, Georg. *The Theory of the Novel*. Boston, MA: MIT Press, 1972.

Maftei, Micaela. *The Fiction of Autobiography*. London: Bloomsbury, 2013.

Magnússon, Gísli. "The Aesthetics of Epiphany in Karl Ove Knausgård's *Min kamp*." *Scandinavian Studies* 92, no. 3 (2020): 348–368.

Malm, Andreas. *The Progress of This Storm: Nature and Society in a Warming World*. London: Verso, 2018.

Marcus, Laura. *Autobiography: A Very Short Introduction*. Oxford: Oxford University Press, 2018.

Marcus, Sharon, Heather Love, and Stephen Best. "Building a Better Description." *Representation* 135 (Summer 2016): 1–21.

Martinsen, Deborah A. *Surprised by Sin: Dostoevsky's Liars and Narrative Exposure*. Athens: Ohio State University Press, 2002.

Mazzoni, Guido. *Theory of the Novel*. Cambridge, MA: Harvard University Press, 2017.

McClanahan, Annie. *Dead Pledges: Debt, Crisis, and 21st Century Culture*. Stanford, CA: Stanford University Press, 2016.

McGurl, Mark. *Everything and Less: The Novel in the Age of Amazon*. London: Verso, 2021.

McKeon, Michael, ed. *Theory of the Novel: A Historical Approach*. Baltimore, MD: Johns Hopkins University Press, 2000.

McQuillan, Martin. *Paul de Man*. London: Routledge, 2011.

Melberg, Arne. "Essä/roman: från Proust via Woolf til Knausgård." In *Så tæt på livet som muligt: Perspektiver på Karl Ove Knausgårds "Min kamp,"* edited by Claus Elholm Andersen, 267–280. Hellerup: Forlaget Spring, 2017.

230 | Bibliography

Melberg, Arne. *Theories of Mimesis*. Cambridge: Cambridge University Press, 1995.

Melberg, Arne. "Vi mangler ord." *Aftenposten*, January 15, 2010.

Menn, Ricarda. "Reading Serial Autofictions—Knausgård and Cusk." Unpublished paper given at the conference Autofiction, University of Oxford, October 2019.

Mieszkowski, Jan. *Labors of Imagination: Aesthetics and Political Economy from Kant to Althusser*. New York: Fordham University Press, 2006.

Miller, D. A. *The Novel and the Police*. Berkeley: University of California Press, 1988.

Miller, J. Hillis. *Ariadne's Thread: Story Lines*. New Haven, CT: Yale University Press, 1995.

Miller, J. Hillis. "The Critic as Host." *Critical Inquiry* 3, no. 3 (Spring 1977): 439–447.

Miller, J. Hillis. "Derrida and Literature." In *Jacques Derrida and the Humanities: A Critical Reader*, edited by Tom Cohen, 58–81. Cambridge: Cambridge University Press, 2001.

Miller, J. Hillis. *On Literature*. London: Routledge, 2002.

Miller, J. Hillis. *Others*. Princeton, NJ: Princeton University Press, 2001.

Miller, J. Hillis. *Reading for Our Time: "Adam Bede" and "Middlemarch" Revisited*. Edinburgh: Edinburgh University Press, 2012.

Mitchell, Josie. "To Endure the Void: On Rachel Cusk's 'Outline' Trilogy. *Los Angeles Review of Books*, August 13, 2018. https://lareviewofbooks.org/article/endure-void-rachel-cusks-outline-trilogy/.

Mitchell, Kaye. *Writing Shame: Gender, Contemporary Literature, and Negative Affect*. Edinburgh: Edinburgh University Press, 2020.

Moi, Toril. "Å lese med innlevelse." *Morgenbladet*, July 21, 2017.

Moi, Toril. "Describing *My Struggle*." *The Point*, December 27, 2017. https://thepointmag.com/criticism/describing-my-struggle-knausgaard/.

Moi, Toril. "Description in *My Struggle* (*Min kamp*): Knausgård's Challenge to Literary Theory." Unpublished paper given at the Modern Language Association conference, New York, January 2018.

Moi, Toril. "Real Characters: Literary Criticism and the Existential Turn." *The Point*, January 28, 2020. https://thepointmag.com/criticism/real-characters-literary-criticism-existential-turn-toril-moi/.

Moi, Toril. "Knausgaard's Ruthless Freedom." *Public Books*, October 26, 2018. https://www.publicbooks.org/knausgaards-ruthless-freedom.

Moi, Toril. "Knausgårds udfordring." *Passage*, no. 78 (Winter 2017): 110–113.

Moi, Toril. *Revolution of the Ordinary: Literary Studies after Wittgenstein, Austin, and Cavell*. Chicago: University of Chicago Press, 2017.

Moi, Toril. "Shame and Openness." *Salmagundi*, no. 177 (Winter 2013): 205–210.

Moi, Toril. "Skam og åpenhet." *Morgenbladet*, July 21, 2011.

Murray, Mitch R. "All Auto All the Time: Artwork, Art Work, and the University." Talk at the University of Florida, April 2022. https://www.mitchrmurray.com/all-auto-all-the-time#_ftn6.

Bibliography | 231

Ngai, Sianne. *Ugly Feelings*. Cambridge, MA: Harvard University Press, 2005.

Nielsen, Henrik Skov. "The Impersonal Voice in First-Person Narrative." *Narrative* 12, no. 2 (2004): 133–150.

Nielsen, Henrik Skov, James Phelan, and Richard Walsh. "Ten Theses about Fictionality." *Narrative* 23, no. 1 (2015): 61–73.

Nørkjær, Hans. "Knausgårds troldspejl." In *Knausgård i syv sind*, edited by David Bugge, Søren R. Fauth, and Ole Morsing, 103–124. Copenhagen: Eksistens, 2016.

Nørkjær Franch, Hans. "Knausgårds absolutte blik og dobbeltrettede længsel." *Dansk Kirketidende*, no. 8 (2019): 22–25.

North, Joseph. *Literary Criticism: A Concise Political History*. Cambridge, MA: Harvard University Press, 2017.

O'Grady, Megan "Rachel Cusk on Her Quietly Radical New Novel, *Outline*." *Vogue*, January 14, 2015. https://www.vogue.com/article/rachel-cusk-new-novel-outline.

Olsen, Stig. "Kan du se englene: Imitation, identitet og narration in Helle Helles *Rødby-Puttgarden*." *Spring*, no. 43 (2018): 69–94.

Ong, Yi-Ping. *The Art of Being: Poetics of the Novel and Existentialist Philosophy*. Cambridge, MA: Harvard University Press, 2018.

Orlemanski, Julie. "Who Has Fiction? Modernity, Fictionality, and the Middle Ages." *New Literary History* 50, no. 2 (2019): 145–170.

Otterbech, Martin Hegstad. "Ut i det åpne." Unpublished master's thesis, University of Bergen, 2020. https://bora.uib.no/bora-xmlui/bitstream/handle/1956/23067/ Ut-i-det--pne---En-komparativ-analyse-av-den-skandinaviske-resepsjonen-av-Karl-Ove-Knausg-rds-Min-kamp.pdf?sequence=1&isAllowed=y.

Øygarden, Geir Angell. *Bagdad Indigo*. N.p.: Pelikanen, 2011.

Parker, Ben. "What Is a Theory of the Novel Good For?" *boundary2*, June 14, 2017. https://www.boundary2.org/2017/06/benjamin-parker-what-is-a-theory-of-the-novel-good-for/.

Parks, Tim. "How Best to Read Auto-Fiction." *New York Review of Books*, NYR Daily, 2018. https://www.nybooks.com/daily/2018/05/25/how-best-to-read-auto-fiction/.

Parks, Tim. "Raise Your Hand if You've Read Knausgaard." *New York Review of Books*, NYR Daily, 2014. https://nybooks.com/daily/2014/07/19/raise-your-hand-if-youve-read-knausgaard/.

Pedersen, Henrik Kayser. "Karl Ove Knausgård bibliografi." http://www.bibliografi. no/kok.pdf.

Phelan, James. *Reading People, Reading Plots*. Chicago: University of Chicago Press, 1989.

Proust, Marcel. *Swann's Way: Remembrance of Things Past*, vol. 1. New York: Henry Holt, 1922. https://www.gutenberg.org/files/7178/7178-h/7178-h.htm.

Radden, Günter, and Zoltán Kövecses. "Towards a Theory of Metonymy." In *The Cognitive Linguistics Reader*, edited by Vyvyan Evans, Benjamin Bergen, and Jörg Zinken, 17–58. London: Equinox, 2007.

232 | Bibliography

Reitan, Rolf. "The Rhetorical of Fictionality: Introduction to Richard Walsh." *Spring*, nos. 31–32 (2011): 22–56.

Renberg, Tore. " 'I røykeavdelingen på havets bunn': Tore Renberg intervjuer Karl Ove Knausgård." *Samtiden*, no. 3 (2010): 20–45.

Riffaterre, Michael. *Fictional Truth*. Baltimore, MD: Johns Hopkins University Press, 1990.

Rohter, Larry. "He Says a Lot, for a Norwegian." *New York Times*, June 18, 2012. https://www.nytimes.com/2012/06/19/books/a-debate-over-karl-ove-knaus-gaards-my-struggle.html?_r=0.

Rothman, Joshua. "Karl Ove Knausgaard Looks Back on 'My Struggle.' " *New Yorker*, November 11, 2018. https://www.newyorker.com/culture/the-new-yorker-interview/karl-ove-knausgaard-the-duty-of-literature-is-to-fight-fiction.

Rothman, Joshua. "Knausgaard's Selflessness." *New Yorker*, April 20, 2016. https://www.newyorker.com/books/page-turner/knausgaards-selflessness.

Rösing, Lilian Munk. "Strindbergs vrede stemme." *K&K* 11, no. 116 (2013): 121–134.

Rottem, Øystein. "Høstens sensasjon." *Dagbladet*, November 25, 1998.

Rühl, Anna: " 'Lite og stygt, men alt som var': Sted og stedløshed i *Min kamp: Tredje bog*." In *Så tæt på livet som muligt: Perspektiver på Karl Ove Knausgårds "Min kamp*," edited by Claus Elholm Andersen, 148–165. Hellerup: Forlaget Spring, 2017.

Ryan, Marie-Laure. *Avatars of Story*. Minneapolis: University of Minnesota Press, 2006.

Saussure, Ferdinand de. "Nature of the Linguistic Sign." In *Modern Criticism and Theory: A Reader*, edited by David Lodge, 10–14. London: Longman, 1988.

Schmitt, Arnaud. "Making the Case for Self-Narration against Autofiction." *a/b: Auto/Biography Studies* 25, no. 1 (2010): 122–137.

Schmitt, Arnaud. *The Phenomenology of Autobiography: Making It Real*. New York: Routledge, 2017.

Schmitt, Arnaud, and Stefan Kjerkegaard. "Karl Ove Knausgaard's *My Struggle*: A Real Life in a Novel." *a/b: Auto/Biography Studies* 31, no. 3 (2016): 553–579.

Schwalm, Helg. "Autobiography." *The Living Handbook of Narratology*. https://www.lhn.uni-hamburg.de/node/129.html.

Schwartz, Camilla. " 'Å skrive handler mer om å ødelegge enn om å skape' Formelle og tematiske splittelses—og reparationsstrategier i *Min kamp*." In *Så tæt på livet som muligt: Perspektiver på Karl Ove Knausgårds "Min kamp*," edited by Claus Elholm Andersen, 95–112. Hellerup: Forlaget Spring, 2017.

Schwartz, Camilla. "Forfatteren som læser: Litteratur i brug hos Karl Ove Knausgård, Tomas Espedal og Pablo Llambías." In *Litteratur i brug*, edited by Anne Marie Mai, 165–183. Hellerup: Forlaget Spring, 2019.

Sedgwick, Eve Kosofsky. *Touching Feeling: Affect, Pedagogy, Performance*. Durham, NC: Duke University Press, 2003.

Bibliography | 233

Sheils, Barry, and Julie Walsh. Introduction to *Shame and Modern Writing*. New York: Routledge, 2018.

Shields, David. *Reality Hunger: A Manifesto*. New York: Vintage Books, 2011.

Shklovsky, Victor. "Art as Technique." In *The Critical Tradition*, 2nd ed., edited by David H. Richter, 717–726. Boston: Bedford St. Martin's, 1998.

Sinykin, Dan. *American Literature and the Long Downturn: Neoliberal Apocalypse*. Oxford: Oxford University Press, 2020.

Sinykin, Dan. "*My Struggle*, Vol. 1." *Post45*. https://post45.org/2016/06/my-struggle-volume-1-dan-june-17/.

Sinykin, Dan. "*My Struggle*, Vol. 2." *Post45: Slow Burn*. https://post45.org/2016/07/my-struggle-vol-2-dan-july-12/.

Sjølyst-Jackson, Peter. "Confession, Shame and Ethics in Coetzee and Knausgård." *Scandinavian Studies* 92, no. 3 (2020): 274–295.

Skei, Hans H. "Mangfoldig, rikt, rystende." *Aftenposten*, September 19, 2009.

Sky, Jeanette. "Et monument over den moderne mannen." *Morgenbladet*, November 30, 1998.

Smith, Zadie. "Man vs. Corpse." *New York Review of Books*, December 5, 2013. https://www.nybooks.com/articles/2013/12/05/zadie-smith-man-vs-corpse/.

Sturgeon, Jonathan. "The Death of the Postmodern Novel and the Rise of Auto-fiction." *Flavorwire*, December 31, 2014. http://flavorwire.com/496570/2014-the-death-of-the-postmodern-novel-and-the-rise-of-autofiction.

Sykes, Rachel. "'Who Gets to Speak and Why?' Oversharing in Contemporary North American Women's Writing." *Signs: Journal of Women in Culture and Society* 43, no. 1 (2017): 151–174.

Taylor, Brandon. "Karl Ove Knausgaard's Haunting New Novel." *New Yorker*, October 16, 2021. https://www.newyorker.com/books/page-turner/karl-ove-knausgaards-haunting-new-novel.

Thurman, Judith. "Rachel Cusk Gut-Renovates the Novel." *New Yorker*, July 31, 2017. https://www.newyorker.com/magazine/2017/08/07/rachel-cusk-gut-renovates-the-novel.

Tomkins, Silvan. *Affect, Imagery, Consciousness: The Complete Edition*. New York: Springer, 2018.

Tomkins, Silvan. *Shame and Its Sisters: A Silvan Tomkins Reader*. Edited by Eve Kosofsky Sedgwick and Adam Frank. Durham, NC: Duke University Press, 1995.

Tønder, Finn Bjørn. "Familien føler sig uthengt i ny Knausgård-roman." *Bergens Tidende*, September 19, 2009.

Valihora, Karen. "She Got Up and Went Away: Rachel Cusk on Making an Exit." *ESC: English Studies in Canada* 45, no. 1 (2019): 19–35.

van de Ven, Inge. "Den monumentale Knausgård: Bag data, et kvantificeret jeg og Proust for Facebook-generationen." In *Så tæt på livet som muligt: Perspektiver på Karl Ove Knausgårds "Min kamp,"* edited by Claus Elholm Andersen, 57–78. Hellerup: Forlaget Spring, 2017.

234 | Bibliography

van de Ven, Inge. "Size Matters: Karl Ove Knausgård's *Min Kamp* and Roberto Bolano's *2666* as (Anti-) Monumental Novels." In *Materializing Memory in Art and Popular Culture*, edited by László Munteán, Liedeke Plate, and Anneke Smelik, 106–122. New York: Routledge, 2017.

van de Ven, Inge. "Guys and Dolls: Gender, Scale, and the Book in Elena Ferrante's Neapolitan Novels and Karl Ove Knausgård's *Min kamp*." *Scandinavian Studies* 92, no. 3 (2020): 296–324.

Vermeulen, Pieter. "Against Premature Articulation: Empathy, Gender, and Austerity in Rachel Cusk and Katie Kitamura." *Critical Critique* 111 (2021): 81–103.

Vermeulen, Pieter. "How Should a Person Be (Transpersonal)? Ben Lerner, Roberto Esposito, and the Biopolitics of the Future." *Political Theory* 45, no. 5 (2017): 659–681.

Vermeulen, Timotheus, and Robin van den Akker. "Notes on Metamodernism." *Journal of Aesthetics and Culture* 2, no. 1 (2010): 56–77.

Vermeulen, Timotheus, and Robin van den Akker. "Periodising the 2000s, or, the Emergence of Metamodernism." In *Metamodernism: Historicity, Affect, and Depth after Postmodernism*, edited by Robin van den Akker, Alison Gibbons, and Timotheus Vermeulen, 1–21. Lanham, MD: Rowman & Littlefield, 2017.

Vermeulen, Timotheus, and Robin van den Akker. "Utopia, Sort of: A Case Study in Metamodernism." *Studia Neophilologica*, no. 87, sup. 1 (2015): 55–67.

Voelz, Johannes. "The American Novel and the Transformation of Privacy: Ben Lerner's *10:04* (2014) and Miranda July's *The First Bad Man* (2015)." In *The American Novel in the 21st Century: Cultural Contexts—Literary Developments—Critical Analyses*, edited by Michael Basseler and Ansgar Nünning, 323–337. Trier: Wissenschaftlicher Verlag, 2019.

Vøllo, Ida Hummel. "The Functions of Autoreception: Karl Ove Knausgård as Author-Critic and Rewriter." Unpublished dissertation, University of Edinburgh, 2019.

Waldman, Katy. " 'Kudos,' the Final Volume of Rachel Cusk's 'Faye' Trilogy, Completes an Ambitious Act of Refusal." *New Yorker*, May 22, 2018. https://www.newyorker.com/books/page-turner/kudos-final-volume-rachel-cusk-faye-trilogy-ambitious-act-of-refusal.

Walsh, Richard. *The Rhetoric of Fictionality*. Athens: Ohio State University Press, 2007.

Wandrup, Frederik. "Engler daler ned i skjul." *Dagbladet*, November 1, 2004.

Wasserman, Sarah. "Critical Darlings, Critical Dogs: Joseph O'Neill and What Contemporary Criticism Doesn't Want." *American Literary History* 34, no. 2 (2022): 561–585.

Watt, Ian. *The Rise of the Novel*. Berkeley: University of California Press, 2001. Originally published 1957.

Weineck, Silke-Maria. *The Tragedy of Fatherhood: King Laius and the Politics of Paternity in the West*. New York: Bloomsbury, 2014.

Bibliography | 235

West, Paul. "Sheer Fiction: The Mind of the Fabulist's Mirage." *New Literary History* 7, no. 3 (1976): 549–561.

Wimsatt, William K. *The Verbal Icon: Studies in the Meaning of Poetry.* Lexington: University of Kentucky Press, 1954.

Winter, Jessica. "Our Autofiction Fixation." *New York Times*, March 14, 2021. https://www.nytimes.com/2021/03/14/books/review/autofiction-my-dark-vanessa-american-dirt-the-need-kate-elizabeth-russell-jeanine-cummins-helen-phillips.html.

Witt-Brattström, Ebba. "En kamp för det första kønet." *Dagens Nyheter*, January 30, 2012.

Wood, James. *How Fiction Works.* New York: Picador, 2018. Originally published 2008.

Wood, James. "Total Recall." *New Yorker*, August 13 and 20, 2012. https://www.newyorker.com/magazine/2012/08/13/total-recall.

Wood, James. "True Lives." *New Yorker*, June 25, 2012. https://www.newyorker.com/magazine/2012/06/25/true-lives-2.

Wood, James, and Karl Ove Knausgaard. "Writing *My Struggle*: An Exchange." *Paris Review*, no. 211 (Winter 2011). https://www.theparisreview.org/miscellaneous/6345/writing-emmy-struggle-em-an-exchange-james-wood-karl-ove-knausgaard.

Worthington, Marjorie. "Fiction in the 'Post-Truth' Era: The Ironic Effects of Autofiction." *Critique* 58, no. 5 (2017): 471–483.

Worthington, Marjorie. *The Story of "Me": Contemporary American Autofiction.* Lincoln: University of Nebraska Press, 2018.

Zhang, Dora. *Strange Likeness: Description and the Modernist Novel.* Chicago: University of Chicago Press, 2020.

Index

10:04 (Lerner), 21, 28, 137, 155–162, 167

16.07.47 (Solstad), 7

Abrahamsen, Morten, 6
Abrams, M. H., 50
Agamben, Giorgio, 27, 84, 212n53
Akhtar, Ayad, 11, 169
alcoholism, 98, 104
Alexievich, Svetlana, 22
"America of the Soul" (Knausgård), 49
Andersen, Hans Christian, 105–106
Anderson, Linda, 42
Angell, Geir, 78, 112, 181n3, 194n60
Angot, Christine, 9
antifiction, 46, 119, 167–168, 186n62, 194n53
Arc, Jonathan, 59
Aristophanes, 88
Aristotle, 50, 127
Attridge, Derek, 41
Aubry, Timothy, 23
authenticity: in *My Struggle*, 1, 24, 51, 52, 60, 63, 72, 76, 83, 123, 154, 168; in other works, 1–2, 15–17, 139–140, 161, 168
autobiography, 7–8, 41–44
"Autobiography as De-facement" (de Man), 27, 41–44

autobiographical pact. *See* pacts, autobiographical and fictional
autofiction, 1–3, 8–20, 69, 136–137, 143, 155, 163–164, 165–169, 173n26, 174n37, 176n52, 192n45; definition of, 1, 8, 14; economics, relationship to, 18–19, 20–21; and gender, 10, 163; and metamodernism, 21–22; and postmodernism, 10, 12, 15, 18–19, 146, 176n63, 177n66, 182n21; and race, 10–11, 163
autofictionalization, 2, 14, 15, 24–27, 168; in *10:04*, 137, 155–162, 167; in *My Struggle*, 25, 69–76, 78, 83, 85, 99, 110, 116, 130, 159–160, 197n86

Back to the Future, 159
Bakhtin, Mikhail, 119
Barthes, Roland, 67, 74, 191n33
Bastien-Lepage, Jules, 158
Batuman, Elif, 19–20
Baudelaire, Charles, 159
Beck-Nielsen, Claus, 7
Behrendt, Poul, 8, 25, 72, 92, 99, 108, 123, 192n44
Benjamin, Walter, 33, 212n53
Bergen, 42, 94, 115, 165, 168, 185n45, 206n43

238 | Index

Best, Stephen, 128
Bewes, Timothy, 26, 39–41, 44, 86, 93
Biles, Jeremy, 51, 58
Bloch, Ernst, 158, 212n53
Bloom, Myra, 14–15, 20, 139
Booth, Wayne, 74
bread, 77
Bronte, Charlotte, 161
Brooks, Cleanth, 23
Brooks, Peter, 33, 59
Bruss, Elizabeth W., 42
Bunch, Mads, 72
Butler, Judith, 58

capital, fictitious, 2, 17–18
capitalism, 2, 17–18, 19, 21, 34, 62,
    111, 112–113, 127–128, 145, 149,
    158, 162, 163, 210n29
Cervantes, Miguel de, 29, 121, 189n17
Chekov, Anton, 71, 194n60
Chihaya, Sarah, 24
Claus Beck-Nielsen (1963–2001), 7
Clemmons, Zinzi, 10–11
Cohn, Dorrit, 2, 26, 46, 66, 67, 70,
    73, 83, 85, 118, 150
Colbert, Stephen, 21
Cole, Teju, 22
Conrad, Joseph, 118
Cooke, Jennifer, 138, 142
Covid-19, 165, 166
crisis: of fiction, 1, 45, 49, 137, 154,
    165, 178n79; financial, of 2008,
    17–18, 20–21, 78, 145, 178n81,
    211n34
Crosthwaite, Paul, 20–21
Cusk, Rachel, 2, 10, 22, 28, 135–137,
    144–155, 163, 166–167, 210n31,
    210n32

De Boever, Arne, 20–21
de Man, Paul, 27, 38, 41–44, 48, 50,
    74, 161, 185n47

de Saussure, Ferdinand, 35–36
death, 31–35, 51–55, 98, 129, 132. *See
    also* Knausgård, Kai-Åge (father),
    death of
deconstruction, 36, 42
defamiliarization, 50, 78, 149, 197n85
Defoe, Daniel, 117
demonic, the (Kierkegaard), 97,
    102–103
Deresiewicz, William, 39
Derrida, Jacques, 58, 182n18
Descartes, René, 58, 62
description, 39–40, 65–66, 75, 78, 82,
    88, 127–133
Det tredje riket (Knausgård), 165
diary, 24, 27, 45–47, 51, 64, 81,
    94–95, 103, 122
diegesis, 43
direct discourse, 39
Dix, Hywel, 9, 10
domesticity, 135–136, 201n44. *See also*
    Knausgård, Karl Ove (character),
    husband and father, as a
Don Quixote, 29, 59, 112, 121, 189n17
Dore, Florence, 23
Dostoyevsky, Fyodor, 59, 124–126,
    206n43
Doubrovsky, Serge, 9, 12, 69
dualism, 27, 58, 61, 62, 71, 83, 93, 165

Eakin, Paul John, 42, 73
Emezi, Akwaeke, 11
Emre, Merve, 152
Engdahl, Horace, 115, 204n17
Ent id for alt. See *A Time for
    Everything*
erasure, 82–85
Ernaux, Annie, 9, 22, 73, 214n7
exclusion, 83, 86, 102

Fagerholm, Monika, 13, 176n56,
    206n42

Index | 239

Farsethås, Ane, 90
Felski, Rita, 46–47, 121
Ferreira-Meyers, Karen, 9
fictional pact. *See* pacts,
   autobiographical and fictional
fictionality, 15, 21, 25–26, 28, 55,
   74–75, 116–118
Fielding, Henry, 117
Figlerowicz, Marta, 72, 156
Fils (Doubrovsky), 9, 12, 69
Flaubert, Gustave, 121, 127, 128
Folarin, Tope, 10–11, 22, 137, 169
formalism, 24–25, 26, 168
free indirect discourse (FID), 25,
   39–41, 184n37, 184n39, 211n39
Freshwater (Emezi), 11
Frey, James, 16, 67, 74
Freytag, Gustav, 143
From the Papers of One Still Living
   (Kierkegaard), 105–106
A Fugitive Crosses His Tracks
   (Sandemose), 85

Gallagher, Catherine, 26, 28, 74,
   116–120
Gasparini, Philippe, 9
gender, 10, 28, 60, 135–138, 139,
   143, 144–145, 149–152, 155, 166,
   174n39, 189n15, 200n33. *See also*
   masculinity
Genette, Gérard, 9, 43, 63, 71, 73,
   131–132, 194n58
genre, 8, 42–44, 61, 168
Gibbons, Alison, 14, 15, 20, 21, 156,
   163
Gombrowicz, Witold, 142, 186n58
Greenaway, Peter, 87–88
Goodnight My Dear Ones (Larsson),
   120
grocery store, 77–78, 126
Gumbrecht, Hans, 72
Gunnar, Uncle. *See* Knausgård, Bjørge

Haarder, Jon Helt, 94
Hägglund, Martin, 25, 46, 72, 100,
   105
Hamsun, Knut, 3, 49, 124, 142
Hartley, Marsden, 147–148
Hauge, Hans, 42
Hawkes, Terence, 36
Heart of Darkness, 118
Hegel, Georg W. F., 50
Heti, Sheila, 2, 8, 10, 15, 21, 22, 28,
   66, 136–144, 163, 167
The Highest Caste (Rydberg), 115
Homeland Elegies (Akhtar), 11, 169
How Should a Person Be? (Heti), 28,
   137–144

identification, 28, 46–47, 120–121,
   125–126
The Idiot (Batuman), 20
imitation, 140–142. *See also* mimesis
Inadvertent (Knausgård), 37, 45, 50,
   182n19, 183n23
indirect discourse, 39–41
irony, 60, 161
itemization, 18, 77–78, 191n37,
   196n83

James, Henry, 24
Jameson, Fredric, 18, 22, 24, 41,
   76–79, 116, 128, 158
Jane Eyre, 161
Joan of Arc (Bastien-Lepage), 158
Johnston, Taylor, 41, 44
Joseph Andrews (Fielding), 117

Karr, Mary, 67
Keyes, Ralph, 17
Kierkegaard, Søren, 97, 102–103,
   105–106
Kim, Annabel L., 14
Kingston-Reese, Alexandra, 35, 48,
   143

240 | Index

Kjaerstad, Jan, 7, 8, 182n21
Kjerkegaard, Stefan, 20, 46, 63, 75–76
Knausgård, Bjørge (Uncle Gunnar),
  66, 75, 78, 107–116, 119, 192n41,
  203n6
Knausgård, Kai-Åge (father), 25,
  27–28, 63, 65, 69–70, 82–83,
  86, 90, 94–99, 129, 132, 201n52;
  alcoholism, 98, 104, 109
death of, 28, 32, 45, 49, 51–55, 66, 98,
  103, 108–110, 194n55; nakedness,
  94–95; and shame, 95–98;
  similarities with son, 27, 53, 96, 97,
  98, 99
Knausgård, Karl Ove (author), 3–6,
  13–14, 137, 165–166, 181n4,
  185n46; crisis of fiction, 1, 5,
  15, 45, 49, 137, 140, 154, 165,
  178n79; form, 49–51, 58, 60–62,
  81, 168–169, 189n3; relationship to
  character, 26, 63–64, 70–73, 76, 84;
  romanticism, 38, 53; shame, 81
Knausgård, Karl Ove (character),
  88–89, 112, 114, 159; children, 99,
  122–124; death, discovery of, 32,
  34, 51–55; dualism, 58; eight-year-
  old, as a, 25, 63, 65, 69–70, 82,
  90, 130–132; exclusion, sense of,
  83–84; father, see Knausgård, Kai-
  Åge; as husband and father, 1, 5,
  99, 103, 122–124, 199n29; mother,
  66–67, 82, 90, 137, 183n24, 201n45,
  205n29; reading, 124–126, 206n41;
  relationship to author, 13–14, 26,
  32, 63–64, 70–73, 76; self-harm,
  57–58, 91, 92; shame, 82–87, 90–91,
  92–93, 94–98; soccer tournament,
  96–97; struggle, 1, 5, 100–101, 105,
  122; truthfulness, 66
Knausgård, Linda Boström (wife), 4,
  5, 57, 60, 63, 71–72, 87, 91–93, 99,

102, 122–123, 124, 150, 194n60,
  199n29, 200n33
Knausgård, Yngve (brother), 51–55,
  57, 69–70, 109, 115
Konstantinou, Lee, 19–20, 60, 178n88
Kornbluh, Anna, 19, 20, 24
Kraus, Chris, 8, 22
Kristiansand (Norway), 46, 54
Kritikerprisen (Critic's Prize), 4
Kudos (Cusk), 135, 210n31
künstlerroman, 139, 143

Laing, Olivia, 22
Larsson, Stig, 7, 120–121, 142, 205n33
laundry, 5, 99, 100, 113
Law of Jante, 85, 198n13, 214n3
Le Guin, Ursula K., 37, 64, 183n23,
  183n24
Lejeune, Philippe, 1, 12, 27, 42, 46,
  51, 58, 64–65, 67, 68–69, 122, 144
Lerner, Ben, 2, 10, 20–21, 22, 28, 94,
  136, 137, 155–163, 167
Levine, Caroline, 24, 51, 55
Levinson, Marjorie, 23
Leypoldt, Günter, 16
Lin, Tao, 22
"Literature and Evil" (Knausgård), 60
Lorentzen, Christian, 12
Lorenzo in Taos (Luhan), 167
Love, Heather, 128
Luhan, Mabel Dodge, 167
Lukács, Georg, 24, 59–62, 127–128,
  131, 168
Lundgren, Maja, 7

Madame Bovary, 60, 121
Malmö, 5, 102, 122
Man Gone Down (Thomas), 10
Man, Paul de. *See* de Man, Paul
Mann, Thomas, 60
Marcus, Sharon, 128

Index | 241

Marshall, Alice, 17
masculinity, 10, 58, 96, 152, 175n42, 198n15. *See also* gender
Mazzoni, Guido, 61–62, 67
Melberg, Arne, 7–8, 94
Melville, Herman, 111
memory, 26, 65–67, 77–78, 87, 89–90, 95, 109, 119, 130, 137
metamodernism, 21–22, 163, 213n67
metonymy, 123–124
Miller, D. A., 86
Miller, J. Hillis, 26, 64, 115
A Million Little Pieces (Frey), 16, 67, 74
mimesis, 41, 61, 67, 77, 141–142
Moi, Toril, 20, 36, 42–43, 105, 120, 128–129, 183n30
Morgenstjernen (Knausgård), 38, 165, 183n22, 202n54
Motherhood (Heti), 167
Munch, Edvard, 37
Murdoch, Iris, 73
Murray, Mitch R., 19–20
My Struggle (Knausgård), 1–3, 5–6, 45–48, 165; and autofictionalization, *see under* autofictionalization; death, treatment of, 31–35, 51–55, 98, 129–132, 180n1, 180n2, 187n83; description, use of, 39–40, 65–66, 75, 78, 82, 88, 127–133; distrust, tone of, 112–113, 116; domesticity, 135–136, 201n44 (*See also* Knausgård, Karl Ove (character), husband and father, as a); dualism, 14, 15, 26, 27, 58, 61–62, 71, 83, 93; form, 24–25, 26, 45, 49–51, 53, 58, 61, 62, 78–79, 81, 89–91, 93, 123, 126, 131; itemization, 18, 77–78, 191n37, 196n83; novel, as a, 48, 55, 68, 193n50; privacy, controversies over, 5–6, 107–108, 202n4; and reality, 14, 22, 26, 32,

35, 37, 54, 107–111, 113–116, 138; shame, 27, 81–87, 90–91, 92–93, 94–98, 109, 198n15

"Narrate or Describe?" (Lukács), 127–128
narration, 25, 40, 46, 72–73, 118, 123–124, 127–133, 159–160. *See also* autofictionalization
Natta de mina (Larsson), 7, 120, 205n33
Nelson, Maggie, 22
New Criticism, 23
New Formalism, 23–24
Ngai, Sianne, 28, 111–112
Nielsen, Henrik Skov, 26, 74
Nietzsche, Friedrich, 34
Nordic Council Literary Prize, 5, 84, 206n42
North, Joseph, 24
novel purchasing program, Norway, 68, 193n49
novel: affordance, 24, 51; characters, 117–120; conflict between inner and outer reality, 57–60, 71, 76; narration, *see* narration; and shame, 93; theory of, 59–62; tone, 111, 203n9; and truth, 116

Offill, Jenny, 22
O'Grady, Megan, 137
Olney, James, 42
On Earth We're Briefly Gorgeous (Vuong), 11
"On the Future" (Knausgård), 32
Ong, Yi-Ping, 106
Only a Fiddler (Andersen, Hans Christian), 105
"Om framtiden" (Knausgård), 32
Out of the World (*Ute av verden*), 3–4, 36–38, 47, 81, 198n15

242 | Index

Outline (novel by Cusk), 144–147,
  149–154
Outline trilogy (Cusk), 28, 135–136,
  144–155, 166

pacts, autobiographical and fictional,
  1, 14, 51, 58, 64–69, 72, 75, 78,
  163; autobiographical, 83, 139, 144,
  156, 168; fictional, 26, 82
Pan (Knut Hamsun), 3–4, 172n11
panfictionality, 74, 195n73
pareidolia, 88, 90
Parker, Ben, 62
A Particular Kind of Black Man
  (Folarin), 11, 169
Phelan, James, 26, 70, 74
Plato, 58, 121
postirony, 60, 178n88, 189n13
postmodernism, 1–2, 10, 12, 15, 18,
  19, 20–22, 60, 76, 79, 182n21
post-truth, 17
poststructuralism, 10, 36, 41–44, 55,
  183n30
privacy, right to, 5–6, 92; violation of,
  86, 105, 107
prolepsis, 71–72
Proust, Marcel, 43, 70, 73, 82, 83,
  89, 94, 115, 118, 131–132, 194n58;
  comparisons of Knausgård to, 3, 4,
  7; influence on Knausgård, 89, 124,
  142, 199n26
Pure Colour (Heti), 167

reading, 2, 60, 64, 120, 124–126,
  163–164, 192n45
Real Life (Taylor), 11, 169
realism, 47, 49, 62, 117, 138, 150
relevance theory, 26, 74–75
Renberg, Tore, 168
Rothman, Joshua, 25, 72
Rühl, Anna, 73, 119
Ryan, Marie-Laue, 21

Rydberg, Carina, 7, 115

Sandemose, Aksel, 85, 198n13, 214n3
Saussure, Ferdinand de, 35–36
Schmitt, Arnaud, 20, 46, 63, 67, 73,
  75–76
Seasons Quartet (Knausgård), 50
Second Place (Cusk), 166
Sedgwick, Eve, 27, 86
self-harm, 57–58, 91, 92
A Severed Head (Murdoch), 73
Shakespeare, William, 88
shame, 4, 27, 81–87, 90–91, 92–93,
  94–98, 109, 198n15
Shklovsky, Victor, 50, 78, 149
Shields, David, 1, 15–17, 48, 55, 143,
  177n76
Sinykin, Dan, 37–38, 41
"Sjelens Amerika" (Knausgård). *See*
  "America of the Soul"
Sjølyst-Jackson, Peter, 72
Smith, Zadie, 120–121
Solstad, Dag, 7
So Much Longing in So Little Space
  (Knausgård), 37
St Aubyn, Edward, 22
Sturgeon, Jonathan, 15

Taylor, Brandon, 11, 22, 169
The Theory of the Novel (Lukács),
  59–61
Thomas, Michael, 10
A Time for Everything (*En tid for alt*),
  4–5, 36, 38, 84, 90, 201n40
Tolstoy, Leo, 125, 127
Tomkins, Silvan, 27, 86–87
The Topeka School (Lerner), 167
Transit (Cusk), 147–148, 166

Ulvene fra evighetens skog
  (Knausgård), 165
Ute av verden. See *Out of the World*

Index | 243

Valihora, Karen, 151
van den Akker, Robin, 21
Vankel, Henrik, 3–5, 38, 90
Vermeulen, Pieter, 156
Vermeulen, Timotheus, 21
Voelz, Johannes, 15
Vuong, Ocean, 11, 22

Waldman, Katy, 135
Walsh, Richard, 26, 74–75
Wasserman, Sarah, 11, 18–19, 20
Watt, Ian, 62
Weineck, Silke-Maria, 96
West, Paul, 8

What We Lose (Clemmons), 11
White, Hayden, 74
Whitman, Walt, 158, 161
Williams, Raymond, 22
window, 46–47, 52–53, 59, 63, 70,
    87, 89, 90, 100, 102, 152,
    194n57
A Wizard of Earthsea (Le Guin), 37,
    64, 183n23
Wood, James, 3, 33, 144
Worthington, Marjorie, 9–10

Zhang, Dora, 128, 132
Zola, Emile, 127, 128, 131, 207n59